Welcome to

zoom Deutsch 1

Corinna Schicker
Marcus Waltl
Chalin Malz

Meet Nina, Ali, Kathi and Nico (in this book and on the *Zoom Deutsch* video).

Share their video blogs and find out more about them.

Symbols and headings you will find in the book: what do they mean?

 VIDEO 1 A video activity

 HÖREN 2 A listening activity

SPRECHEN 3 A speaking activity

LESEN 4 A reading activity

SCHREIBEN 5 A writing activity

 Do this with a partner

 Work with a group

 **Grammatik → p.000** Grammar information

 **?** Think about this!

Important words or phrases

Challenge ◉ A challenge

Extra Star / Plus	Reinforcement and extension activities
Sprachlabor	Grammar, strategies, pronunciation
Testseite	Test yourself
Vokabular	Unit vocabulary list
Lesen	Reading pages
Grammatik	Grammar reference
Vokabular	Glossary

OXFORD
UNIVERSITY PRESS

Inhalt

Unit	Contexts/Language	Grammar	Learning strategies and pronunciation
Los geht's! Page 4	Introduction to the *Zoom Deutsch* video characters Facts about German-speaking countries Classroom language	Gender and the indefinite article (*ein/eine*)	Use German for classroom communication Pronunciation of *ä, ö, ü* and *ß*
0 Hallo! Page 8	**Introducing yourself** Greetings: say your name and spell it Numbers 1–31 Say how old you are and the month of your birthday Countries and languages	The German alphabet The *ich* and *du* forms of *sein* and *haben*	Compare German and English words Work out language rules Work out meaning Identify links between spelling and pronunciation Pronunciation of umlauts (*ä, ö, ü*), *w* and letter combinations
1A Meine Familie Page 24	**Family** Family members Brothers and sisters Pets and colours Describe yourself, your pets, friends and family members	Possessive adjectives: *mein(e)/dein(e)* (my/your) *Ich habe einen/eine/ein …* Negatives: *ich habe keinen/keine/kein …* Noun plurals Subject pronouns: *er, sie, es*	Think about language patterns Learn words and their plurals Work out meaning Use a bilingual dictionary Pronunciation of *v, ei, ü* and *sch*
1B Meine Schule Page 40	**School** Classroom objects and items in your school bag School subjects and your opinions of them Tell the time; say when you have different subjects Days of the week Talk about your timetable	Gender: *der, die, das* The *wir* form of *haben* Use 'verb second' word order	Use question words Work out the meaning of unknown words Pronunciation of *ö*
2A Freizeit und Hobbys Page 56	**Free time and hobbies** Sports and musical instruments Your favourite hobbies Opinions of computer games Say how often you do something	*Gern, nicht gern, lieber, am liebsten* Present tense (regular and irregular verbs) Time expressions Use *denn*	Listen for intonation Use words you already know to work out the meaning of new words Keep a record of new language Pronunciation of *a* and *ä* Pronunciation of words which are similar in English and German
2B Wo wohnst du? Page 72	**Home** Say where you live and what the weather is like Describe your house or flat and your own room Numbers up to 100	*Ich wohne in einem/einer/einem …* *Es gibt einen/eine/ein …* Prepositions + *dem/der/dem*	Adapt familiar language Work out language patterns Read for sense and extract information from texts Techniques for learning new words Pronunciation of *ch*

Inhalt

Unit	Contexts/Language	Grammar	Learning strategies and pronunciation
3A Guten Appetit! Page 88	**Food and drink** Say what food and drink you like and don't like; say what you eat for different meals Order food in a café or snack bar Buy food in a shop Numbers up to 1000 Talk about healthy eating Order a meal in a restaurant	Use 'verb second' word order *Ich möchte* + noun *Man soll … essen/trinken* Negatives: *gern, nicht gern; keinen/keine/kein*	Use familiar language in a new context Use polite language Identify language patterns Work out meaning Build longer sentences using linking words (*und, denn, aber, oder*) Pronunciation of long *u* and short *u*
3B Mein Zuhause Page 104	**Local area** The places in a town Say what you can do in a place Ask for and give directions Buy tickets and presents Understand tourist information	*Es gibt einen/eine/ein …* *Es gibt keinen/keine/kein …* Modal verbs: *können* and *wollen* Give instructions (*du* and *Sie* forms) Ask questions	Evaluate and improve your work Work out language patterns Listening strategies: deal with unfamiliar language Identify formality of language Pronunciation of *v* and *w*
4A Modestadt Berlin! Page 120	**Fashion and shopping** Talk about clothes and give your opinion of them Talk about what you wear and what you'd like to wear Go shopping for clothes Talk about problems with clothes Designer clothing and school uniform	Singular noun + *ist*, plural noun + *sind* Adjective endings in the accusative case *Ich möchte* + infinitive How to say 'it' (*ihn/sie/es*) and 'them' (*sie*) Future tense (*werden* + infinitive) Comparisons	True and false friends Recycle familiar language (adjectives) in a new context Identify grammar patterns Prepare for and evaluate language tasks Evaluate and improve your written work Pronunciation of *ich*, *ig* and *isch*
4B Zu Besuch Page 136	**Going on a trip** Talk about holidays (where you go, how you travel, where you stay and for how long) Talk about what you can do on holiday and what you're going to do Talk about past holiday experiences	Prepositions + the dative case Modal verbs (*können, wollen*) Future tense (*werden* + infinitive) Perfect tense (with *haben* and *sein*)	Identify language patterns Work out the meaning of compound nouns Give your opinion Recycle familiar words and phrases in different tenses Listening strategies Pronunciation of word endings
Lesen Page 152–160	Extra reading practice for each unit		
Grammatik Page 161–169	Grammar reference section		
Vokabular Page 170–175	German–English glossary		

Willkommen!

Vocabulary: greetings; names of towns and countries
Grammar: name people using *das ist* ...
Skills: learn words by listening and repeating

  Hör zu und lies.
Listen and read.

Das ist Nina.

Hallo!

Das ist Ali.

Guten Tag!

Das ist Kathi.

Wie geht's?

Das ist Nico.

Hallo!

  Hör noch einmal zu.
Listen again and find three different greetings.

? Think

How do you say 'this is' in German?

Deutschland, Österreich und die Schweiz

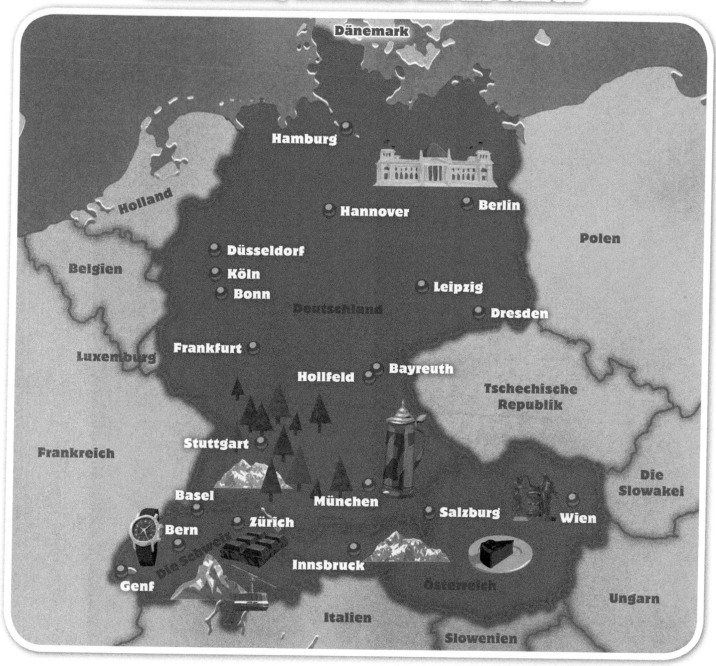

Dänemark

Hamburg

Holland

Hannover

Berlin

Polen

Belgien

Düsseldorf

Köln

Bonn

Leipzig

Deutschland

Dresden

Luxemburg

Frankfurt

Hollfeld

Bayreuth

Tschechische Republik

Frankreich

Stuttgart

Basel

München

Die Slowakei

Bern

Zürich

Salzburg

Wien

Genf

Die Schweiz

Innsbruck

Österreich

Ungarn

Italien

Slowenien

Hör zu und wiederhole.
Listen and repeat the names of the towns.
Point to them on the map.

Germany is a large country right in the centre of Europe. 82 million people live there, making it the largest nation in Europe in terms of population. German is spoken in Germany, Austria and Switzerland. The other languages spoken in Switzerland are French, Italian and Romansh (spoken by a very small minority). German is also spoken in small parts of Belgium and in Northern Italy.

Was ist das?

Vocabulary: talk about symbols of Germany; use classroom language
Grammar: gender
Skills: use German for classroom communication; pronounce ä, ö, ü and ß

1 Lies die Fragen. Was ist richtig?
Read the questions. Which answer is correct?

Beispiel: **1 b**

Zoom-Deutsch-Quiz

1 ⓐ Das ist England.
ⓑ Das ist Deutschland.

2 ⓐ Das ist ein Auto.
ⓑ Das ist ein Bus.

3 ⓐ Das ist eine CD.
ⓑ Das ist ein Sportschuh.

4 ⓐ Das ist Fußball.
ⓑ Das ist Hockey.

5 ⓐ Das ist Berlin.
ⓑ Das ist London.

2 🎧 Ist alles richtig? Hör zu. (1–5)
Is everything correct? Listen to check your answers.

? Think

Look at the German nouns in the quiz. What do you notice about the way they are written? How is this different from English?

⚙ Grammatik → p.162

ein/eine
All German nouns have a 'gender': they are either masculine, feminine or neuter. This means that German has more than one word for 'a', depending on the noun's gender:

ein + masculine nouns → **ein Bus**
eine + feminine nouns → **eine CD**
ein + neuter nouns → **ein Auto**

Hör zu und lies. (1–10)
Listen and read. Which phrases can you guess the meaning of?

 Was passt zusammen?
Match the English to the German.

Beispiel: **a** *7*

a 'Kuli'? What does that mean?
b How do you spell that?
c I don't know.
d Here you go.
e Sorry? Pardon?
f Quiet, please!
g What's the word for 'biro' in German?
h 'Biro' is 'Kuli' in German.
i Thank you.
j I don't understand.

? Think

German has one letter that doesn't exist in English: ß (called *Eszett*). It is pronounced like a double 's': *Ich weiß es nicht.*

Umlauts (two dots) are used in German on the letters *ä*, *ü* and *ö*. Listen to the way they change the sounds:

s**a**gen (*to say*) → s**ä**gen (*to saw*)
r**u**fen (*to call*) → **ü**ben (*to practise*)
sch**o**n (*already*) → sch**ö**n (*pretty*)

0.1 Wie heißt du?

> Vocabulary: greetings; say your name and spell it
> Grammar: use the German alphabet
> Skills: compare German and English words; imitate German sounds

1 Finde die Paare.
Match up the English expressions with the German.

Beispiel: **a 3**

a Goodbye!	**d** My name is Alex.
b Good evening!	**e** Bye!
c What's your name?	**f** Good morning!

? Think

Some words in German and English look quite similar. See if you can guess the meanings of some of these words – use the pictures to help.

1 Guten Morgen!

4 Guten Abend!

2 Ich heiße Alex.

5 Tschüs!

3 Auf Wiedersehen!

6 Wie heißt du?

2 🎧 Hör zu (a–f). Welches Bild?
Listen and choose the correct picture in activity 1 each time.

Beispiel: **a 4**

3 👥 Macht zwei Dialoge. A ↔ B.
Take turns making a short dialogue to introduce yourself to your partner.

Beispiel: **A** Guten Morgen!
B Hallo!
A Wie heißt du?
B Ich heiße …

? Think

Look at the German alphabet. Which letters do you think you will find most difficult to pronounce? Then listen and check whether you were right.

A B C D E F G H
I J K L M N O P
Q R S T U V W
X Y Z Ä Ö Ü ß

4 🎧 Hör zu und wiederhole.
Listen to the German alphabet and repeat each letter.

5 👥 Was folgt? A ↔ B.
What comes next? **A** says a letter in German and **B** says which letter comes next.

Beispiel: **A** f
B g

Hör zu (1–8). Was fehlt?
Listen. Which letter is missing?

Beispiel: **1** C

Hör zu und lies.
Listen and read.

NC 1–2

Nico: Hallo! Wie heißt du?
Kathi: Hallo! Ich heiße Kathi.
Nico: Wie schreibt man das?
Kathi: Das schreibt man K-A-T-H-I.

? **Think**

Can you remember what the German ß sounds like?

Look back at page 7 for a reminder.

 Sieh dir das Video an. Schreib Ninas Nachnamen auf.
Watch the video. Write down Nina's surname.

Nina

? **Think**

Look at this German keyboard. How does it compare to the keyboard on your computer? What is the same? What is different? What additional keys are there?

Kathi

Nico

Challenge

Make a short dialogue with a partner with questions and answers introducing yourself, and saying how your name is spelled.

Beispiel: **A** Guten Morgen. Wie heißt du?
B Hallo. Ich heiße Marcus.
A Wie schreibt man das?
B Das schreibt man M-A-R-C-U-S.

NC 1–2

0.2 Wie alt bist du?

Vocabulary: use the numbers 1–20; say how old you are
Grammar: use the *ich* and *du* forms of *sein* (to be)
Skills: use knowledge you already have to work out language rules

0 null	6 sechs
1 eins	7 sieben
2 zwei	8 acht
3 drei	9 neun
4 vier	10 zehn
5 fünf	

 HÖREN 1 🎧 **Hör zu und wiederhole.**
Listen and repeat.

? Think

Listen carefully to the words *fünf* and *acht* and practise their pronunciation.

 SPRECHEN 2 👥 **A sagt eine Zahl. B sagt die Buchstaben. A ⟷ B.**
A says a number. **B** says which letters appear on that button on the telephone.

Beispiel: **A** Fünf
B   J, K, L

When you phone Germany you have to dial the international dialling code 0049 first. For Austria you dial 0043 and for Switzerland 0041.

 SPRECHEN 3 👥 **A buchstabiert eine Zahl. B schreibt die Zahl auf. A ⟷ B.**
A spells a number from 1 to 10. **B** writes down which number it is.

Beispiel: **A** Z-W-E-I
B   2

 HÖREN 4 🎧 **Hör zu (1–6). Welches Handy ist das?**
Listen. Which mobile phone is it?

Beispiel: **1** *d*

Wie geht's? *How are you?*	
☺	☹
Mir geht's gut!	Mir geht's schlecht!
Sehr gut!	Nicht so gut!
Fantastisch!	Nicht gut!

a
An: **Kati**
Speed-Dial: 4
Hallo, wie geht's?

b
An: **Werner**
Speed-Dial: 29
Werner, mir geht's schlecht.

c
An: **Clemens**
Speed-Dial: 11
Guten Morgen! Mir geht's fantastisch!

d
An: **Sabine**
Speed-Dial: 132
Gruß aus Berlin!

e
An: **Jenny**
Speed-Dial: 435
Es ist super in Hamburg!

f
An: **Aische**
Speed-Dial: 632
Hallo, wie geht's? Mir geht's gut!

5 **Sieh dir das Video an. Schreib die Telefonnummern auf.**
Watch the video. Write down the last four digits of Nina's and Kathi's telephone numbers.

Nina   0176 29 04 _ _ _ _

Kathi   0181 98 87 _ _ _ _

You know the numbers 1–10 already. Can you use your existing knowledge to work out the rule for forming the numbers 13–19?

You form the numbers 13 to 19 by taking the first ▬▬▬ letters of the numbers ▬▬▬ to ▬▬▬ and adding the word ▬▬▬ on the end.

 6 **Was passt zusammen?**
Match the words with the numbers and put them in the correct order.

Beispiel: **11** *elf,* **12** *zwölf*

11 12 13 14 15 16 17 18 19 20

neunzehn   vierzehn
elf   dreizehn   zwanzig
zwölf   achtzehn
siebzehn   fünfzehn
sechzehn

Try to count backwards from 20 to 1, then try only counting the even numbers.

 7 🎧 **Hör zu und wiederhole.**
Listen and repeat the numbers.

 8 **Lies den Dialog.**
Read the dialogue.

Esther: Hallo, ich heiße Esther. Ich bin zwölf Jahre alt. Und du, Konrad? Wie alt bist du?

Konrad: Ich bin vierzehn Jahre alt. Hallo, Karim. Wie geht's? Wie alt bist du?

Karim: Ich bin dreizehn Jahre alt. Und du, Sonja? Wie alt bist du?

Sonja: Ich bin elf Jahre alt. Tschüs, Karim!

⚙ Grammatik → p.166

Ich bin   *I am*
Du bist   *You are*
Wie alt **bist du**?   *How old **are you**?*
Ich bin zwölf Jahre alt.
  I am twelve years old.

Challenge

Take turns making up dialogues.

Beispiel: **A** *Hallo. Wie heißt du?*
  B *Ich heiße Johannes.*
  A *Wie alt bist du?*
  B *Ich bin siebzehn Jahre alt.*
  A *Tschüs, Johannes.*
  B *Tschüs.*

 Johannes 17

 Claudia 15

 Benjamin 9

 Anja 20

NC 1–2

0.3 Ich habe Geburtstag!

Vocabulary: learn the months and numbers 21 to 31
Grammar: learn how to say 'I have' and 'you have' using *haben*
Skills: work out the meaning of new words

 SCHREIBEN 1 **Was ist die richtige Reihenfolge?**
Put the months of the year into the right order.

Beispiel: Januar, …

März Dezember April Oktober

Februar Januar September Mai

Juli Juni November August

 ? Think

Sometimes you can work out the meaning of new words because their spelling is similar or the same as in English. Try this with activity 1.

 HÖREN 2 🎧 **Hör zu. Wann hast du Geburtstag?**
Listen. When do these five people have their birthdays?

a Kirsten

Ich habe im zeDebemr Geburtstag.

b Ralf

Hallo. Ich habe im ärzM Geburtstag.

c Seema

Guten Tag. Ich habe im iMa Geburtstag.

d Silvia

Ich habe im iuJl Geburtstag.

e Markus

Guten Morgen! Ich habe im Fberrua Geburtstag.

HÖREN 3 🎧 **Hör zu. Ein Interview im Radio.**
Listen to this radio interview. Note down the month of each person's birthday in English.

Beispiel: **1** *Claudia: October*

1 Claudia	**4** Klaus
2 Julian	**5** Martina
3 Rebecca	

SPRECHEN 4 👥 **Macht Dialoge. A ↔ B.**
In pairs, take turns to make dialogues.

NC 1–2

Beispiel: **A** *Niklas, wann hast du Geburtstag?*
B *Ich habe im Mai Geburtstag.*

Schreib die Dialoge auf.

NC 1–2

Write down your dialogues from activity 4. Extend them by adding some of the things you learned earlier in the unit.

Beispiel: **A** *Guten Morgen! Ich heiße Andreas.*
B *Hallo! Ich bin Luisa.*
A *Wann hast du Geburtstag? ...*

🎧 Hör zu und wiederhole.
Listen to the numbers 21 to 31 and repeat.

🎧 Welche Zahl hörst du? (a–f)
Which number do you hear? Pick the correct one each time.

Beispiel: **a** *28*

a	26 28	**d**	27 30
b	21 29	**e**	21 31
c	22 23	**f**	24 27

👥 Schreib eine Zahl von 21–31 auf. A ↔ B.
A writes down a number between 21 and 31. **B** guesses what the number is in German.

Beispiel: **B** *Ist das einundzwanzig?*
A *Nein.*
B *Ist das ...*

Wie heißt du?

Wie schreibt man das?

Wie alt bist du?

? Think

What is the pattern for forming the numbers 21 to 31 in German? Can you guess how you would say the numbers 32–39? What do you think the word *und* means?

21	einundzwanzig
22	zweiundzwanzig
23	dreiundzwanzig
24	vierundzwanzig
25	fünfundzwanzig
26	sechsundzwanzig
27	siebenundzwanzig
28	achtundzwanzig
29	neunundzwanzig
30	dreißig
31	einunddreißig

Challenge

Write sentences.

Beispiel: **a** *Ich heiße Anna. Ich bin achtzehn Jahre alt. Ich habe im Januar Geburtstag.*

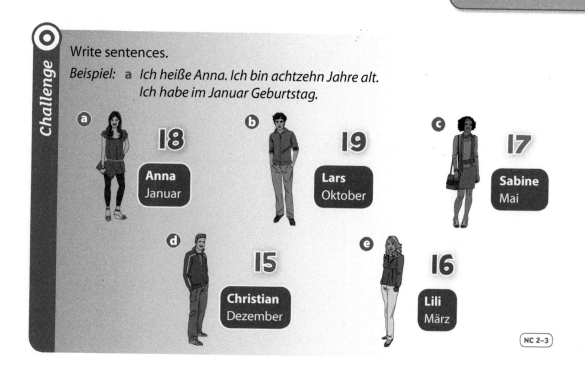

a 18 Anna Januar

b 19 Lars Oktober

c 17 Sabine Mai

d 15 Christian Dezember

e 16 Lili März

NC 2–3

Vocabulary: learn the names for different countries and languages
Grammar: *das ist* (that is), *ich spreche* (I speak), *ich komme aus* (I come from), *ich wohne* (I live)
Skills: identify links between spelling and pronunciation

 LESEN 1

Lies den Text. Mach eine Liste.
Read the text. Make a list of the countries and the languages in German and English.

Beispiel: **Land**	*Country*	**Sprache**	*Language*
Deutschland	*Germany*	Deutsch	*German*

a

Das ist Großbritannien. Ich heiße Jenny. Ich komme aus Großbritannien. Ich spreche Englisch.

b

Das ist Deutschland. Ich heiße Nico. Ich wohne in Deutschland. Ich spreche Deutsch.

c

Das ist Polen. Ich heiße Tomasz. Ich wohne in Polen und ich spreche Polnisch.

h

Hier ist Frankreich. Ich heiße Beatrice. Ich wohne in Frankreich. Ich spreche Französisch.

d

Das ist Österreich. Ich heiße Kathi. Ich komme aus Österreich. Ich spreche Deutsch.

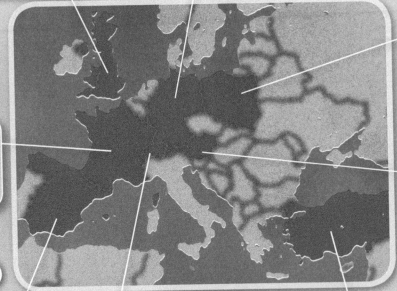

g

Das ist Spanien. Ich heiße Miguel. Ich komme aus Spanien und ich spreche Spanisch.

f

Das ist die Schweiz. Ich heiße Sandra. Ich wohne in der Schweiz. Ich spreche Deutsch, Französisch und Italienisch.

e

Hier ist die Türkei. Ich heiße Ali. Ich komme aus der Türkei, aber ich wohne in Deutschland. Ich spreche Türkisch und Deutsch.

HÖREN 2 🎧 **Hör zu. Wiederhole.**
Listen and repeat.

a *Deutschland*    **e** *Türkei*

b *Österreich*   **f** *Polen*

c *Frankreich*   **g** *Schweiz*

d *Großbritannien*   **h** *Spanien*

? Think

Listen to the pronunciation of the country names. The letter *w* in German is pronounced like a *v* in English and *ei* sounds like the English word *I*. How is *ien* as in *Großbritannien* pronounced?

 SCHREIBEN 3 **Füll die Lücken aus.**
NC 1–2
Copy and complete the paragraph with words from the box.

Hallo. Ich (**a**) _heiße_ Nina. Ich komme aus (**b**)▩▩ . Ich (**c**)▩▩ in Berlin. Ich bin (**d**)▩▩ Jahre alt. Ich habe im Mai (**e**)▩▩ . Ich spreche (**f**)▩▩ und (**g**)▩▩ .

> 14   Englisch   Deutsch   Geburtstag   heiße   wohne   Deutschland

 VIDEO 4 🎥 **Sieh dir das Video an. Wähle die richtige Antwort.**
Watch the video. Kathi and Nina introduce themselves. Choose the correct answers.

a Kathi is from …   **1** Germany   **2** Austria.
b Nina …   **1** is from Berlin   **2** is not from Berlin.

 SCHREIBEN 5 **Schreib Sätze.**
NC 2
Write a short paragraph about yourself like the one in activity 3. Mention the following points:

- what your name is
- how old you are
- the month of your birthday
- where you live (you can put a country, area, city or town here)
- where you come from
- what languages you speak

> Ich heiße …
> Ich bin … Jahre alt.
> Ich habe im … Geburtstag.
> Ich wohne in …
> Ich komme aus …
> Ich spreche …

Challenge
Try to find five more countries and languages in a dictionary. Write a paragraph like the one in activity 3 for a famous person, using one of the countries and languages you have found.
Beispiel: Ich heiße Christiano Ronaldo. … NC 2

Vocabulary: say what date your birthday is; give personal information
Grammar: use correct endings for numbers
Skills: identify language patterns

1

NC 1–2

Schreib Sätze.
Write a sentence for each person using the numbers grid below.

Beispiel: **a** *Thomas*: *Ich habe am vierten Januar Geburtstag.*

a
Thomas,
4. Januar

b
Rita,
28. Juni

c
Werner,
15. August

d
Sonja,
3. Oktober

Ich habe am			Geburtstag.
	ersten (1.)	Januar	
	zwei**ten (2.)**	Februar	
	dritten (3.)	März	
	vier**ten (4.)**	April	
	fünf**ten (5.)**	Mai	
	sechs**ten (6.)**	Juni	
	siebten (7.)	Juli	
	achten (8.)	August	
	neun**ten (9.)**	September	
	zehn**ten (10.)**	Oktober	
	elf**ten (11.)**	November	
	…	Dezember	
	zwanzig**sten (20.)**		
	einundzwanzig**sten (21.)**		
	zweiundzwanzig**sten (22.)**		
	dreißig**sten (30.)**		

? **Think**

Look at the pattern for saying the date of your birthday and make up a rule to describe it.

When I say the date of my birthday, I usually add the letters ▬▬▬ to the numbers 1–19. The exceptions are the numbers ▬▬ , ▬▬ , ▬▬ and ▬▬ . For the numbers 20 – 31 I add ▬▬ .

2 **Hör zu (1–5). Wähle den richtigen Geburtstag.**
Listen. Choose the correct birthday.

Beispiel: **1** *d*

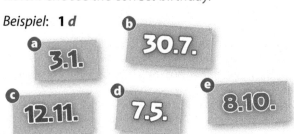

a 3.1.   **b** 30.7.   **c** 12.11.   **d** 7.5.   **e** 8.10.

3 **Macht eine Umfrage in der Klasse: „Wann hast du Geburtstag"?**

NC 1–2

Do a survey in class: 'When is your birthday?'

Beispiel: **A** *Wann hast du Geburtstag?*
B *Ich habe am zwölften März Geburtstag.*

Kathi Kool

Info   Pinnwand   Fotos   +

Blog-Name:	Kathi Kool
Land:	Deutschland und Österreich
Alter:	14
Geburtstag:	4. Mai
Idol:	Heidi Klum (Model)

NC 2

Sieh dir das Video an. Füll die Lücken aus.
Watch the video and complete Kathi's sentences.

a   Ich heiße __Kathi__ .
b   Das schreibt man K ▨▨▨ .
c   Ich bin ▨▨▨ Jahre alt.
d   Ich habe am vierten ▨▨▨ Geburtstag.
e   Ich wohne in ▨▨▨ .
f   Ich spreche ▨▨▨ , ▨▨▨ und ▨▨▨ .
g   Meine Nummer ist 030 38 ▨▨▨ .

NC 2

Füll die Lücken aus.
Fill in the gaps using the word box on the right.

heiße   Jahre   Geburtstag   Deutsch   gut
geht's   wohne

Hallo, wie (**a**) _geht's_ ?
Ich (**b**) ▨▨▨ Heidi Klum.
Ich habe am 1. Juni (**c**) ▨▨▨ .
Ich bin 40 (**d**) ▨▨▨ alt.
Ich (**e**) ▨▨▨ in Amerika.
Ich spreche (**f**) ▨▨▨ und
Englisch. Das ist sehr (**g**) ▨▨▨ .

Challenge

Write answers to Kathi's questions for your own video blog.

Beispiel: Ich heiße …

• Wie heißt du?
• Wie ist dein Nachname? (*last name*)
• Wann hast du Geburtstag?
• Wo wohnst du?
• Was ist deine Telefonnummer?

NC 2

0.6 Sprachlabor

Word order, *sein* and *haben*

sein (*to be*)
You will frequently use the verb *sein* (to be). It is important that you learn the different forms of the verb as you go along:

Ich bin	*I am*
Du bist	*You are*

Very often you will use the *du* form in a question:

Bist du …?	*Are you …?*
Wie alt bist du?	*How old are you?*

haben (*to have*)
Another very important verb to know well is *haben* (to have):

Ich habe	*I have*
Du hast	*You have*

If you want to ask a question, you say:
Hast du …? *Do you have …?*
Wann hast du Geburtstag?
When is your birthday? (When do you have your birthday?)

1 Put the words in the right order.

Beispiel: **a** *Hallo Franziska. Wie alt bist du?*
Hallo Natalie. Ich bin zwölf Jahre alt.

a
alt du Hallo bist? Wie Franziska
Natalie Hallo bin Ich zwölf alt Jahre

b
Martin Hallo du alt bist Wie?
Klaus vierzehn Ich Jahre bin alt Hallo

c
Hallo? Sabrina alt Wie bist du
Hallo Ich alt Jahre bin dreizehn Bernd

2 Fill in the gaps with the correct form of *haben*.

a Ich ____ im Mai Geburtstag.
b Wann ____ du Geburtstag?
c ____ du im Juni oder im Juli Geburtstag?
d Hallo. Ich ____ im Juli Geburtstag.

Identifying words from the same family

3 Match the flag (a–g) with the country (1–7) and the language (i–vi). Watch out: more than one language is spoken in two of these countries.

Beispiel: ***a* + 3 + *vi***

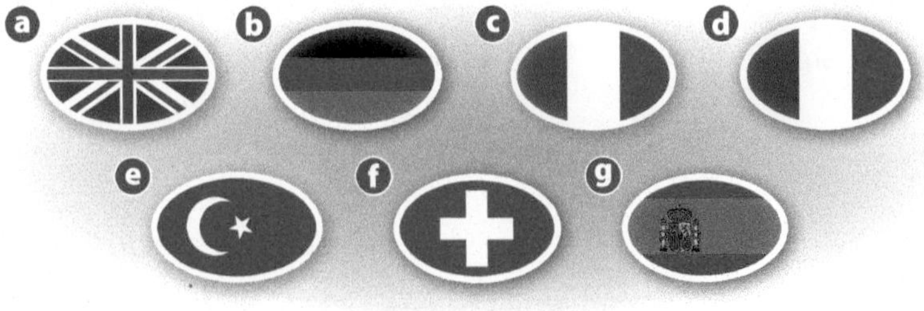

Länder *countries*
1 die Schweiz
2 Italien
3 Großbritannien
4 Frankreich
5 Spanien
6 die Türkei
7 Deutschland

Ich spreche …
i Französisch
ii Italienisch
iii Deutsch
iv Spanisch
v Türkisch
vi Englisch

Das ist + *country*; Ich spreche + *language*

Das ist …   *That is …*
Ich spreche …   *I speak …*

The words you use for countries are not the same as the words you use for the language you speak there:

Das ist **Deutschland**.   Ich spreche **Deutsch**.

4 **Look at the numbers for the countries in activity 3 and roll a dice. A ↔ B.**

Beispiel: **A**   **B** *Das ist Italien. Ich spreche Italienisch.*

Pronunciation of umlauts (*ä, ö, ü*), letter combinations and *w*

5 🎧 **Listen carefully to the following words.**

a fünf **b** zwölf **c** Bär **d** Ich **e** heiße **f** dreißig
g Griechenland **h** schlecht **i** gute Nacht **j** Tschüs
k Wie? **l** Wann?

6 👥 **A says a word in activity 5. B points at the word. A ↔ B.**

7 🎧 **Listen to the words (a–f) and try to spell them correctly.**

Beispiel: **a** *h e i ß e*

8 🎧 **First try to pronounce these words. Then listen to check.**

a Spanien **b** Wien **c** zwei **d** wie **e** dreißig **f** schreiben

Letter combinations
Certain sounds in German are always spelled with the same letter combinations:
  ei in *drei* sounds like 'I'
  ie in *wie* sounds like 'ea' in 'tea'
  sp in *spreche* sounds like 'shp'
  w in *was* sounds like 'v' in 'vest'

Bär	*bear*
dreißig	*thirty*
Griechenland	*Greece*
gute Nacht	*good night*
Wien	*Vienna*
schreiben	*to write*

Vocabulary: practise language from the unit
Grammar: identify parts of *haben* and *sein*
Skills: work out meaning

SCHREIBEN 1

NC 1

Fill in the gaps to complete the numbers.

Beispiel: **a** *eins*

a e_ns   **b** si_ben   **c** ac_t   **d** _ehn   **e** e_f
f sie_zehn   **g** ne_nzehn   **h** _wanzi_

LESEN 2

NC 1

Which are positive ☺ and which are negative ☹?

Beispiel: gut ☺

gut   super   fantastisch   schlecht   nicht gut   nicht so gut   sehr gut

SCHREIBEN 3

NC 1–2

Match the questions and answers and write out the dialogue.

Beispiel: Wie heißt du?
Ich heiße Claudia Schiffer.
...

Wie geht's?	Ich heiße Claudia Schiffer.
Wann hast du Geburtstag?	Ich bin 41 Jahre alt.
Wie heißt du?	Ich habe im August Geburtstag.
Wie alt bist du?	Sehr gut. Danke.

LESEN 4

NC 1–2

Match the calendar pages with sentences a–f.

Beispiel: **a** 4

1 12.4.   **2** 7.6.   **3** 27.7.   **4** 3.10.   **5** 30.11.   **6** 24.12.

a Ich habe im Oktober Geburtstag.
b Ich habe im April Geburtstag.
c Ich habe im Dezember Geburtstag.
d Ich habe im Juni Geburtstag.
e Ich habe im November Geburtstag.
f Ich habe im Juli Geburtstag.

Vocabulary: practise language from the unit
Grammar: learn forms for nationalities
Skills: use knowledge of grammar to work out meaning

Was ist die Lösung?

NC 1

Calculate the sums and write down the solution.

Beispiel: **a** *sechzehn*

a vierundzwanzig minus acht = ?
b fünf plus sechs = ?
c achtundzwanzig minus sieben = ?
d vierzehn plus neun = ?
e acht plus fünf plus drei minus eins = ?
f zwei plus drei plus zwanzig minus zwei minus sechs = ?

 **Think**

Nationalität

You can use your knowledge of word endings to help you work out meaning.

masculine	feminine
Ich bin Engländ**er**.	Ich bin Engländer**in**.
Ich bin Österreich**er**.	Ich bin Österreicher**in**.
Ich bin Schweiz**er**.	Ich bin Schweizer**in**.
Ich bin Deutsch**er**.	Ich bin Deutsch**e**.

The male version ends in -*er*; the female version in -*e* or -*in*.

Schreib Sätze für die Bilder.

Beispiel: **a** *Ich bin Engländerin.*

a **b** **c** **d** **e** **f** **g**

Lies den Text. Richtig oder falsch?

NC 2

Beispiel: **a** *richtig*

a Franka is an actress.
b Franka is from France.
c Franka's birthday is on 23rd July.
d She speaks English and German in her films.
e She does not like English.

Schreib einen kurzen Absatz.

NC 2

Write a short paragraph about yourself.

Beispiel: *Ich heiße … Ich bin …*

Hallo. Wie geht's? Ich heiße Franka Potente. Ich bin Schauspielerin und ich komme aus Deutschland. Ich habe am zweiundzwanzigsten Juli Geburtstag. Ich spreche Deutsch. Ich spreche auch Englisch in meinen Filmen. Das ist sehr gut. Englisch ist super. Tschüs.

die Schauspielerin *actress*

1 Listen (1–6). Who speaks about a–f? (See pages 8–15.)

NC 1–2 *Beispiel*: **1** *d*

a their age	**d** the country they come from
b their birthday	**e** the way they spell their name
c the languages they speak	**f** how they feel

2 Unscramble the word order in these sentences. (See pages 12–15.)

NC 1–2 *Beispiel*: **a** *Wann hast du Geburtstag?*

a Geburtstag Wann du hast ?
b habe Ich im Juni Geburtstag
c Karin heiße Ich
d spreche Italienisch und Ich Deutsch
e komme Ich aus Frankreich
f England wohne in Ich

3 Match sentences 1–6 in the box below with a–f.
(See pages 10–15.)

NC 1–2 *Beispiel*: **a** *4*

Which sentence …
a talks about the languages this person speaks?
b talks about the age of the person?
c says that Berlin is great?
d mentions a birthday?
e says where the person comes from?
f says where the person lives?

> **1** Ich bin dreizehn Jahre alt.
> **2** Ich habe im März Geburtstag.
> **3** Ich wohne in Deutschland, in Berlin.
> **4** Ich spreche Deutsch, Türkisch und Französisch.
> **5** Ich komme aus der Türkei.
> **6** Berlin ist toll.

4 Make up an interview with a partner, asking the
following questions (a–e). Match up the answers (1–5)
first to help you. (See pages 8–13.)

NC 1–2

Beispiel: **a** *5*

a Wie heißt du?
b Wie schreibt man das?
c Wie geht's?
d Wie alt bist du?
e Wann hast du Geburtstag?

> **1** Das schreibt man …
> **2** Sehr gut.
> **3** Ich bin (dreizehn) Jahre alt.
> **4** Ich habe im (Januar) Geburtstag.
> **5** Ich heiße (Tina/Max).

Vokabular

Von 1 bis 31	*From 1 to 31*
eins	*one*
zwei	*two*
drei	*three*
vier	*four*
fünf	*five*
sechs	*six*
sieben	*seven*
acht	*eight*
neun	*nine*
zehn	*ten*
elf	*eleven*
zwölf	*twelve*
dreizehn	*thirteen*
vierzehn	*fourteen*
fünfzehn	*fifteen*
sechzehn	*sixteen*
siebzehn	*seventeen*
achtzehn	*eighteen*
neunzehn	*nineteen*
zwanzig	*twenty*
einundzwanzig	*twenty-one*
zweiundzwanzig	*twenty-two*
dreiundzwanzig	*twenty-three*
vierundzwanzig	*twenty-four*
fünfundzwanzig	*twenty-five*
sechsundzwanzig	*twenty-six*
siebenundzwanzig	*twenty-seven*
achtundzwanzig	*twenty-eight*
neunundzwanzig	*twenty-nine*
dreißig	*thirty*
einunddreißig	*thirty-one*

Wie alt bist du?	*How old are you?*
Ich bin … Jahre alt.	*I am … years old.*
Ich habe am … Geburtstag.	*My birthday is on the …*
Ich habe im … Geburtstag.	*My birthday is in …*
Wann hast du Geburtstag?	*When is your birthday?*
am ersten/zweiten/dritten/ vierten	*on the first/second/third/fourth*
am zwanzigsten	*on the twentieth*

Monate	*Months*
Januar	*January*
Februar	*February*
März	*March*
April	*April*
Mai	*May*
Juni	*June*
Juli	*July*
August	*August*
September	*September*
Oktober	*October*
November	*November*
Dezember	*December*

Wie geht's?	*How are you?*
Mir geht's gut	*I feel good, I'm well*
sehr gut	*very good*
fantastisch	*fantastic*
nicht so gut	*not so good*
schlecht	*bad*

Hallo	*Hello*
Guten Tag	*Hello/Good day*
Guten Morgen	*Good morning*
Guten Abend	*Good evening*
Auf Wiedersehen	*Good bye*
Tschüs	*Bye*

Wie heißt du?	*What's your name?*
Ich heiße …	*My name is/I am called …*
Wie schreibt man das?	*How do you spell that?*
Das schreibt man …	*That is spelled …*

Länder	*Countries*
Ich komme aus …	*I come from … (+ country)*
Ich wohne in …	*I live in … (+ country)*
Deutschland	*Germany*
die Schweiz	*Switzerland*
die Türkei	*Turkey*
Frankreich	*France*
Österreich	*Austria*
Polen	*Poland*
Spanien	*Spain*

Sprachen	*Languages*
Ich spreche …	*I speak … (+ language)*
Deutsch	*German*
Englisch	*English*
Französisch	*French*
Italienisch	*Italian*
Spanisch	*Spanish*

I can...

- say my name and how old I am
- say when my birthday is
- use the German alphabet
- pronounce the letters *ä, ö, ü, ß, w* and *ch* correctly
- count from 1–31
- use the verbs *haben* and *sein* in the *ich* and *du* forms
- name a few countries and languages

1A.1 Das ist meine Familie!

> Vocabulary: say who there is in your family
> Grammar: use *meine(e)/dein(e)* (my/your)
> Skills: think about language patterns

HÖREN 1 🎧 Hör zu. Was passt zusammen?

Listen and match the correct pictures to the sentences.

Beispiel: **a 4**

a   Das ist meine Mutter.

b   Das ist mein Vater.

c   Das ist meine Oma.

d   Das ist mein Opa.

e   Das ist meine Schwester.

f   Das ist mein Bruder Ulli.

g   Das ist mein Bruder Ralf.

SPRECHEN 2 Wer ist das? A ←→ B.

A points to a picture and asks who it is,
B answers as if he or she is Nico.

Beispiel: **A** *Wer ist das?*
        B *Das ist meine Schwester!*

? Think

Can you find the odd one out in each group?

1 meine Mutter	mein Bruder	meine Schwester
2 mein Vater	meine Mutter	mein Opa
3 meine Tante	meine Oma	meine Großeltern

Hör zu. Welcher Name passt?
Listen and match the correct names to the family members.

Beispiel: meine Großeltern – Elisabeth + …

Anna	Elisabeth
Franz	Karl
Kathi	Markus
Peter	Sandra

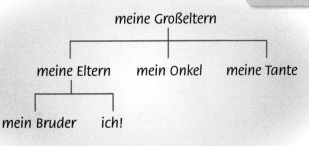

meine Großeltern

meine Eltern   mein Onkel   meine Tante

mein Bruder   ich!

  Mein Stammbaum. A ↔ B.
Write your own family tree as in activity 3.
Then take turns to ask each other questions.

NC 1–2

Beispiel: **A** *Wer ist Susan?*
 B *Das ist meine Mutter.*

Wer ist das?	
Das ist	mein/dein Vater/Opa/Bruder/Onkel.
	meine/deine Familie/ Mutter/Oma/ Schwester/Tante.
Das sind	meine/deine Eltern/Großeltern.
Er/sie heißt … Sie (pl.) heißen …	

 Mein oder meine?
Fill in the gaps with either *mein* or *meine*.

Beispiel: _mein_ Vater

a ▓▓▓ Tante   **b** ▓▓▓ Bruder   **c** ▓▓▓ Großeltern
d ▓▓▓ Schwester   **e** ▓▓▓ Opa   **f** ▓▓▓ Familie
g ▓▓▓ Onkel

 Think

When would you use *mein/meine*
and when *dein/deine* when talking
about family members?

 **Lies Toms Nachricht.**
Read Tom's message and answer the questions in English.

Hallo!
Ich heiße Tom und ich bin vierzehn
Jahre alt. Mein Vater heißt Uwe
und meine Mutter heißt Vera.
Meine Schwester heißt Klara. Mein
Bruder heißt Sebastian. Und meine
Großeltern? Mein Opa heißt Walter und
meine Oma heißt Ruth.

a What are the names of Tom's parents?
b What are his brother and sister called?
c What are the names of his grandparents?

Challenge

Write a message like Tom's
about your own family.
Try to write three sentences.

NC 2

1A.2 Ich habe einen Bruder

Vocabulary: talk about brothers and sisters
Grammar: *ich habe eine(n)/keine(n)* ...
Skills: work out new language and plural patterns

 VIDEO 1

 Sieh dir Nicos Videoblog an. Was passt zu Nico?
Watch Nico's video blog. Which set of photos matches his family?

VIDEO 2

Sieh dir das Video an. Was passt zu Ali und Kathi?
Watch the video. Which sentence matches Ali, and which Kathi?

a Ich habe einen Bruder.

b Ich habe eine Schwester.

c Ich habe eine Schwester und zwei Brüder.

d Ich habe zwei Schwestern.

e Ich bin Einzelkind – ich habe keine Geschwister.

f Ich habe zwei Brüder.

Ali

Kathi

 HÖREN 3

NC 2

 Hör zu. Geschwister. Was passt?
Listen. Which picture matches Maren, Alex, Sandra and Carsten?

Beispiel: Maren 4

1   2   3   4

? Think

You know that *eine* is feminine and *ein* masculine – can you figure out what *einen* means?

Das ist **eine** Schwester.
→ Ich habe **eine** Schwester.

Das ist **ein** Bruder.
→ Ich habe **einen** Bruder.

⚙ Grammatik → p.162, p.167

Ich habe einen/keinen ...
The German word for 'a' (*ein*) sometimes changes in a sentence – but only for masculine nouns:

m   ein Bruder   → Ich habe ein**en** Bruder. (ein + -en)
f   eine Schwester   → Ich habe eine Schwester.

If you want to say you **don't** have something, you use *keinen/keine* in the same way:

m   Ich habe kein**en** Bruder. (kein + -en)
f   Ich habe keine Schwester.
pl   Ich habe keine Geschwister.

Füll die Lücken aus.

Fill in the gaps with *eine/einen* (✓) or *keine/keinen* (✗).

Ich habe …

Beispiel: __eine__ Mutter ✓

a ▨▨▨ Schwester. ✗   d ▨▨▨ Schwester. ✓

b ▨▨▨ Bruder. ✓   e ▨▨▨ Bruder. ✗

c ▨▨▨ Geschwister. ✗

Umfrage: Hast du Geschwister?

NC 2

Do a survey: Do you have siblings?
Make notes of your classmates' answers.

Beispiel:

A *Hast du Geschwister?*
B *Ja, ich habe einen Bruder.*

> James: 1 Bruder

Ratespiel: Wer ist das?

A chooses a student from the group survey in activity 5,
B guesses who it is.

Beispiel:

A *Ich habe zwei Schwestern.*
B *Das ist Sarah!*

Füll die Lücken aus.

NC 2

Read the sentences and fill in the gaps.

 Think

What is the difference between:
Bruder and *Brüder*?
Schwester and *Schwestern*?
When would you use the second words instead of the first ones?

Hast du	Geschwister? einen Bruder? eine Schwester?
Ja, ich habe	einen Bruder. eine Schwester. zwei Brüder. zwei Schwestern.
Nein, ich habe	keinen Bruder. keine Schwester. keine Geschwister.
Nein, ich bin	Einzelkind.

Ich heiße Joe Jonas und ich bin 21 Jahre alt. Ich habe ▨▨▨ ▨▨▨ – Nick und Kevin.

Ich heiße Serena Williams. Ich bin 28 Jahre alt. Ich habe ▨▨▨ ▨▨▨ – Venus.

Ich heiße Harry Potter. Ich bin 18 Jahre alt. Ich habe ▨▨▨ ▨▨▨ – ich bin ▨▨▨.

Challenge

Write a speech bubble about yourself, or pretend you are your favourite star, and read it to the class.

NC 2

1A.3 Hast du ein Haustier?

> Vocabulary: talk about pets and colours
> Grammar: use *er/sie/es* and noun plurals correctly
> Skills: strategies for learning new words and their plurals

HÖREN 1 🎧 **Hör zu. Was passt zusammen?**
Listen and match the pictures (1–9) with the pets (a– i).

Ich habe …
Beispiel: **a 7**

a einen Hund
b einen Fisch
c einen Wellensittich
d eine Katze
e eine Maus
f eine Schildkröte
g ein Meerschweinchen
h ein Pferd
i ein Kaninchen

SPRECHEN 2 👥 **Was hast du? A ←→ B.**
What do you have? **A** says a picture number, **B** says the answer.

Beispiel: **A** *Nummer 3!*
B *Ich habe eine Katze.*

> **? Think**
> Which letter do you add to *eine* to say 'I **don't** have a cat'?

HÖREN 3 🎧 **Hör zu und lies. Farben.**
Listen and read. Colours.

 blau braun gelb grau grün orange rot schwarz weiß

HÖREN 4 🎧 **Hör zu und lies.**
Listen and read.

 a
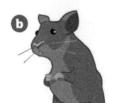 b
 c

a Das ist ein Huhn. **Es** ist gelb.
b Das ist ein Hamster. **Er** ist braun.
c Das ist eine Schlange. **Sie** ist grün.

> ⚙️ **Grammatik →** p.35
>
> Unlike in English, animals are called 'he', 'she' or 'it' depending on which gender they are.
>
> | masculine | feminine | neuter |
> |---|---|---|
> | ein Hund → **er** | eine Katze → **sie** | ein Pferd → **es** |

SCHREIBEN 5 **Schreib Sätze.**
Choose six pets from activity 1 and write sentences.
NC 2–3
Beispiel: Das ist eine Katze. Sie ist weiß und schwarz.

HÖREN 6 🎧 **Hör zu und lies.**
Listen and read.

Ich habe zwei Hunde, drei Katzen, vier Kaninchen, fünf Schildkröten, sechs Wellensittiche, sieben Hamster, acht Mäuse und neun Fische!

⚙️ **Grammatik →** p.162

German nouns form their plurals (more-than-one form) in different ways:

ein Hund → zwei Hund**e**
eine Katze → zwei Katze**n**
ein Kaninchen → zwei Kaninchen(-)
eine Maus → zwei M**ä**us**e**

Each time you learn a new noun, try to learn its plural too!

SCHREIBEN 7 **Finde die Pluralformen.**
Find the plurals for these words on the Vocabulary page or in the Glossary.

Beispiel: eine Katze – zwei Katzen

a ein Huhn
b ein Meerschweinchen
c eine Schlange
d ein Pferd

 SPRECHEN 8 👥 **Was ist die Pluralform? A ↔ B.**
A names a pet and B gives the plural.

Beispiel: **A** *ein Hund!*
           B *zwei Hunde!*

 **Challenge**

Memory game. Name as many pets as possible, first on your own, then with a partner, and then share your list with the rest of the class!

Beispiel:
A *Ich habe einen Hund …*
B *Ich habe einen Hund und eine Katze …*

NC 1–2

1A.4 Wie bist du?

> Vocabulary: describe yourself, your friends and family
> Grammar: *ich bin/du bist/er ist/sie ist* + adjectives
> Skills: learn how to pronounce the *ü* and *sch* sounds in German; work out the meaning of new words

 LESEN 1

Wie heißt das auf Englisch?

Find the English translations for the adjectives below. Do as many as you can, then use the Vocabulary page or the Glossary to help you.

Beispiel: klein – small

 ? Think

You can work some words out because they look like English words. Check the others on the Vocabulary page.

a Ich bin klein, nett und romantisch.

b Ich bin intelligent und fleißig.

c Ich bin musikalisch und laut.

d Ich bin sportlich.

e Ich bin faul und frech.

f Ich bin groß und schüchtern.

 SCHREIBEN 2

👥 Positiv oder negativ?

Are the adjectives positive or negative? Write two lists. Then compare your lists with a partner.

Beispiel: <u>positive</u>   <u>negative</u>
          nett   …

 SPRECHEN 4 · NC 2

👥 Ist alles richtig?

A chooses a person from activity 3.
B answers for him or her.

Beispiel: **A** Kathi, wie bist du?
          B Ich bin …

 HÖREN 3 · NC 2

🎧 Hör zu. Wie bist du?

Listen and write down the adjectives that apply to Kathi, Ali, Nina and Nico.

Beispiel: Kathi – groß, …

Wörter mit ü.
Listen and repeat.

Wörter mit sch.
Take it in turns to read out the *sch* phrases.

a Das ist eine Schildkröte.   c Susi Schuhmann ist schüchtern.
b Das ist eine Schlange.   d Meine Schwester ist schrecklich!

Hör zu und lies.
Listen and check your pronunciation of a–d in activity 6.

Wie bist du?
NC 1–2
What are you like? Choose three adjectives and write sentences.

Beispiel: Ich bin groß. Und ich bin ...

sehr	= ✓✓
ziemlich	= ✓
nicht	= ✗
gar nicht	= ✗✗

Hör zu und lies.
Listen and read.

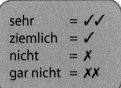
Das ist mein Freund Andi.
Er ist sehr laut – und er ist
gar nicht musikalisch ...

Das ist meine Freundin Lisa.
Sie ist nicht romantisch –
aber sie ist ziemlich sportlich!

Think

The word *und* means 'and' and is used to link words and
sentences together. Can you guess what the linking word *aber*
in activity 9 means?

Hör zu und mach Notizen. (a–d)
NC 2
What are Sven, Anne, Markus and Tanja like? Listen and make
notes (adjective + ✓✓, ✓, ✗ or ✗✗).

Beispiel: **a** *Sven   klein ✓ faul ✗✗*

Challenge
Describe your family
members to a partner.

Beispiel:
A *Wie ist deine Mutter?*
B *Sie ist sehr nett, aber ...* NC 2

Vocabulary: zoo animals

Grammar: *ich habe ein(e)(n)/kein(e)(n)* ...; *das ist ein(e)* + animal; *er/sie/es ist* + adjective

Skills: learn how to pronounce *v* and *ei*

Ni&Co

Info | Pinnwand | Fotos | +

Blog-Name:	Ni&Co
Land:	Deutschland
Alter:	14
Geburtstag:	13. September
Idol:	Isaac Boakye (Fußballer)

VIDEO 1

NC 2

Sieh dir das Video an. Richtig (✓) oder falsch (✗)?

Watch the video. Which sentences are true (✓) and which are false (✗)?

Beispiel: **a ✓**

a I'm 14 years old.
b I live in Bremen.
c I have a sister and two brothers.
d Ulli is 16 years old.
e Ulli is tall, musical and shy.
f Ralf is sporty and intelligent – and lazy.
g Britta is 19 years old.
h Britta is naughty, loud and not very nice.

2 **Wie sagt man das?**

Look at the words and try to guess how they are pronounced.

a ein Vogel   b ein Affe   c ein Bär   d ein Delfin

e ein Elefant   f eine Giraffe   g ein Löwe   h ein Nashorn

i ein Papagei   j ein Tiger

? **Think**

The sound *v* in *Vogel* is pronounced like the English *f* in 'for'.

The sound *ei* in *Papagei* is pronounced like the *y* in 'my' or *ie* in 'pie'.

3 **Was passt zusammen?**

Match the words (a–j) in activity 2 with the pictures (1–10).

Beispiel: **a 9**

4 🎧 **Hör zu (1–10). Ist alles richtig?**

Listen and check your answers – and your pronunciation!

5 🎧 **Hör zu (1–10). Wie ist er/sie/es?**

NC 1–2

Listen and look at the pictures above. Describe the animal.

Beispiel: **1** *ein Delfin – er ist sportlich.*

6 👥 **Macht Dialoge! A ↔ B.**

NC 1–2

A says a number. **B** says which animal it is and what it is like.

Beispiel: **A** *Nummer 1!*
       B *Das ist ein Delfin. Er ist sportlich!*

Challenge

Describe your pets.

Beispiel: Ich habe zwei Hunde – Benno und Snoopy. Benno ist sehr klein. Snoopy ist ziemlich frech.

NC 2

Possessive adjectives, gender and negatives

mein/meine, dein/deine

Possessive adjectives like *mein* (my) and *dein* (your) show who or what something belongs to (my dog, your brother etc.).

| Das ist **meine** Schwester. | *That is my sister.* |
| Ist das **dein** Vater? | *Is that your father?* |

They come before the noun they describe in place of *ein/eine/ein*:

	masculine (m)	feminine (f)	neuter (n)	plural (pl)
my	mein Vater	meine Katze	mein Pferd	meine Eltern
your	dein Vater	deine Katze	dein Pferd	deine Eltern

1 Fill in the gaps with the correct forms of *mein(e)* or *dein(e)*.

Beispiel: Ist das d*ein* Vater?

a Das ist m____ Mutter.

b Wie ist d____ Freund?

c Das sind m____ Großeltern.

d Ist das d____ Tante?

e Das ist m____ Hamster.

f Wie ist d____ Schwester?

2 Choose the correct form of *ein(e)(n)*.

Beispiel: Ich habe eine/*einen* Hund. (m)

a Ich habe ein/einen Wellensittich. (m)
b Ich habe ein/eine Schildkröte. (f)
c Ich habe einen/ein Meerschweinchen. (n)
d Ich habe eine/einen Fisch. (m)
e Ich habe ein/einen Hamster. (m)
f Ich habe einen/ein Kaninchen. (n)

Ich habe einen/eine/ein …

The German word for 'a' sometimes changes in a sentence – but this change only happens for masculine nouns:

m	Das ist ein Hund.	→ Ich habe einen Hund.
f	Das ist eine Katze.	→ Ich habe eine Katze.
n	Das ist ein Pferd.	→ Ich habe ein Pferd.

3 Fill in the gaps with the correct negatives.

Beispiel: Ich habe keine Katze. (f)

- **a** Ich habe _____ Maus. (f)
- **b** Ich habe _____ Hamster. (m)
- **c** Ich habe _____ Wellensittich. (m)
- **d** Ich habe _____ Huhn. (n)

Negatives (ich habe keinen/keine/kein …)
To say you don't have something, you need a negative: *kein*. This follows the same pattern as *ein*:

m ein Hund → Ich habe keinen Hund.
f eine Katze → Ich habe keine Katze.
n ein Pferd → Ich habe kein Pferd.

4 Write down *er*, *sie* or *es* for these nouns.

Beispiel: ein Hund er

- **a** eine Schildkröte
- **b** ein Meerschweinchen
- **c** ein Kaninchen
- **d** ein Wellensittich

er/sie/es
All German nouns are masculine (*Maskulinum*), feminine (*Femininum*) or neuter (*Neutrum*). This is called their gender. The words for 'he', 'she' and 'it' depend on the gender of the noun they replace:

m ein Hund → er
f eine Katze → sie
n ein Pferd → es

Using a bilingual dictionary

5 Look at extract a from a bilingual dictionary. Where does it say …

- **a** … what the gender of the noun is?
- **b** … what the plural of the noun is?

a
der **Stiefvater** (*plural* die **Stiefväter**)
stepfather

6 Now look at b. Where does it say …

- **a** … if the word is a verb?
- **b** … if the word is an adjective?

b
schön *adjective*
1 **beautiful**
2 **nice**

spielen *verb* (*perfect* **hat gespielt**)
1 **to play**
2 **to gamble**
3 **to act**

7 Use a dictionary to translate the underlined words.

- **a** *This is a polar bear.* → Das ist ein _____ .
- **b** *My brother is very thin.* → Mein Bruder ist sehr _____ .
- **c** *We have a rat as a pet.* → Wir haben eine _____ als Haustier.

Pronunciation – *ü* and *sch*

8 The German sound *ü* is called an umlaut. Listen carefully: do you hear *ü* or not? (1–8)

9 Listen. How many *sch* sounds can you hear – more than two?

Vocabulary: practise words for colours, pets and family
Grammar: revise some of the grammar of the unit
Skills: practise reading skills

1 Match the colours.

LESEN

NC 1

Beispiel: **a** 4

a braun   **d** blau
b rot   **e** gelb
c grün   **f** schwarz

2 Write out these words correctly.

NC 1

Beispiel: **a** eine *Katze*

eine AZKET   ein MTSAHRE   ein DREFP   ein HCNAKINNE   ein NUHD   ein HICFS

3 Match the pictures.

LESEN

NC 1

Beispiel: **a** 5

a Ich bin frech!
b Ich bin sportlich!
c Ich bin groß!
d Ich bin musikalisch!
e Ich bin klein!
f Ich bin faul!

4 Look at Anja's family tree and read her statements. Can you fill in the gaps?

LESEN

NC 1–2

Beispiel: Meine <u>Oma</u> heißt Ilse.

a Mein Vater heißt ▆▆▆▆.
b Meine ▆▆▆▆ heißt Susi.
c Mein Opa heißt ▆▆▆▆.
d Ich habe eine ▆▆▆▆.
e Ich habe zwei ▆▆▆▆.

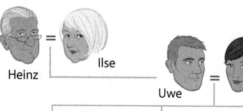

Heinz = Ilse

Uwe = Susi

Anja   Julia   Tim   Daniel

Vocabulary: practise words for family, colours and pets
Grammar: practise using *er/sie/es*, *eine(n)* and *keine(n)*
Skills: practise reading skills

Was passt zusammen?

NC 2

Beispiel: **a 3**

a   Wie heißt du?
b   Hast du Geschwister?
c   Ist das deine Tante?
d   Wie ist dein Freund?
e   Hast du ein Haustier?
f   Wie bist du?

1   Ja, ich habe einen Hund.
2   Er ist sportlich und nett.
3   Ich heiße Sascha.
4   Nein, ich bin Einzelkind.
5   Ich bin musikalisch und fleißig.
6   Nein, das ist meine Mutter.

Haustiere und Farben – schreib Sätze.

NC 2

Beispiel:  *Das ist eine Katze. Sie ist schwarz.*

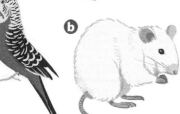

Geschwister – Ich habe eine(n)/keine(n) …

NC 2

Write sentences about siblings.

Beispiel: → *Ich habe einen Bruder.*

a   b   c   d   e

Richtig oder falsch?

NC 2

Read David's text and his statements below. Are they true or false?

a   Ich habe keine Großeltern.
b   Ich bin kein Einzelkind.
c   Ich habe drei Geschwister.
d   Ich habe ein Haustier.

Ich heiße David. Ich habe eine Oma und einen Opa. Meine Mutter heißt Katja und mein Vater heißt Jens. Ich habe auch eine Tante und einen Onkel. Ich habe zwei Brüder und eine Schwester. Und ich habe einen Wellensittich und eine Maus.

1 Listen (a–f) and match the pictures. (See pages 24–28.)

NC 1–2 *Beispiel:* **a** 4

2 Unscramble the word order in these sentences. (See pages 24–31.)

NC 1–2
a keine habe Geschwister ich.
b ist Schwester meine Tanja das.
c einen habe Bruder ich.

d ein ist Meerschweinchen das.
e Vater nett sehr ist mein.
f habe Wellensittich einen ich.

3 A asks questions a–e. B looks at the pictures and answers in full sentences. (See pages 26–31.)

NC 1–2

A	B
a Hast du Geschwister?	Ja, ich habe …
b Wie ist dein Bruder?	Er ist …
c Wie ist deine Schwester?	Sie ist …
d Hast du Haustiere?	Ja, ich habe …
e Wie ist dein Haustier?	Es ist …

4 Read the email and answer the questions. (See pages 24–31.)

NC 2

a How many grandparents does Hannah have?
b How many siblings does she have?
c What does she say her brother is like?
d How does she describe her sisters?
e What pets does she have?
f What does she say about (a) her first pet and (b) her second pet?

Hannah

Ich heiße Hannah. Ich habe keine Großeltern – leider. Ich habe einen Bruder und zwei Schwestern. Mein Bruder ist sehr frech, aber meine Schwestern sind sehr nett. Ich habe auch Haustiere – ich habe einen Hamster und eine Katze. Mein Hamster heißt Karli. Er ist sehr schüchtern. Meine Katze heißt Pauli. Sie ist weiß.

Meine Familie	*My family*
Wer ist das?	*Who's that?*
Ist das dein/e (Vater/Mutter)?	*Is that your (father/mother)?*
Sind das deine (Großeltern)?	*Are these your (grandparents)?*
Hast du Geschwister?	*Do you have siblings?*
Das ist mein/e (Bruder/ Schwester).	*This is my (brother/sister).*
Das sind (meine Brüder).	*These are (my brothers).*
Ja, ich habe (einen Bruder).	*Yes, I have (a brother).*
Nein, ich bin Einzelkind.	*No, I'm an only child.*
Er/sie heißt (Jens/Julia).	*He/she is called (Jens/Julia).*
ein Bruder(-üder)	*a brother*
ein Onkel(-)	*an uncle*
ein Opa(-s)	*a granddad*
ein Vater(-äter)	*a father*
eine Familie(-n)	*a family*
eine Mutter(-ütter)	*a mother*
eine Oma(-s)	*a grandmother*
eine Schwester(-n)	*a sister*
eine Tante(-n)	*an aunt*
Eltern	*parents*
Großeltern	*grandparents*

Haustiere	*Pets*
ein Fisch(-e)	*a fish*
ein Hamster(-)	*a hamster*
ein Huhn(-ühner)	*a chicken*
ein Hund(-e)	*a dog*
ein Kaninchen(-)	*a rabbit*
eine Katze(-n)	*a cat*
eine Maus(-äuse)	*a mouse*
ein Meerschweinchen(-)	*a guinea pig*
ein Pferd(-e)	*a horse*
eine Schildkröte(-n)	*a tortoise*
eine Schlange(-n)	*a snake*
ein Wellensittich(-e)	*a budgie*

Tiere im Zoo	*Zoo animals*
ein Affe(-n)	*a monkey*
ein Bär(-en)	*a bear*
ein Delfin(-e)	*a dolphin*
ein Elefant(-en)	*an elephant*
eine Giraffe(-n)	*a giraffe*
ein Löwe(-n)	*a lion*
ein Nashorn(-örner)	*a rhino*
ein Papagei(-en)	*a parrot*
ein Tiger(-)	*a tiger*
ein Vogel(-ögel)	*a bird*

Wie bist du?	*What are you like?*
faul	*lazy*
fleißig	*hard-working*
frech	*naughty*
groß	*tall, big*
intelligent	*intelligent*
klein	*small*
laut	*loud, noisy*
musikalisch	*musical*
nett	*nice*
romantisch	*romantic*
schüchtern	*shy*
sportlich	*sporty*
gar nicht	*not at all*
nicht	*not*
ziemlich	*quite*
sehr	*very*

Farben	*Colours*
blau	*blue*
braun	*brown*
gelb	*yellow*
grau	*grey*
grün	*green*
orange	*orange*
rot	*red*
schwarz	*black*
weiß	*white*

I can…

- ask who someone is
- say who the members of my family are
- say the words for 'my' and 'your' – *mein(e)/dein(e)*
- talk about brothers and sisters
- use *Ich habe eine(n)/keine(n) …*
- use the correct words for more than one (plurals)
- talk about pets
- say what colours pets are
- use *er/sie/es* correctly
- describe myself
- describe my friends and family

Vocabulary: say what's in your classroom and what you have in your school bag

Grammar: use *der/die/das*

Skills: use question words

LESEN 1

Was passt zusammen?

Match the words to the pictures.

Beispiel: **a 2**

a der/ein Lehrer
b der/ein Schreibtisch
c der/ein Schüler
d der/ein Stuhl
e die/eine Lehrerin
f die/eine Schülerin
g die/eine Tafel
h das/ein Klassenzimmer

①  **②**  **③**  **④**

⑤  **⑥**  **⑦**  **⑧**

HÖREN 2

 Hör zu (1–8). Ist alles richtig?

Listen and look at the pictures again. Is everything correct?

> **? Think**
>
> ein/eine/ein = *a*
> der/die/das = …?

SPRECHEN 3

 Wer/Was ist das? A ⟷ B.

Who/What is it? **A** says a picture number and **B** says what it is.

Beispiel: **A** *Nummer 1 – was ist das?*
B *Das ist die Tafel!*

> **Wer/Was ist das?**
>
> | Das ist | der Lehrer. |
> |---|---|
> | | die Tafel. |
> | | das Klassenzimmer. |

⚙ Grammatik → p.162

der/die/das

Remember that all German nouns have a gender: masculine, feminine or neuter. Just as there is more than one word for 'a' (*ein/eine/ein*), there is also more than one word for 'the':

m **der** Lehrer
f **die** Schülerin
n **das** Klassenzimmer

> **? Think**
>
> Look at the words *Wer*? (Who?) and *Was*? (What?) in activity 3. What other question words do you know? Start a list.

SCHREIBEN 4

Füll die Lücken aus.

Fill in the gaps.

a ___die___ Lehrerin b ▓▓▓ Stuhl c ▓▓▓ Schüler
d ▓▓▓ Tafel e ▓▓▓ Klassenzimmer f ▓▓▓ Schreibtisch

VIDEO 5

 **Sieh dir das Video an. Was ist die richtige Reihenfolge?**
Watch the video. What is the correct order of the school equipment?

Beispiel: *h*, ...

a einen Bleistift   **b** ein Schulbuch   **c** einen Füller

d ein Heft   **e** einen Kuli   **f** ein Lineal   **g** einen Ordner   **h** eine Schultasche   **i** einen Taschenrechner

> **Grammatik** → p.162, p.167
>
> **Ich habe einen/eine/ein ...**
> **m** ein/der Füller
> → Ich habe **einen/keinen** Füller.
> **f** eine/die Schultasche
> → Ich habe **eine/keine** Schultasche.
> **n** ein/das Lineal
> → Ich habe **ein/kein** Lineal.

SPRECHEN 6

 Was hast du? A ↔ B.
What do you have? Take it in turns to play the roles for **A** and **B**.

Beispiel: **A** *Hast du ein Lineal?*
B *Ja, ich habe ein Lineal. Hast du ...?*

LESEN 7 NC 1–2

Lies den Text. Was passt zusammen?
Read the text and find the right school bag for Ben.

1    **2**

> Ich habe ein Lineal. Ich habe einen Bleistift. Ich habe auch ein Buch und ich habe eine Federtasche. Ich habe einen Ordner. Ich habe auch ein Heft.

eine Federtasche   *a pencil case*

SCHREIBEN 8 NC 1–2

 Was hat Ben nicht?
What equipment does Ben not have? Write sentences for him using the equipment in the other picture.

Beispiel: *Ich habe keinen Füller, ...*

Challenge
Write six sentences saying which school equipment you have in your bag today and which you don't have.
Beispiel: *Ich habe ein Lineal.*
Ich habe auch ...
Ich habe keinen Kuli. NC 2

1B.2 Schulfächer

> Vocabulary: say which school subjects you have
> Grammar: use adjectives to give your opinion on school subjects
> Skills: work out the meaning of unknown words

 HÖREN 1 🎧 **Hör zu und lies.**
Listen and read.

a  Deutsch
b Englisch
c Erdkunde
d Französisch
e Geschichte
f Informatik
g Kunst

h  Latein
i Mathe
j Musik
k Religion
l Spanisch
m Sport
n Naturwissenschaften (Biologie, Chemie, Physik)

 LESEN 2 **Was passt zusammen?**
Match the English to the German words.

Beispiel: **interessant** *interesting*

Mathe/Musik ist …	
interessant	langweilig
einfach	prima
fantastisch	doof
furchtbar	schwer
gut	super

Maths/Music is …	
boring	difficult
super	interesting
stupid	great
fantastic	easy
good	awful

? Think

Work out the meaning of unknown words
Try these three steps for working out the meaning of new words.
1 Pick out any words which are similar to English.
2 Make sensible predictions for the rest.
3 Check any remaining words in the Glossary.

 HÖREN 3 🎧 **Hör noch einmal zu (a–n). Positiv (+) oder negativ (–)?**

Beispiel: **a** *Deutsch +*

 SPRECHEN 4 👥 **Partnerarbeit. A ⟷ B.**
A points to a subject in activity 1, **B** gives an opinion of it.

Beispiel: **A** **B** *Mathe ist gut!*

 HÖREN 5 🎧 **Hör zu und wiederhole: ö.**
Listen and repeat the sentence: **ö.**

HÖREN
6 🎧 **Hör zu und lies.**
Listen and read.
NC 2

> Ich finde Erdkunde sehr langweilig. Ja, Erdkunde ist schlecht! Ich mag Deutsch. Deutsch ist prima! Mein Lieblingsfach ist Mathe. Mathe ist super! Aber Sport … Sport ist furchtbar! Und ich finde Biologie nicht gut.

Kathi

Wie findest du …?
Ich finde Mathe toll/nicht toll.
Magst du Erdkunde?
Ich mag Naturwissenschaften.

Ich mag Englisch nicht.
Was ist dein Lieblingsfach?
Mein Lieblingsfach ist Deutsch.

? *Think*
- Find three new ways of saying you like a subject.
- Which words do you use to say you **don't** like a subject?

HÖREN
7 🎧 **Hör zu. Mach Notizen.**
Note whether they like the subject – and why (not).
NC 2–3

	Subject	Like (✓) Dislike (X)	Reason
a David	*history*	*X*	*boring*
b Bianca			
c Jens			
d Jana			
e Thomas			
f Suse			

SPRECHEN
8 👥 **Umfrage: Schulfächer**
Survey: find out the favourite/least favourite school subjects in your class. Look at the table for activity 7 and show your results in the same way.
NC 2–3

Beispiel: **A** *Tony, wie findest du Mathe?*
B *Ich mag Mathe nicht. Mathe ist schwer.*
A *Katy, magst du Kunst?*
D *Ja, Kunst ist mein Lieblingsfach.*

Challenge ◎ Read the text and then write three sentences for yourself – what your favourite subject is and which subjects you like and dislike. NC 2–3

> Ich finde Englisch super. Englisch ist interessant. Ich mag auch Mathe. Der Lehrer ist sehr nett. Aber ich mag Latein nicht. Latein ist schwer. Und ich finde Musik nicht gut. Ich bin nicht musikalisch. Und was ist mein Lieblingsfach? Mein Lieblingsfach ist Geschichte. Geschichte ist super!

1B.3 Wie spät ist es?

Vocabulary: tell the time; ask and say when you have different subjects
Grammar: use *wir haben*
Skills: use question words

 HÖREN 1 🎧 **Hör zu und lies.**

Wie spät ist es?

Viertel vor acht.

Es ist zehn Uhr.

Zehn Uhr? Oh nein – wir haben Mathe …

Es ist halb eins.

Super – wir haben Sport!

Wie spät ist es?
Es ist …

| neun Uhr | halb neun | Viertel **vor** neun | Viertel **nach** neun | Mittag | Mitternacht |

 HÖREN 2 🎧 **Hör zu (1–6). Was passt zusammen?**
Listen and find the correct watch (a–f) for each time.

Beispiel: **1 d**

 SPRECHEN 3 👥 **Wähle die richtige Uhrzeit. A ↔ B.**
A says the time, **B** points to the correct watch.

Beispiel: **A** *Es ist Viertel vor sechs.*
B

4 Hör zu und lies.
Listen and read.

Nico Um wie viel Uhr haben wir Informatik?
Ali Um Viertel vor neun.
Nico Und wann haben wir Erdkunde?
Ali Um elf.
Nico Und Geschichte – wann haben wir Geschichte?
Ali Um Viertel vor eins.
Nico Und um wie viel Uhr haben wir Französisch?
Ali Um halb zwei.

5 Schreib die Uhrzeiten für Nico auf.
NC 2
Write down the times for Nico's timetable above.

Beispiel: Informatik: 8.45

? Think

You know *Ich habe* … means 'I have …'
What do you think *Wir haben* … means?

6 Füll die Lücken aus.
Fill in the gaps.

Beispiel: **a** *haben*

a Wann ha▇▇ wir Mathe?
b Ich ha▇▇ Sport.
c Wann ha▇▇ du Geschichte?
d Sie ha▇▇ Erdkunde.

⚙ Grammatik → p.166

haben (*to have*)
Ich **habe** Deutsch.
Du **hast** Deutsch.
Er/sie **hat** Deutsch.
Wir **haben** Deutsch.

7 Hör zu. Richtig oder falsch?
NC 2
Listen to Kathi updating her timetable. Then read the sentences.
Are they true or false?

Beispiel: **a** *richtig*

a Mathe beginnt um 8 Uhr.
b Französisch beginnt um 9 Uhr 15.
c Deutsch beginnt um 10 Uhr 30.
d Sport beginnt um 11 Uhr.
e Geschichte beginnt um 12 Uhr 15.
f Religion beginnt um 14 Uhr 30.

Wann haben wir Mathe?
Um wie viel Uhr beginnt Kunst?
Wir haben um zehn Uhr Sport.

8 „Wann haben wir …?" A ↔ B.
NC 2
'When do we have …?' Take turns giving the times for
these school subjects.

Beispiel: **A** *Wann haben wir Englisch?*
B *Um ein Uhr.*

Challenge
Write sentences with
the information given in
activity 8.
Beispiel: **a** *Englisch beginnt*
um ein Uhr.
NC 2

a
13:00

b
11:30

c
8:15

d
10:45

e
12:30

1B.4 Mein Schultag

Vocabulary: say the days of the week; ask and say on what day you have different subjects

Grammar: write a sentence where the verb comes second

Skills: work out meaning; identify language patterns

 LESEN 1

Lies die Wörter. Wie heißen sie auf Englisch?
Read the words. What are they in English?

Beispiel: **Montag** *Monday*

 **Think**

What do you think *Tag* means? (Mon**tag**, Diens**tag**, ...)

| Montag | Dienstag | Mittwoch | Donnerstag | Freitag | Samstag | Sonntag |

 HÖREN 2

🎧 **Hör zu. Ist alles richtig?**
Listen. Is everything correct?

 HÖREN 3

🎧 **Hör zu. Was passt zusammen?**
Listen. Match the pictures (1–7) with the sentences you hear (a–g).

Beispiel: **a 6**

Think

In these sentences, what do you notice about the position of the verb *haben*?

Am Montag **habe** ich Musik.

Am Dienstag **habe** ich Erdkunde.

Grammatik → p.167–8

In German sentences, only one element can come before the verb – the verb is always the second piece of information:

1	2	3		1	2	3	4
Ich	**habe**	Deutsch.	→	Am Montag	**habe**	ich	Deutsch.

4 **Schreib neue Sätze.**
Write new sentences.

Beispiel: Ich habe Physik. (Am Dienstag) → *Am Dienstag habe ich Physik.*

a Ich habe Sport. (Am Freitag)
b Ich habe Englisch. (Am Montag)
c Ich habe Kunst. (Am Mittwoch)
d Ich habe Französisch. (Am Donnerstag)
e Ich habe Naturwissenschaften. (Am Samstag)
f Ich habe keine Schule. (Am Sonntag)

5 **Hör zu. Finde die passenden Bilder.**

NC 2

Which subjects do they have on which day? Choose the correct two pictures.

Beispiel:

a Katja	2, 5
b Markus	
c Vera	
d Thorsten	
e Anne	
f Ralf	

6 **Was hast du wann? Schreib fünf Sätze.**

NC 2

Look at your own timetable and write one sentence for each school day.

Beispiel: Am Montag habe ich Deutsch. Am Dienstag habe ich … .

7 **Gedächtnisspiel.**

NC 2

Memory game. Pick a day from your timetable and take turns adding one subject at a time.

Beispiel: **A** *Am Montag habe ich Mathe.*
B *Am Montag habe ich Mathe und Kunst.*

Challenge

Expand your sentences for activity 6 – give your opinion as well!

Beispiel: Am Montag habe ich Deutsch. Deutsch ist mein Lieblingsfach.

NC 2–3

Vocabulary: talk about school subjects and times
Grammar: use the correct word order
Skills: use context to find out the meaning of words such as *um*

Super–Nina

| Info | Pinnwand | Fotos | + |

Blog-Name: **Super-Nina**
Land: **Deutschland**
Alter: **14**
Geburtstag: **24. Mai**
Idol: **Heike Makatsch (Schauspielerin)**

VIDEO 1

NC 2–3

Sieh dir Ninas Videoblog an. Wähle die richtige Antwort.
Watch Nina's video diary. Select the correct answer for her each time.

Beispiel: a 1

a What day is it?
   1 Dienstag
   2 Donnerstag

b What time is it?
   1 acht Uhr
   2 sieben Uhr

c What is your favourite subject?
   1 Latein
   2 Italienisch

d At what time does your favourite subject start?
   1 um halb zwölf
   2 um Viertel vor neun

e What other subjects do you like?
   1 Mathe und Musik
   2 Medienwissenschaften und Turnen

f What subjects don't you like?
   1 Latein und Kochen
   2 Geschichte und Mathe

HÖREN 2
NC 2

🎧 **Hör zu (1–9). Was passt zusammen?**
Listen and find the matching pictures (a–i) and times.

Beispiel: **1** *8:00* **d**

| 8:45 | 13:00 | 10:45 | 10:00 | 9:30 | 13:45 | 8:00 | 12:15 | 11:30 |

a Italienisch **b** Sport **c** Kunst **d** Mathe **e** Pause

f Musik **g** Latein **h** Mittagspause **i** Chemie

 SPRECHEN 3
NC 2

👥 **Was haben wir? A ←→ B.**
Take turns asking questions using the timetable on the right.

Beispiel: **A** *Was haben wir um halb zehn?*
          B *Um halb zehn haben wir Pause.*

⚙ Grammatik → p.167–8

| 1 | 2 | 3 | | 1 | 2 | 3 | 4 |
| Wir | **haben** | Latein. | → | Um acht Uhr | **haben** | wir | Latein. |

 SCHREIBEN 4
NC 2

Schreib neue Sätze.
Write new sentences.

Beispiel: Wir haben Chemie. (Um Viertel nach elf)
          → *Um Viertel nach elf haben wir Chemie.*

a Wir haben Sport. (Um zehn)
b Wir haben Musik. (Um halb zwölf)
c Wir haben Italienisch. (Um ein Uhr)
d Wir haben Kunst. (Um halb elf)
e Wir haben Pause. (Um zwölf)

Am … Montag		Deutsch.
Dienstag	habe ich	Englisch.
Mittwoch	haben wir	Spanisch.
Donnerstag		
Freitag		
Um zehn Uhr		

Montag

8:00	Sport
8:45	Musik
9:30	Pause
10:00	Italienisch
10:45	Kunst
11:30	Latein
12:15	Mittagspause
13:00	Chemie
13:45	Mathe

◎ **Challenge**

Write sentences for one of
your school days.

Beispiel: *Am Mittwoch haben
wir Spanisch. Um
acht Uhr …*

NC 2–3

der/die/das, wir and word order

der/die/das
Articles (the German words for 'the' in front of a noun) have to match the gender of the noun (masculine, feminine or neuter):

m der Schüler
f die Lehrerin
n das Heft

1 Choose the correct articles.

Beispiel: der/die Tisch

a das/der Stuhl
b die/der Lehrer
c der/das Klassenzimmer
d die/das Lehrerin
e der/die Schreibtisch
f das/die Tafel

2 Find the articles for these words (der/die/das) in a dictionary.

Beispiel: Unterricht → *der* Unterricht

a Bibliothek
b Direktor
c Pause
d Schulhof
e Projekt
f Prüfung

wir
The word *wir* (we) is another small word that is used to replace a noun – and like *ich/du/er/sie/es* it has a different verb form:

ich habe	*I have*
du hast	*you have*
er/sie/es hat	*he/she/it has*
wir haben	*we have*

3 Translate the sentences into German.

Beispiel: You have art. → *Du hast Kunst.*

a You have French.
b She has English.
c We have history.
d I have music.
e He has maths.
f We have geography.

Word order

In German sentences, the verb is always the second piece of information – only one element can go in front of it:

1	2	3		1	2	3	4
Wir	**haben**	Physik.	→	Am Mittwoch	**haben**	wir	Physik.

4 Write new sentences.

Beispiel: Am Dienstag: Deutsch → *Am Dienstag haben wir Deutsch.*

a Am Montag: Sport
b Am Freitag: Informatik
c Am Donnerstag: Spanisch

d Am Mittwoch: Englisch
e Am Samstag: Kunst
f Am Dienstag: Biologie

Guessing the meaning of unknown words

Don't panic when you come across some unknown words in a text! Use these strategies to work out their meaning:

- Do they look like an English word? Then they probably mean the same.

- What do the other words in the sentence mean? You can often guess the meaning of the unknown word from the context.

- Can you recognise a part/some parts of the word? Many German words are made up of shorter words – if you know what a part of the word means you can often work out the rest.

- Are there any other clues (pictures, headings or titles)? They can also help you to work out the meaning of an unknown word.

5 What English words do the underlined ones resemble?

a Ich habe einen <u>Rucksack</u>.
b Ich spreche <u>Dänisch</u>.
c Das ist mein <u>Telefon</u>.

6 What do the underlined words mean?

a Meine Schule ist <u>groß</u>: sie hat 600 Schüler und Schülerinnen.
b Am Sonntag habe ich <u>frei</u> – ich habe keine Schule.
c Meine Federtasche ist <u>bunt</u>: grün, rot, gelb, blau, braun und orange!

7 Can you work out what each whole word means?

a ein Schulkind
b ein Musikzimmer
c eine Englischlehrerin

Pronunciation of the *ö* sound

8 Listen and note how many *ö* sounds you can hear. (1–9)

You already know that adding an umlaut to *u* makes it sound different: **u → ü**.
Adding an umlaut to *o* also changes it.

Vocabulary: know the words for school subjects, equipment and times
Grammar: use the correct word order
Skills: practise common spellings

1 **Find eight school subjects.**

Beispiel: Deutsch …

DEUTSCHMATHEINFORMATIKGESCHICHTEKUNSTENGLISCHERDKUNDEFRANZÖSISCH

2 **Fill in the gaps.**

Beispiel: **a** *ein Heft*

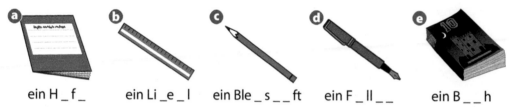

ein H _ f _   ein Li _ e _ l   ein Ble _ s _ _ ft   ein F _ ll _ _   ein B _ _ h

3 **Match each time (a–f) with a picture (1–6).**

NC 2   *Beispiel:* **a 5**

a   Es ist ein Uhr.   c   Es ist halb eins.   e   Es ist elf Uhr.
b   Es ist Viertel vor vier.   d   Es ist Viertel nach neun.   f   Es ist Viertel vor acht.

4 **Unscramble the word order in these sentences.**

NC 2   *Beispiel:* habe Am ich Deutsch Mittwoch.
           → *Am Mittwoch habe ich Deutsch.*

a   ich Montag Spanisch Am habe.   d   ich Am Geschichte Samstag habe.
b   Sport habe Am Freitag ich.   e   habe Religion Am ich Donnerstag.
c   Dienstag ich Kunst habe Am.   f   Am ich habe Informatik Mittwoch.

- Vocabulary: talk about school subjects and timetables
- Grammar: use the correct word order
- Skills: write new sentences following an example

SCHREIBEN 1

Schreib die Schulfächer auf.
Write down the school subjects.

Beispiel: Sport

 a   b  c  d   e   f

SCHREIBEN 2

NC 2

Schreib die richtige Zeit auf.
Write down the correct time.

Beispiel: *Es ist Viertel vor neun.*

 a  b  c   d  e

LESEN 3

NC 2–3

Lies. Welches Bild passt?
Read the text. Which picture (a or b) matches?

Am Montag habe ich Deutsch, Mathe und Kunst. Um acht Uhr habe ich Deutsch und um Viertel vor neun habe ich Mathe. Kunst beginnt um halb zehn. Ich mag Deutsch und Mathe, aber ich finde Kunst langweilig. Und um zehn Uhr habe ich Geschichte. Geschichte ist schwer.

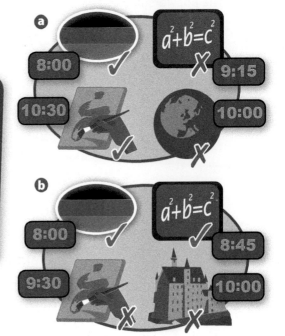

SCHREIBEN 4

NC 3

Schreib Sätze für das andere Bild.
Now write sentences for the other picture.

Beispiel: Am ... habe ich...

HÖREN 1

NC 2–3

🎧 **Listen (a–f) and match the pictures to the words. Listen again and choose ✓ or ✗ for each. (See pages 42–43 and 46–47.)**

Beispiel: a + 6 + ✗

a Montag	b Dienstag	c Mittwoch
d Donnerstag	e Freitag	f Samstag

SPRECHEN 2

NC 2

Say the following times. (See pages 44 and 45.)

Beispiel:

  Es ist acht Uhr.

LESEN 3

NC 2–3

Read Andi's message and write down the answers in English. (See pages 42–45.)

a What are the subjects he has today?
b At what times do they start?
c What is his opinion of them?

> Ich habe heute Biologie, Deutsch, Kunst, Religion und Französisch. Biologie ist um Viertel vor neun. Biologie ist mein Lieblingsfach!
>
> Deutsch beginnt um halb zehn. Aber ich finde Deutsch langweilig. Wir haben um Viertel vor elf Kunst. Ich mag Kunst – Kunst ist prima!
>
> Religion beginnt um halb zwölf. Ich finde Religion sehr interessant. Wir haben um ein Uhr Französisch. Französisch ist schwer, und die Lehrerin ist nicht nett.

SCHREIBEN 4

NC 2–3

Answer these questions for yourself. (See pages 41–49.)

a Was ist dein Lieblingsfach?
Mein Lieblingsfach ist …

b Wie findest du Englisch?
Ich finde Englisch …

c Magst du Mathe?
Ja/nein, ich mag …

d Was hast du um halb zehn?
Ich habe …

e Was hast du am Dienstag? (*name one subject*)
Am Dienstag …

f Was hast du in deiner Schultasche?
(*name two objects*) *Ich habe …*

Mein Klassenzimmer	**My classroom**
das Klassenzimmer	classroom
der Lehrer	teacher (male)
die Lehrerin	teacher (female)
der Schreibtisch	desk
der Schüler	pupil (male)
die Schülerin	pupil (female)
der Stuhl	chair
die Tafel	board, chalkboard

Schulsachen	**School equipment**
der Bleistift	pencil
die Federtasche	pencil case
der Filzstift	felt-tip pen
der Füller	fountain pen
das Heft	exercise book
der Kuli	ballpoint pen
das Lineal	ruler
der Ordner	file
der Radiergummi	eraser
das Schulbuch	school book
die Schultasche	school bag
der Taschenrechner	calculator

Schulfächer	**School subjects**
Deutsch	German
Englisch	English
Erdkunde	geography
Französisch	French
Geschichte	history
Informatik	IT
Kochen	cookery
Kunst	art
Latein	Latin
Mathe	maths
Medienwissenschaften	media studies
Musik	music
Naturwissenschaften	sciences
(Biologie, Chemie, Physik)	(biology, chemistry, physics)
Religion	religion, RE
Spanisch	Spanish
Sport	PE
Turnen	gymnastics

Meinungen	**Opinions**
Wie findest du (Mathe)?	What do you think of (maths)?
Ich finde (Mathe) toll.	I think (maths) is great.
Ich finde (Mathe) nicht toll.	I don't think (maths) is great.
Magst du (Kunst)?	Do you like (art)?
Ich mag (Kunst).	I like (art).
Ich mag (Kunst) nicht.	I don't like (art).

Was ist dein Lieblingsfach?	What's your favourite subject?
Mein Lieblingsfach ist (Sport).	My favourite subject is (sport).
einfach	easy
interessant	interesting
fantastisch	fantastic
furchtbar	awful
gut	good
langweilig	boring
prima	great
doof	stupid
schwer	difficult
super	super

Wie spät ist es?	**What time is it?**
Es ist ...	It is ...
neun Uhr	nine o'clock
halb neun	half past eight
Viertel vor neun	quarter to nine
Viertel nach neun	quarter past nine
Mittag	12 o'clock (noon)
Mitternacht	12 o'clock (midnight)

Wann haben wir Mathe?	**When do we have maths?**
Um wie viel Uhr beginnt Kunst?	At what time does art begin?
Wir haben um zehn Uhr Mathe.	We have maths at ten o'clock.
Kunst beginnt um halb zwölf.	Art begins at half past eleven.

Wochentage	**Days of the week**
Montag	Monday
Dienstag	Tuesday
Mittwoch	Wednesday
Donnerstag	Thursday
Freitag	Friday
Samstag	Saturday
Sonntag	Sunday

I can...

- say what's in my classroom and in my school bag
- use der/die/das and einen/eine/ein correctly
- say which school subjects I have
- give my opinion on my school subjects
- tell the time
- say the days of the week
- say when I have school subjects

Vocabulary: say what sports and instruments you like and don't like playing

Grammar: use *gern*; learn about verb endings

Skills: pronounce words which look alike in English and German

HÖREN 1 🎧 **Hör zu und wiederhole. (1–10)**

LESEN 2 **Lies die Sätze. Was passt zusammen?**

Match the sentences (a–h) to the pictures above (1–10).
For two sentences you will need two pictures.

Beispiel: **a 4**

a Ich spiele gern am Computer.
b Ich spiele nicht gern Klavier.
c Ich spiele gern Fußball.
d Ich spiele gern Geige.
e Ich spiele gern Flöte.
f Ich spiele nicht gern Gitarre.
g Ich spiele nicht gern Federball, aber ich spiele gern Schlagzeug.
h Ich spiele nicht gern Tennis und ich spiele nicht gern Basketball.

SPRECHEN 3 **Macht Dialoge. A ⟷ B.**

NC 2

Discuss whether you like doing the activities above.

Beispiel:

A *Spielst du gern (am Computer)?*
B *Ja, ich spiele gern (am Computer).*
A *Spielst du gern (Klavier)?*
B *Nein, ich spiele nicht gern (Klavier).*

? Think

In activity 2 (a–h), which sports and musical instruments look the same as or similar to English words? Do you pronounce them in the same way?

⚙ Grammatik → p.167

gern/nicht gern

Use *gern* or *nicht gern* with a verb to say what you like or don't like to do. The words *gern/nicht gern* come after the verb:

Ich spiele **gern** Tennis.
I like playing tennis.
Ich spiele **nicht gern** Basketball.
I don't like playing basketball.

LESEN 4

NC 2–3

Lies den Text. Finde die passenden Bilder.

What do they all do? Find the matching pictures for Ulrike, Achim, Diane and their parents.

Beispiel: Ulrike 3

Ich heiße Ulrike. Ich wohne in München. Ich spiele gern Volleyball. Ich spiele auch Basketball. Ich bin sehr sportlich.

Ich habe einen Bruder. Er heißt Achim. Er spielt nicht gern Volleyball, aber er spielt gern Fußball, Gitarre und Schlagzeug. Er ist in einer Band und sehr musikalisch. Ich habe auch eine Schwester. Sie heißt Diane. Sie spielt gern am Computer. Sie ist ziemlich faul. Und meine Eltern? Sie spielen oft Tennis.

Und du? Spielst du Volleyball oder ein Instrument?

1   **2** 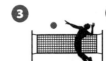 **3**   **4**   **5**   **6**   **7**

SCHREIBEN 5

Füll die Lücken aus.

Look at the grammar box and fill in the gaps.

All forms of the verb ___spielen___ have the same stem. The stem of regular verbs is formed by taking the infinitive form (*spielen*) and removing the *-en* ending (*spiel~~en~~*). The following endings are then added to the stem: *ich* ▨▨▨; *du* ▨▨▨; *er/sie/es* ▨▨▨. The ▨▨▨, ▨▨▨ and ▨▨▨ forms are the same. They end in ▨▨▨. The *ihr* form ends in ▨▨▨.

Grammatik → p.165

spielen (*to play*)
ich spiel**e** *I play*
du spiel**st** *you play (singular)*
er/sie/es spiel**t** *he/she/it plays*
wir spiel**en** *we play*
ihr spiel**t** *you play (plural, when talking to more than one)*
sie spiel**en** *they play*
Sie spiel**en** *you play (formal)*

SCHREIBEN 6

Schreib Sätze mit *spielen*.

Write sentences using the verb *spielen*.

Beispiel: **a** *Ich spiele gern/nicht gern Gitarre.*

a Ich

b Du

c Er

d Wir

e Ihr

f Sie (they)

Challenge

Write five sentences about what you and your friends and family like and don't like doing. Use *spielen* in each sentence. Use a dictionary to find the words for other sports and musical instruments.

NC 3

Vocabulary: say what your favourite hobbies are

Grammar: talk about your favourite activities using *lieber* and *am liebsten*; use some irregular verbs

Skills: listen for intonation

🎧 **Was passt zusammen? Hör zu. Ist alles richtig?**

Match the sentences (1–9) with the pictures (a–i). Then listen to check.

Beispiel: **a 5**

1 Ich besuche gern meine Freunde.   2 Ich chatte gern im Internet.   3 Ich sehe gern fern.
4 Ich gehe gern ins Kino.   5 Ich fahre gern Skateboard.   6 Ich lese gern.
7 Ich gehe gern einkaufen.   8 Ich fahre gern Rad.   9 Ich höre gern Musik.

Welches Hobby ist das?

Look at the pictures in activity 1 and note what each person below likes to do, prefers, and what their favourite activity is.

Beispiel: *Richard – likes* **h**

❤ gern
❤❤ lieber
❤❤❤ am liebsten

Richard: Ich fahre gern Rad, aber ich chatte lieber im Internet. Ich fahre am liebsten Skateboard!

Alenka: Ich höre gern Musik, aber ich lese lieber. Mein Bruder und ich sehen am liebsten fern!

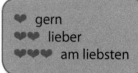

Hannes: Ich gehe am liebsten ins Kino! Ich gehe auch gern einkaufen – aber ich besuche lieber meine Freunde.

VIDEO 3

NC 3–4

Sieh dir Alis Videoblog an. Füll die Tabelle aus.

gern ♡	lieber ♡♡	am liebsten ♡♡♡
reading		

Ich	spiele		Fußball/Gitarre/Rugby/ am Computer.
	fahre	gern	Skateboard/Rad.
	sehe	lieber	fern.
	gehe	am liebsten	ins Kino.

SCHREIBEN 4

NC 2–3

Schreib Sätze für die Bilder.
Write a sentence for each picture.

Beispiel: **a** *Sie spielt gern Fußball.*

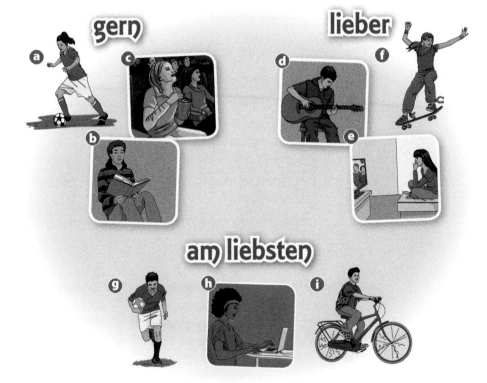

gern

lieber

am liebsten

SPRECHEN 5

NC 2–3

Macht eine Umfrage.
Carry out a survey of six people in your class.

Beispiel:

Was machst du gern? *Ich (sehe gern fern).*
Was machst du lieber? *Ich (gehe lieber ins Kino).*
Was machst du am liebsten? *Ich (fahre am liebsten Skateboard).*

 Think

Can you tell from someone's voice whether they are happy or unhappy? In Ali's video blog, what else helps you to work out what he is talking about?

 Grammatik → p.165

Some verbs are irregular. They change some letters in the *du* and *er/sie/es* forms:

fahren
 to go/travel
ich fahre
du f**ä**hrst
er/sie/es f**ä**hrt

sehen
 to see
ich sehe
du s**ie**hst
er/sie/es s**ie**ht

lesen
 to read
ich lese
du l**ie**st
er/sie/es l**ie**st

Challenge

Write sentences about what you and other people like doing, using *gern*, *lieber* and *am liebsten*.

Beispiel: Ich … gern, aber ich … lieber …
Anna … gern, …

NC 3

2A.3 Ich liebe Computerspiele

Vocabulary: give opinions of different types of computer games
Grammar: use *sie* to say 'them'; use *denn*
Skills: use words you know to work out the meaning of new words

SCHREIBEN 1

Was ist das?

Fill in the types of games from the box on the right.

Beispiel: **a** *das Quizspiel*

das **Lern**spiel	das **Abenteuer**spiel
das **Musik**spiel	das **Sport**spiel
das **Quiz**spiel	das **Tanz**spiel

a

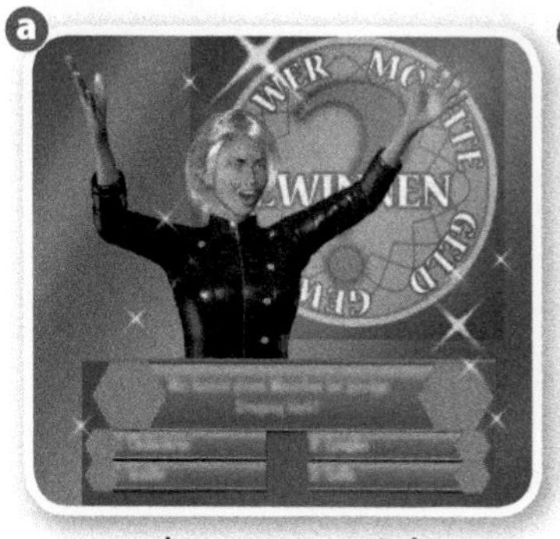

das ______spiel

b

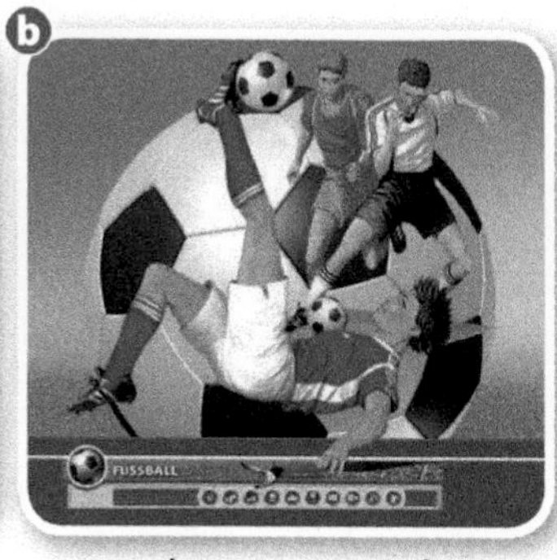

das ______spiel

c

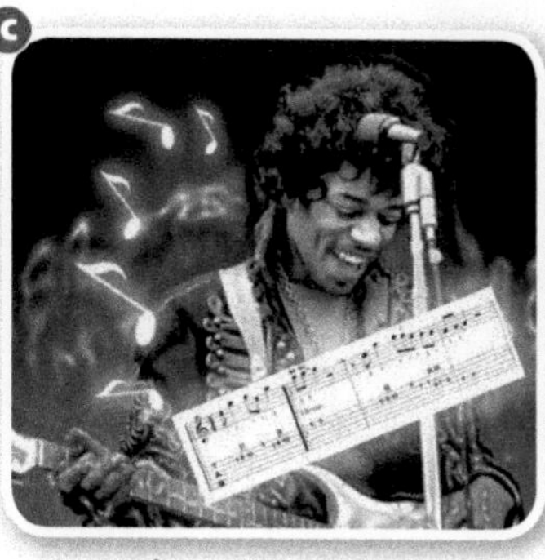

das ______spiel

d

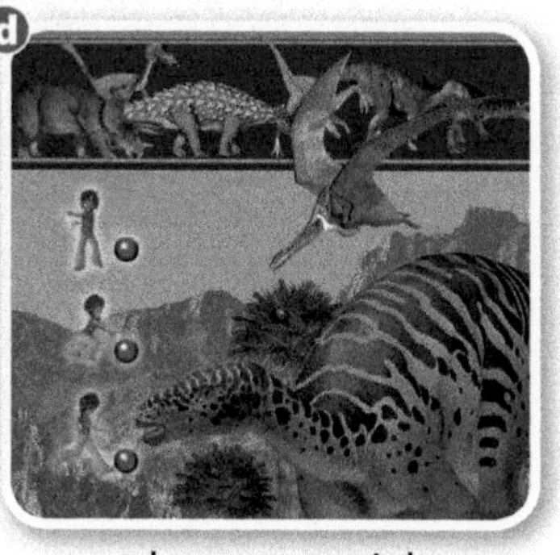

das ______spiel

e

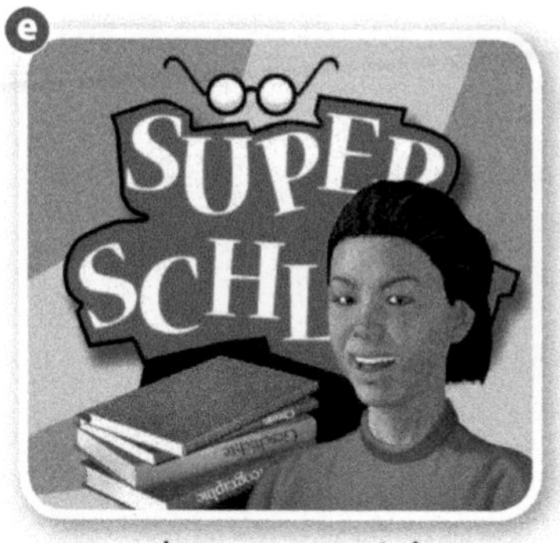

das ______spiel

f

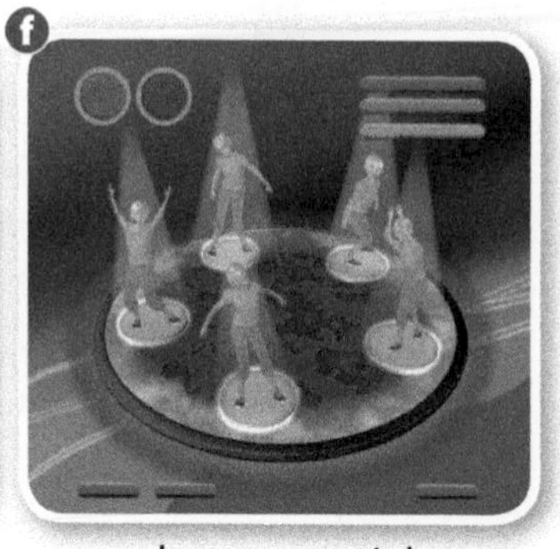

das ______spiel

? Think

Many words in German are made by putting two words together:
Sport + Spiel = das Sportspiel (sports game).
If *Tanzspiel* means 'dance game', what does *tanzen* mean?

HÖREN 2

Hör zu (a–f). Ist alles richtig?

Listen to check your answers.

LESEN 3

Lies und beantworte die Fragen.

NC 2–3

Read the speech bubbles and answer the questions.

Who …

- **a** finds music games funny?
- **b** finds quiz games awful?
- **c** likes dance games because they are great?
- **d** likes sports games because they are exciting?
- **e** finds educational games useful?
- **f** finds adventure games cool?

Mareike: Ich finde Quizspiele schrecklich.

Meltem: Ich mag Sportspiele. Sie sind spannend.

Birte: Ich mag Musikspiele, denn sie sind lustig.

Rainer: Ich finde Abenteuerspiele cool.

Barbara: Ich finde Lernspiele nützlich.

Werner: Ich mag Tanzspiele, denn sie sind klasse.

Schreib eine Liste.
Make a list of the adjectives from activity 3 in German and English.
Look them up in the Glossary if you don't know what they mean.

Beispiel: schrecklich *awful*

Hör zu (1–6). Welches Spiel ist das?
Which games do these six young people mention?
Do they like (✓) or dislike (✗) them?

NC 3

Beispiel: **1** *quiz games* ✓

> Wie findest du **Quizspiele**? *How do you find **quiz games**?*
> Ich mag **sie** nicht, **denn** ich finde **sie** langweilig.
> *I don't like **them**, **because** I find **them** boring.*

Schreib die Wörter richtig auf.
Write the words correctly, putting the letters in the right order.

a Ich mag SRPOETESPIL, denn sie sind ASDNPNEN.
b Ich finde LLENSRIPEE GTU.
c Ich finde QIIPZSUELE SPURE.
d Ich mag MSIEPKSIUEL nicht, denn sie sind CRHCEKLISCH.
e Ich finde ATBENUELRSPIEEE LTUSGI.
f Ich mag ANZITSLPEE sehr gern, denn sie sind KEASLS.

Wie findest du Computerspiele? A ←→ B.
What do you think of computer games? Try to give a reason for your opinion, using *denn*.

NC 2–3

Beispiel: **A** Wie findest du Quizspiele?
　　　　　　B Ich finde Quizspiele nicht gut, denn sie sind langweilig.
　　　　　　　　 Wie findest du Quizspiele?

Magst du (Lernspiele)? Wie findest du (Abenteuerspiele)?		
Ich mag	Lernspiele Tanzspiele Musikspiele Sportspiele Quizspiele Abenteuerspiele	(nicht).
Ich finde sie	gut, … sehr gut, … nicht gut, …	
denn sie sind	lustig. spannend. langweilig. schrecklich.	
(Lernspiele) sind (klasse). (Abenteuerspiele) sind (cool).		

Challenge
Write five sentences saying which video and computer games you like and don't like, and give reasons.

NC 3

Vocabulary: say how often you do something
Grammar: use the correct word order with expressions of time
Skills: use previously learned language to create new expressions

HÖREN 1

Hör zu (1–6). Was passt zusammen?
Listen and match the sentences you hear (1–6) with the pictures (a–f).

Beispiel: **1 c**

Ich spiele einmal in der Woche Gitarre.

Ich schwimme am Montag.

Ich sehe am Abend fern.

Ich spiele jeden Tag am Computer.

Ich gehe am Wochenende ins Kino.

Ich gehe am Nachmittag ins Café.

LESEN 2

Wie sagt man ...?
Find these expressions in activity 1.

a   on Monday   b   at the weekend   c   in the afternoon
d   once a week   e   in the evening   f   every day

? Think

Extend your vocabulary by combining words you already know with new ones. If *am Donnerstag* means 'on Thursday', how would you say 'on Friday'? How would you say 'three times a week'?

HÖREN 3

Hör zu und füll die Lücken aus. (a–f)
Listen and fill in the gaps.

Beispiel: **a** *jeden Tag*

a   Ich spiele ▨▨▨ Fußball.   d   Sie fährt ▨▨▨ Skateboard.
b   Ich schwimme ▨▨▨ .   e   Wir hören ▨▨▨ Musik.
c   Er geht ▨▨▨ ins Kino.   f   Sie sehen ▨▨▨ fern.

LESEN 4

Lies die Wörterschlange.
How many new expressions of time and frequency can you find in this word snake? What do they mean?

jedesJahramMorgenjedenMonatamDonnerstagjedeWochezweimalinderWoche

SPRECHEN
5
NC 2

👥 **A sagt einen Buchstaben und eine Zahl. B sagt die passenden Sätze. A ↔ B.**
A says a letter and a number. **B** says the matching sentences.

Beispiel: **A** b und drei.
B Ich schwimme jeden Tag.

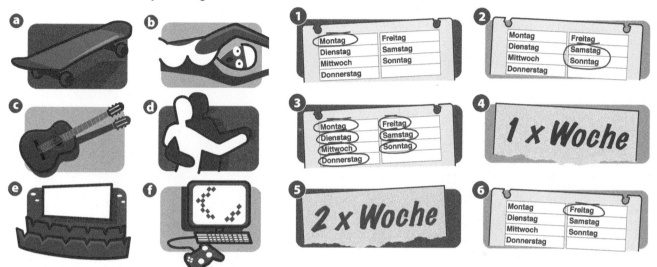

SCHREIBEN
6
NC 2–3

Schreib Sätze.
Use your answers from activity 5 to write six different sentences. Use each of the activities and expressions of time once.

Beispiel: **e+6** Ich gehe am Freitag ins Kino.

VIDEO
7
NC 3–4

🎥 **Sieh dir das Video an. Beantworte die Fragen.**
Watch the video and answer the questions.

a What excuses does Ali have for not meeting Nina on Monday, Tuesday, Wednesday and Friday?
b What hobby do Nina and Ali have in common?

Ich spiele Er/sie spielt	am Montag/Dienstag/…	Gitarre/Fußball/ am Computer.
Ich gehe Er/sie geht	am Morgen/Nachmittag/Abend am Wochenende	ins Kino.
Ich fahre Er/sie fährt	einmal/zweimal in der Woche jeden Tag	Skateboard.
Ich sehe Er/sie sieht		fern.
Ich schwimme Er/sie schwimmt	am Montag/… am Wochenende	
Ich tanze Er/sie tanzt	am Morgen/… einmal/zweimal in der Woche jeden Tag	

Challenge

Imagine you've been asked to the cinema but you don't want to go. Write five excuses, saying what you're doing each day. Add details of how often you do each activity.

Beispiel: Ich spiele am Montag Fußball …

NC 3

2A.5 ⟫⟫ Am Wochenende ⟫⟫

Vocabulary: talk about leisure activities
Grammar: use expressions of time; use irregular verbs
Skills: pronounce *a* and *ä* correctly

Chatpartner gesucht!

  Kathi ist freundlich und besucht oft ihre Freunde. Sie fährt gern Rad, aber sie geht lieber einkaufen.

  Nina sieht gern jeden Abend fern, aber sie hört lieber Musik. Sie geht am liebsten aus, zum Beispiel in Cafés.

  Nico ist sehr sportlich. Er fährt gern Rad, aber er fährt lieber Skateboard. Am liebsten spielt Nico Fußball in einer Mannschaft. Er spielt am Wochenende.

  Ali ist ein Allrounder. Er liebt Mathe. Er spielt gern Sudoku und er liest am liebsten Bücher.

 LESEN 1

Lies den Text.
Read the text and find examples of irregular verbs.

Beispiel: fährt

 SCHREIBEN 2

Lies den Text oben noch einmal. Füll die Lücken aus.
Read the text above again and fill in the gaps.

Beispiel: **a** *fährt*

a Kathi f■hrt gern Rad.
b Nina hör■ gern Musik.
c Nina s■ht gern fern.
d Nico ■■■■ gern Skateboard.
e Ali ■■■■ gern Bücher.

 Grammatik → p.165

Remember that some verbs are irregular and change some letters in the *du* and *er/sie/es* forms:
ich fahre → du fährst, er/sie fährt
See page 59 for a reminder.

? **Think**

Can you remember how to pronounce the *ahr* sound in *fahre*, and *ähr* in *fährst* and *fährt*? The *ahr* sound is a bit like the English word 'are', but *ähr* sounds more like 'air'.

Montag	Dienstag	Mittwoch	Donnerstag	Freitag	Samstag	Sonntag

3

NC 2–3

Sieh dir Sabines Kalender an. Schreib Sätze.

Look at Sabine's diary above. Write sentences to say what she does each day. Make up an activity for Sunday!

Beispiel: *Sabine spielt am Montag Fußball.*
Sie ▒▒▒▒ *am Dienstag* ▒▒▒▒ .

4

NC 2–3

 Macht eine Umfrage in der Klasse.

Do a survey in your class.

Welchen Sport...	magst du und warum?	magst du nicht und warum?	machst du?	siehst du dir im Fernsehen an?
1	*Fußball*			
2				
3				

Ich mag	Tennis/Basketball/Fußball/...		(nicht)
..., denn ich finde	(Tennis)	(nicht) gut/langweilig/anstrengend. spannend/klasse/toll.	
Ich spiele	gern nicht gern	Tennis/Basketball/...	
Ich fahre		Ski/Rad/Skateboard/...	
Ich sehe mir		Fußball/Volleyball/Rugby/...	im Fernsehen an.
Ich schwimme Ich tanze	gern. nicht gern.		
Ich mache das	einmal/zweimal in der Woche		
Ich sehe mir das	jeden Tag/am Wochenende/am Abend/...		im Fernsehen an.

5

Vergleicht eure Antworten.

In a group, compare your survey answers. How often do you do each activity?

Beispiel: **A**   *Wie oft machst du das?*
B   *Ich mache das ...*

Challenge

Write an internet profile like on page 64, describing your hobbies. Use the correct verb endings and vowel changes for irregular verbs.

Beispiel: Katrina hört gern Musik, aber sie chattet lieber im Internet ...

NC 3–4

Regular and irregular endings for verbs, word order

1 Match the German and the English.

Beispiel: ich – I

ich
du
er/sie/es
wir
ihr
sie
Sie

we
they
you (formal)
you (plural)
he/she/it
you (singular)
I

ich spiele, du spielst
Verbs in German have different endings depending on the person they refer to. Make sure you learn these endings as you will have to use them all the time. Try to pronounce them clearly, including the final 'e'.

ich spiel**e** *I play*
du spiel**st** *you play (singular)*
er/sie/es spiel**t** *he/she/it plays*

wir spiel**en** *we play*
ihr spiel**t** *you play (plural, when talking to more than one)*
sie spiel**en** *they play*
Sie spiel**en** *you play (formal)*

2 Choose the correct form of the verb *spielen*.

Beispiel: a spiele

a Ich spiele/spielt gern Musik.
b Er spielt/spielen lieber Tennis.
c Sie (*they*) spielen/spielst am liebsten mit Freunden Fußball.
d Spiele/Spielst du lieber Karten oder Schach?
e Spiele/Spielt ihr am Wochenende mit der Band?
f Sie (*she*) spielt/spielst oft am Computer.

ich fahre, du fährst
Some verbs in German are irregular. Their spellings change for the *du* and *er/sie/es* forms. You must learn them as they are used very often.

ich fahre	ich sehe	ich lese
du f**ä**hrst	du s**ie**hst	du l**ie**st
er/sie/es f**ä**hrt	er/sie/es s**ie**ht	er/sie/es l**ie**st

3 Fill in the missing letters in these verb forms.

Beispiel: a sieht

a Sie si_ht am Wochenende acht Stunden lang fern.
b Katrin l_est jede Woche ein Buch.
c Ich f_hre gern im Park Rad.
d Boris f_hrt lieber Skateboard.
e Wir l_sen oft Bücher.
f Lisa, s_ _hst du gern fern?

4 Read the captions for pictures a and b. Put the words in the right order.

Beispiel: a Er ...

a spielt liebsten Schlagzeug am Er.

b Skateboard gern Sie fahren. fährt lieber Rad Er.

Keeping a record of new language

5 **Put these words into positive (+) or negative (-) columns.**

Beispiel:

+	–
toll	nicht gut

toll   nicht gut   langweilig   schlecht   gern

nicht gern   mag   mag nicht   spannend

furchtbar   lustig

6 **Find other adjectives from this unit and add them to your list.**

 Think

Put adjectives into positive and negative categories when you learn them – this will help you to remember what they mean.

Try to match different activities to each word on your list. This will help you to remember them together.

langweilig – Fußball, Quizspiele

spannend – ins Kino gehen,
Skateboard fahren

Pronouncing words which look like English words

Many words in German look like English words and have the same meaning. But watch out – they need to be pronounced differently. Here are some tips to help you pronounce words accurately:

- always sound the letter *e* at the end of a word, e.g. *ich chatte*
- make sure you pronounce all vowel sounds correctly:
  - the letter *a* is a short sound in German, as in *Handball*
  - *u* sounds like *oo*, as in *Fußball*
  - *i* is a long sound, as in *Musik*
- remember that *z* sounds like *tz*, as in *tanzen*
- remember that *sch* is pronounced like *sh* in English, as in *Schule*.

7 **Listen to these words and note the difference between the English and German pronunciation.**

a Basketball
b Sofa
c Auto
d Musik
e Radio
f Handball
g Magazin
h Station
i Butter
j Marmelade

8 **First try to pronounce the following words. Then listen to check.**

a Flöte
b Gitarre
c Supermarkt
d Lampe
e Mathematik
f Jacke
g Englisch
h Banane
i CD-Spieler
j Joghurt

Vocabulary: practise words for hobbies
Grammar: practise using *gern, lieber, am liebsten*
Skills: read for gist and detail

 SCHREIBEN 1 **Fill in the missing letters.**

a Fu_ball   c Vol_e_ball   e Kla_ier

b Gei_e   d Gita_re

 LESEN 2 **Match the sentences with the pictures.**

NC 1–2 *Beispiel:* **a 2**

a Ich spiele gern Schlagzeug.
b Ich spiele nicht gern am Computer.
c Ich spiele nicht gern Tennis.
d Ich spiele gern Rugby.
e Ich spiele nicht gern Flöte.
f Ich spiele nicht gern Federball.

 LESEN 3 **Mark each sentence in activity 2 with + or – to show whether it is positive or negative.**

NC 1–2

Beispiel: **a +**

LESEN 4 **Match the sentence halves.**

NC 1–2 *Beispiel:* **a 4**

a Ich sehe gern …
b Ich chatte …
c Ich finde Sportspiele …
d Ich spiele …
e Ich gehe oft …

1 … mit Freunden.
2 … Klavier.
3 … einkaufen.
4 … fern.
5 … toll.

 SCHREIBEN 5 **Write a sentence for each picture, using the jumbled-up phrases in the box.**

NC 2

Beispiel: **a** *Ich chatte gern mit Freunden.*

♥ gern
♥♥ lieber
♥♥♥ am liebsten

- Skateboard am ich liebsten fahre
- spiele ich Gitarre lieber
- gern ich Freunden mit chatte
- am ich Fußball liebsten spiele
- gehe ich einkaufen gern
- ich lieber lese

Vocabulary: talk about hobbies
Grammar: use *denn*; use correct word order with time expressions
Skills: build longer sentences

 SCHREIBEN 1

NC 3

Schreib Sätze für die Bilder.

Write a sentence for each picture. Use *denn* to add a reason for each opinion.

Beispiel: **a** *Ich spiele gern Fußball, aber ich spiele lieber Rugby, denn es ist toll.*

a aber  toll

d anstrengend, aber klasse

b langweilig

e gut, aber interessant

c  super, aber schwierig

f interessant, aber  toll

 LESEN 2

NC 3–4

Lies den Text. Richtig oder falsch?

Read the text. Are the sentences true or false?

Beispiel: **a** *Richtig*

a Svenja lives in Austria.
b Svenja does not cycle.
c Svenja likes skiing more than cycling.

d Svenja goes swimming with her parents and her brother.
e Svenja goes to the cinema on her own.
f Svenja likes computer games.

Ich heiße Svenja und ich wohne in Wien. Wien ist in Österreich.
Ich fahre gern Rad. Das ist lustig. Im Winter fahre ich Ski.
Ich fahre gern Rad, aber ich fahre lieber Ski.
Im Sommer gehen meine Eltern, mein Bruder und ich schwimmen.
Mein Bruder und ich gehen gern am Wochenende ins Kino.
Meine Freunde mögen Computerspiele, aber ich spiele nicht gern am Computer, denn es ist langweilig.
Und du? Was machst du?

 SCHREIBEN 3

NC 3–4

Wie oft machst du das? Wie findest du es, und warum?

Choose six activities pictured on pages 68 and 69. Write a sentence for each activity, saying how often you do it. Then add your opinion, using *denn*. (If you can't see six activities that you do, use your own ideas!)

Beispiel: *Ich schwimme zweimal in der Woche.*
Ich finde das toll, denn ich bin sehr sportlich.

HÖREN 1 NC 3

🎧 **Listen to Samira. Copy and complete the grid with the information you hear. (See pages 56–65.)**

	Activity	When	Opinion
Samira	*plays volleyball*	*at the weekend*	
Samira's brother			*great*
Samira's mother			*interesting*
Samira's father	*sees movies*		

LESEN 2 NC 3

Read Bernhard's email and answer the questions below in English. (See pages 56–65.)

Hallo, ich heiße Bernhard. Ich wohne in Salzburg in Österreich. Salzburg ist super.

Ich fahre oft Rad mit meinen Freunden. Ich mache das sehr gern, denn ich finde Radfahren toll.

Mein Bruder fährt nicht gern Rad, denn er findet das total langweilig. Er fährt am Dienstag, Donnerstag und Samstag Skateboard.

Im Winter fahre ich Ski. Ich schwimme auch fünfmal in der Woche. Das ist viel, aber ich finde es gut.

Beispiel: **a** cycling

- **a** What does Bernhard do with his friends?
- **b** What does he think about it?
- **c** What does his brother think about this activity?
- **d** What does his brother do three times a week?
- **e** What does Bernhard do in winter?
- **f** How often does he go swimming?
- **g** How does he find it?

SPRECHEN 3 NC 3

👥 **Discuss your hobbies with a partner. (See pages 56–65.)**

a Was machst du in deiner Freizeit?
  Ich (spiele) gern ...
  Ich (schwimme) gern.

b Wann machst du das?
  Ich mache das ...

c Wie findest du das?
  Ich finde das ...

d Was machst du nicht gern?
  Ich (spiele) nicht gern (Rugby).

Mark, 14

SCHREIBEN 4 NC 3

Look at the picture and imagine you are Mark. Write a few sentences saying what you do in your spare time. (See pages 56–65.)

Ich spiele (nicht) gern …	I (don't) like playing …
Spielst du gern …?	Do you like playing …?
Basketball	basketball
Federball	badminton
Fußball	football
Rugby	rugby
Tennis	tennis
Volleyball	volleyball
Flöte	flute
Geige	violin
Gitarre	guitar
Klavier	piano
Schlagzeug	drums
am Computer	on the computer
in einer Band	in a band
Karten	cards
Schach	chess

Das mache ich am liebsten	That's what I like doing most of all
Ich besuche gern meine Freunde.	I like visiting my friends.
Ich chatte gern im Internet.	I like chatting on the internet.
Ich sehe gern fern.	I like watching TV.
Ich gehe gern ins Kino.	I like going to the cinema.
Ich gehe gern ins Café.	I like going to the café.
Ich gehe gern einkaufen.	I like going shopping.
Ich fahre gern Rad.	I like cycling.
Ich fahre gern Skateboard.	I like skateboarding.
Ich fahre gern Ski.	I like skiing.
Ich höre gern Musik.	I like listening to music.
Ich lese gern.	I like reading.
Ich tanze gern.	I like dancing.
Ich schwimme gern.	I like swimming.
Ich sehe lieber fern.	I prefer watching TV.
Ich spiele am liebsten Rugby.	Most of all I like playing rugby.
Ich sehe mir gern (Rugby) im Fernsehen an.	I like watching (rugby) on TV.

Ich liebe Computerspiele	I love computer games
das Abenteuerspiel	adventure game
das Lernspiel	educational game
das Musikspiel	music game
das Quizspiel	quiz game
das Sportspiel	sports game
das Tanzspiel	dance game
Magst du (Sportspiele)?	Do you like (sports games)?
Wie findest du (Quizspiele)?	How do you find (quiz games)?
Ich mag … (nicht).	I (don't) like …
…, denn ich finde sie …	…, because I find them …

anstrengend	tiring, strenuous
cool	cool
klasse	great
interessant	interesting
langweilig	boring
lustig	funny
nützlich	useful
schrecklich	awful, terrible
schwierig	difficult
spannend	exciting
toll	great

Wie oft machst du das?	How often do you do that?
am Montag, Dienstag, …	on Monday, Tuesday, …
am Wochenende	at the weekend
am Morgen	in the morning
am Nachmittag	in the afternoon
am Abend	in the evening
jeden Tag	every day
jeden Monat	every month
jede Woche	every week
jedes Jahr	every year
einmal/zweimal/dreimal in der Woche	once/twice/three times a week
Ich höre jeden Tag Musik.	I listen to music every day.

I can…

- say what sports and instruments I like and don't like playing
- talk about my favourite hobbies using *gern*, *lieber, am liebsten*
- use some regular and irregular verbs
- give opinions of computer games
- use *sie* to mean 'them'
- use *denn*.
- say how often I do something
- use the correct word order with expressions of time
- pronounce words which look alike in English and German

Vocabulary: say where you live and whether you like it; say what the weather is like in your region

Grammar: use adjectives to describe the weather

Skills: learn how to pronounce the *ch* sound

🎧 **Hör zu (1–4). Wer spricht?**

Listen. Who's speaking? Write down the names in the order you hear them.

Beispiel: Lukas, …

Anne

Ich komme aus Österreich. Ich wohne in Wien. Das ist im Osten.

Lukas

Ich komme aus Deutschland. Ich wohne in Köln. Das ist im Westen.

Bremen

Berlin

Köln

Dresden

München

Zürich

Wien

Bern

Salzburg

Genf

Suse

Ich komme aus der Schweiz. Ich wohne in Zürich. Das ist im Norden. Es gefällt mir nicht.

Markus

Ich komme aus Deutschland. Ich wohne in München. Das ist im Süden. Es gefällt mir gut.

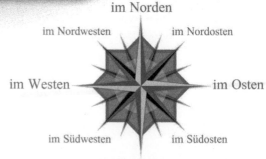

im Norden

im Nordwesten   im Nordosten

im Westen   im Osten

im Südwesten   im Südosten

im Süden

👥 **Ratespiel! Wo wohnst du? A ↔ B.**

NC 2

Look again at the map. **A** says where he or she comes from and **B** guesses which town it is.

Beispiel: **A** *Ich komme aus Deutschland. Ich wohne im Norden.*
B   *Du wohnst in Bremen!*

Wo wohnst du? Schreib Sätze.

NC 2–3

Write a speech bubble for yourself or your favourite celebrity.

Beispiel: *Ich heiße Monica Miller und ich komme aus England. Ich wohne in Manchester. Das ist im Norden. Es gefällt mir gut.*

 **Think**

In German, *ch* is pronounced like in the Scottish word *loch*.

LESEN 4

Was passt zusammen?
Match the sentences (a–l) with the pictures (1–12).

Beispiel: **a 2**

Wie ist das Wetter?

a Es ist sonnig. **b** Es ist kalt. **c** Es ist heiß. **d** Es ist neblig. **e** Es ist windig. **f** Es ist wolkig.
g Es ist schön. **h** Es ist warm. **i** Es regnet. **j** Es schneit. **k** Es gewittert. **l** Es friert.

HÖREN 5

 🎧 **Hör zu (1–12). Ist alles richtig?**
Look again at the pictures in activity 4. Listen and check.

SCHREIBEN 6

NC 2

Schreib Sätze.
What is the weather like in …? Look at the weather map and write a report.

Beispiel: *In Hamburg: Es regnet.*
Im Westen: Es …

SPRECHEN 7

NC 2

 👥 **Gedächtnisspiel! A ↔ B.**
Memory game. Take turns adding another weather condition.

Beispiel: **A** *Es ist warm.*
B *Es ist warm und windig.*
A *Es ist warm, windig und es regnet.*

SCHREIBEN 8

NC 2–3

Schreib Sätze.
What's the weather like in your area today? Do you like it?
Write a few sentences.

Beispiel: *Es ist schön und es regnet nicht. Es gefällt mir gut.*

> Ich komme aus (Deutschland). Ich wohne in (Bremen).
> Wo ist das? Das ist im (Norden).
> Gefällt es dir?
> Ja, es gefällt mir gut./Nein, es gefällt mir nicht.

Challenge

Look at the map of Europe on page 14 and choose a country. Now write a weather report for 'your' country for a blog, including whether or not you like it.

Beispiel: *Ich heiße Ryan und ich wohne in Barcelona in Spanien. Das ist im Nordosten. Wie ist das Wetter in Barcelona? Es ist sehr heiß und …*

NC 3

2B.2 Hier wohne ich

Vocabulary: describe your house or flat and where you live
Grammar: use adjectives to describe where you live;
use *Ich wohne in* ... correctly
Skills: adapt language you know to build new sentences

HÖREN 1 🎧 **Hör zu und lies.**

Jana: Ich wohne in der Stadt.

Tobias: Ich wohne in einem Dorf.

Sandra: Ich wohne am Stadtrand.

Ulf: Ich wohne in einer Wohnsiedlung.

Katrin: Ich wohne auf dem Land.

SPRECHEN 2 👥 **Wo wohnst du? A ↔ B.**
Look at the photos in activity 1 and take turns asking questions.

Beispiel: **A** Wo wohnst du, Jana?
B Ich wohne ...

? Think

In Unit 2A, you learned the phrase *Ich spiele gern Tennis* (I like playing Tennis).

How would you say that you like or don't like **living** somewhere using *gern*?

LESEN 3 **Was passt zusammen?**
Match the German adjectives with the English ones.

Beispiel: **a 3**

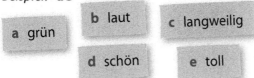

- a grün
- b laut
- c langweilig
- d schön
- e toll

1 beautiful **2** great **3** green **4** noisy **5** boring

SCHREIBEN 4 **Lies Saschas Nachricht. Schreib eine Antwort.**
Read Sascha's message and write an answer.

NC 3

Beispiel: Ich heiße ...

Ich heiße Sascha und ich komme aus Österreich. Ich wohne auf dem Land.

Ich wohne gern auf dem Land, denn es ist schön und grün, und es ist nicht laut. Das finde ich toll!

Aber es ist manchmal langweilig. Das ist nicht gut.

LESEN 5 **Was passt zusammen?**
Match each person to the place where they live.

Beispiel: **Nina** 4

Nina: Ich wohne in einer Wohnung.

Ali: Ich wohne in einem Reihenhaus.

Anna: Ich wohne in einem Doppelhaus.

Maik: Ich wohne in einem Bungalow.

Nico: Ich wohne in einem Einfamilienhaus.

1 

2 

3 

4 

5 

Grammatik → p.162–3

Ich wohne in einem/einer/einem

m ein Bungalow
Ich wohne in ein**em** Bungalow.

f eine Wohnung
Ich wohne in ein**er** Wohnung.

n ein Haus
Ich wohne in ein**em** Haus.

HÖREN 6 **Hör zu. Ist alles richtig?**
Listen. Is everything correct?

SCHREIBEN 7 **Füll die Lücken aus.**

Beispiel: **a** *einem*

Ich wohne in …

a ____ Doppelhaus.
b ____ Bungalow.
c ____ Wohnung.
d ____ Reihenhaus.
e ____ Dorf.
f ____ Wohnsiedlung.

Ich wohne	in der Stadt. in einem Dorf. in einer Wohnsiedlung. am Stadtrand. auf dem Land.
Ich wohne (nicht) gern …, denn es ist …	
ich wohne du wohnst er/sie wohnt	wir wohnen ihr wohnt sie/Sie wohnen

HÖREN 8 **Hör zu. Wo wohnen Jens, Maria, Jonas, Lene und Sven? Mach Notizen.**
NC 2–3
Where do they all live? Listen and make notes.

Beispiel: **Jens**: *Reihenhaus – Stadtrand*

SCHREIBEN 9 **Schreib Sätze für Jens, Maria, Jonas, Lene und Sven.**
NC 2
Use your notes and write sentences for the people in activity 8.

Beispiel: *Jens wohnt in einem Reihenhaus am Stadtrand.*

SPRECHEN 10 **Wo wohnst du? Macht Dialoge.** A ↔ B.
NC 2–3

Beispiel: ***A*** *Wo wohnst du, Louis?*
B *Ich wohne in einem Bungalow am Stadtrand. Und du?*
A *Ich wohne ...*

Challenge

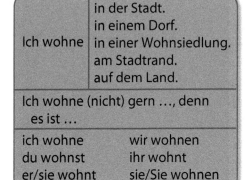

Write a description of where you live giving as many details as you can. You can invent as many details as you like! (Look back over pages 72–75 to help you.)
NC 3

2B.3 Mein Haus

Vocabulary: describe the rooms in your house or flat and where they are

Grammar: learn the numbers up to 100

Skills: use knowledge you already have to work out language rules

 HÖREN 1 🎧 **Hör zu – was kommt danach?**

Listen, then repeat the number and say the next one before you hear it.

Beispiel: zwanzig, einundzwanzig …

20	21	22	23	24	25
zwanzig	einundzwanzig	zweiundzwanzig	dreiundzwanzig	vierundzwanzig	fünfundzwanzig

26	27	28	29	30	31
sechsundzwanzig	siebenundzwanzig	achtundzwanzig	neunundzwanzig	dreißig	einunddreißig

 HÖREN 2 🎧 **Hör zu und lies.**

40	50	60	70
vierzig	fünfzig	sechzig	siebzig

80	90	100
achtzig	neunzig	hundert

? Think

You already know the numbers 1–31. Can you use your existing knowledge to work out the numbers 32–99?

 HÖREN 3 🎧 **Hör zu und finde die passenden Zahlen.**

Listen and find the matching numbers.

44 87 51 39 62 74
93 65 46 32 84 57

 SPRECHEN 4 👥 **Was kommt danach? A ↔ B.**

A says a number, B says the number that follows.

Beispiel: **A** vierundvierzig!
B fünfundvierzig!

SPRECHEN 5 👥 **Wo wohnst du? A ↔ B.**

Take turns asking and answering.

Beispiel: **A** Wo wohnst du?
B Nummer zweiundvierzig.

6 🎧 **Hör zu. Was passt zusammen?**

Listen and match the words (a–j) with the rooms in the house.

Beispiel: **a** *der Balkon – 8*

a	der Balkon
b	der Garten
c	der Keller
d	die Dusche
e	die Garage
f	die Küche
g	das Badezimmer
h	das Esszimmer
i	das Schlafzimmer
j	das Wohnzimmer

7 🎧 **Hör noch einmal zu. Wie sind die Zimmer im Haus? Mach Notizen.**

NC 3

Listen again. What are the rooms in the house like? Make notes.

Beispiel: **1** *die Küche – schön*

8 👥 **Was ist das? Wie ist das? A ↔ B.**

NC 2–3

Take turns asking each other what the rooms are like.

Beispiel: **A** *Nummer 1 – was ist das?* **B** *Das ist die Küche.*
A *Wie ist die Küche?* **B** *Die Küche ist schön.*

9 **Lies den Dialog. Wo sind die Zimmer?**

NC 2

Read the dialogue. Where are the rooms? Write **E** (Erdgeschoss), **1** (im 1. Stock) or **2** (im 2. Stock).

Beispiel: *die Küche – E*

Ali Also, die Küche ist im Erdgeschoss.

Kathi Und wo ist das Wohnzimmer?

Ali Das Wohnzimmer ist im ersten Stock. Das Esszimmer ist auch im ersten Stock.

Kathi Und wo ist das Badezimmer?

Ali Das Badezimmer ist im ersten Stock, und die Dusche ist im zweiten Stock. Die Schlafzimmer sind auch im zweiten Stock.

Kathi Und wo ist der Balkon?

Ali Der Balkon ist im ersten Stock – im Wohnzimmer.

Das ist …

cool	klein	schön
groß	laut	super
kalt	praktisch	

im Erdgeschoss
  on the ground floor
im ersten/zweiten Stock
  on the first/second floor

◎ **Challenge**

Draw a plan for a house. Write at least five sentences saying where everything is and what it is like.

Beispiel: Das …zimmer ist im Erdgeschoss. Es ist …

NC 3

2B.4 Mein Zimmer

Vocabulary: say what is in your room and where things are

Grammar: use *es gibt einen/eine/ein*; use prepositions; change 'the' after a preposition

Skills: check you've used the correct words for 'the' and 'a'

HÖREN 1

🎧 **Hör zu. Was passt zusammen?**

Listen. Match the words (a–k) with the furniture (1–11).

Beispiel: **a 2**

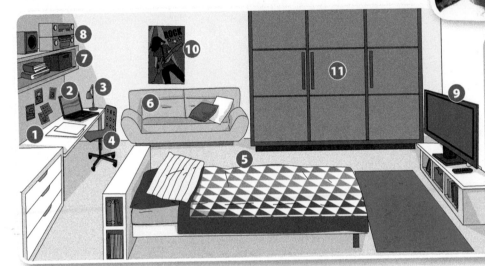

Es gibt …/In meinem Zimmer gibt es …

a einen Computer
b einen Fernseher
c einen Kleiderschrank
d einen Schreibtisch
e einen Stuhl
f eine Lampe
g eine Stereoanlage
h ein Bett
i ein Poster
j ein Regal
k ein Sofa

SCHREIBEN 2

Füll die Lücken aus.

In meinem Zimmer gibt es …

a *ein* Sofa.
b ▭ Schreibtisch.
c ▭ Computer.
d ▭ Stereoanlage.
e ▭ Bett.
f ▭ Kleiderschrank.

SPRECHEN 3
NC 2

👥 **Macht Sätze. A ⟷ B.**

Point at items in the picture. Take turns making sentences.

Beispiel: **A** Nummer 1!
B *In meinem Zimmer gibt es einen Schreibtisch.*

SCHREIBEN 4
NC 2

Was gibt es in deinem Zimmer? Schreib sechs Sätze.

What is there in your room? Write six sentences.

Beispiel: *In meinem Zimmer gibt es …*

VIDEO 5

🎥 **Sieh dir das Video an. Was ist die richtige Reihenfolge?**

Watch the video. Note the order in which the items of furniture are mentioned.

? Think

For masculine nouns, the word for 'a' changes after *es gibt* or *gibt es* (there is):

ein Stuhl →
In meinem Zimmer gibt es ein**en** Stuhl.
In my room there is a chair.

Does the word 'a' change for feminine or neuter nouns? Check those listed in activity 1 (a–k).

wardrobe		chair	
desk		bed	1
lamp			

Grammatik → p.163

in, auf, neben, unter, …

Prepositions tell you where something or someone is (in, on, under, next to, etc.). The article 'the' (*der/die/das*) changes after a preposition:

m	der Schreibtisch	→ Das Buch ist auf **dem** Schreibtisch.
f	die Lampe	→ Die CD ist neben **der** Lampe.
n	das Bett	→ Der Fußball ist unter **dem** Bett.

auf	*on*
hinter	*behind*
in	*in*
neben	*next to*
unter	*under*
vor	*in front of*
zwischen	*between*

6 Schreib die richtigen Wörter auf.

Give the prepositions and the correct forms of 'the' for the masculine, feminine and neuter words.

a Das Sofa ist ▨▨ ▨▨ Bett. (*next to*)
b Der Fernseher ist ▨▨ ▨▨ Schreibtisch. (*on*)
c Das Buch ist ▨▨ ▨▨ Lampe. (*behind*)
d Die Katze ist ▨▨ ▨▨ Kleiderschrank. (*in*)
e Der Stuhl ist ▨▨ ▨▨ Regal. (*under*)
f Das Buch ist ▨▨ ▨▨ Stuhl. (*under*)

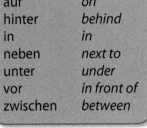

? Think

When you use the preposition *in* with the article *dem*, you usually say *im* instead of *in dem*:

Er ist **im** Bett.

7 Wo ist alles in Alis Zimmer? Schreib Sätze.

NC 2

Where is everything? Look at the picture of Ali's room on page 78 (activity 1) and write sentences.

Beispiel: Die Lampe ist auf dem Schreibtisch.

8 👥 Ist alles richtig? A ↔ B.

NC 2

Beispiel: **A** *Wo ist die Lampe?*
B *Die Lampe ist …*

9 Lies den Text. Wo sind die Möbel?

NC 2

Read the description. Identify each item of furniture (1–7) on the plan.

Beispiel: **1** *bed*

In meinem Zimmer gibt es ein Bett und einen Schreibtisch. Der Schreibtisch ist neben dem Bett. Ich habe auch einen Stuhl. Er ist vor dem Schreibtisch.

In meinem Zimmer gibt es auch eine Lampe und einen Computer. Die Lampe ist auf dem Schreibtisch. Der Computer ist neben der Lampe.

Ich habe auch einen Kleiderschrank. Er ist zwischen dem Schreibtisch und dem Sofa. Ich mag mein Zimmer, denn es ist ziemlich groß und modern.

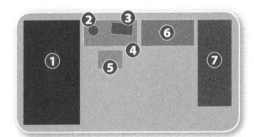

Challenge

Write a description of a room, saying where everything is and giving your opinion of each piece of furniture (use the adjectives on page 77).

Beispiel:
Im Schlafzimmer gibt es …

NC 3

Vocabulary: describe your house and your dream house
Grammar: revise the grammar points covered in this unit
Skills: read for sense and extract information from texts

Kathi Kool

Info | Pinnwand | Fotos | +

Blog-Name: Kathi Kool
Land: Deutschland und Österreich
Alter: 14
Geburtstag: 4. Mai
Idol: Heidi Klum (Model)

 VIDEO 1
NC 3–4

🎥 Sieh dir das Video an. Wähle die richtigen Antworten.
Watch Kathi's video diary. Choose the correct answers for her.

Beispiel: **a 1**

a Wo wohnst du?
1 in Berlin   **2** in Österreich

b Wo ist dein Haus in Wien?
1 in der Stadtmitte   **2** am Stadtrand

c Wie ist das Haus?
1 Es ist sehr groß und schön.
2 Es ist klein und modern.

d Was spielst du im Garten?
1 Ich spiele Fußball.   **2** Ich spiele Tennis.

e Wo ist dein Zimmer?
1 Im dritten Stock.   **2** Im zweiten Stock.

f Wie viele Stühle gibt es in deinem Zimmer?
1 zwei   **2** drei

 SPRECHEN 2
NC 3–4

👥👥 Wo wohnst du? Macht Dialoge.
A ↔ B.

Beispiel: **A** Wo wohnst du?
        B Ich wohne in London.
        A Wo ist dein Haus?
        B In der Stadtmitte.
        A Wie ist das Haus?
        B …

3 HÖREN
NC 3–4

Hör zu und lies. Richtig oder falsch?
Listen and read. Are the sentences below true or false?

Beispiel: **a** *false*

Nina: Mein Traumhaus ist ein Haus in Kalifornien. Das ist in Amerika. Das Haus ist in Los Angeles – es ist ein Haus am Meer.

Das Haus ist total groß und es gibt einen Garten. Es gibt auch ein großes Schwimmbad im Garten – in Los Angeles ist es immer sonnig und heiß, und ich schwimme jeden Tag!

Es gibt ein Kinozimmer im Erdgeschoss. Dort schaue ich mit meinen Freunden und Freundinnen Filme und DVDs. Es gibt auch ein Musikzimmer im Keller – ich spiele dort Gitarre und Schlagzeug, und ich singe.

a Nina's dream house is in Austria.
b The house doesn't have a garden.
c It doesn't snow in Los Angeles and it's not cold.
d Nina likes to swim a lot in her pool.
e Nina likes watching movies.
f Nina makes music in the cellar.

> Kalifornien *California*
> am Meer *by the sea*
> ein Schwimmbad *swimming pool*

4 SCHREIBEN
Füll die Lücken aus.
Fill in the gaps with the words below.

Mein Traumhaus ist ___ein Bungalow___ in Berlin. Das ist im ▒▒▒ von Deutschland. Dort ist es manchmal ▒▒▒, aber es ▒▒▒ oft. Mein Traumhaus ist sehr ▒▒▒. Es gibt vier ▒▒▒ und eine ▒▒▒. Es gibt auch einen ▒▒▒.

> Garten   regnet   Osten   Schlafzimmer   schön
> Küche   ein Bungalow   sonnig

Challenge

Draw a picture of your dream house or find a photo of it. Write a short description of it.

Beispiel:

- Wo? ... *mein Traumhaus ist in den Bergen/am Meer/in der Stadt/auf dem Land*
- Wetter? ... *es ist heiß/kalt, es regnet/schneit*
- Wie? ... *es ist klein/groß/ schön*
- Was gibt es alles? ... *es gibt ein Wohnzimmer/zwei Schlafzimmer*
- Was machst du dort? ... *ich schwimme/fahre Ski/ mache Sport*

NC 3–4

2B.6 Sprachlabor

Prepositions, using *es gibt*

Ich wohne in …
Words like *in* in front of a noun tell you where something or someone is. They always change the endings of the article (*ein/eine/ein*) which goes with the noun:

m	ein Bungalow	→ Ich wohne **in einem** Bungalow.
f	eine Wohnung	→ Ich wohne **in einer** Wohnung.
n	ein Dorf	→ Ich wohne **in einem** Dorf.

---

1 Fill in the gaps with the correct articles.

    a Ich wohne in ___einem___ Doppelhaus. (das)
    b Ich wohne in ▨▨▨ Einfamilienhaus. (das)
    c Ich wohne in ▨▨▨ Wohnsiedlung. (die)
    d Ich wohne in ▨▨▨ Reihenhaus. (das)
    e Ich wohne in ▨▨▨ Stadt. (die)

In meinem Zimmer gibt es …
After *es gibt* or *gibt es*, the word for 'a' changes for masculine nouns:

m	ein Stuhl	→ In meinem Zimmer gibt es **einen** Stuhl.
f	eine Lampe	→ In meinem Zimmer gibt es **eine** Lampe.
n	ein Bett	→ In meinem Zimmer gibt es **ein** Bett.

---

2 Choose the correct article.

    a In meinem Zimmer gibt es eine/**ein** Regal. (das)
    b In meinem Zimmer gibt es ein/**einen** Kleiderschrank. (der)
    c In meinem Zimmer gibt es **einen**/eine Fernseher. (der)
    d In meinem Zimmer gibt es eine/**ein** Poster. (das)
    e In meinem Zimmer gibt es ein/**einen** Computer. (der)
    f In meinem Zimmer gibt es ein/**eine** Stereoanlage. (die)

3 Complete the sentence with the furniture on the right.
Give the correct article each time (see page 78).

Beispiel: In meinem Zimmer gibt es ein Sofa, …

---

in, auf, hinter, neben, vor, unter, zwischen
Prepositions tell you where something or someone is, and they change the ending of the article (*der/die/das*) which goes with the noun:

m	der Schreibtisch	→ Die CD ist **auf dem** Schreibtisch.
f	die Lampe	→ Die CD ist **neben der** Lampe.
n	das Bett	→ Die CD ist **unter dem** Bett.

---

4 True or false? Write the false sentences correctly in German.

Beispiel: **a** *Falsch. Die Lampe ist auf dem Schreibtisch.*

a Die Lampe ist neben dem Schreibtisch.
b Das Buch ist unter dem Bett.
c Die Schultasche ist auf dem Kleiderschrank.

d Das Bett ist zwischen dem Kleiderschrank und dem Sofa.
e Der Stuhl ist hinter dem Schreibtisch.
f Die Stereoanlage ist auf dem Stuhl.

Techniques for learning new words

Learning new words

It's important to use a range of techniques for memorising new words. Some strategies work better than others. Reorder these in order of priority for you.

1 Colour-code them according to gender (masculine, feminine, neuter).

2 Group them into categories, e.g. in alphabetical order.

3 Group them into words that are like English and those that aren't.

4 Copy each new word five times.

5 Practise saying each new word aloud five times.

Checklist for learning a new word

1 Do you understand it (when listening or reading)?

2 Can you say it (so that others will understand your pronunciation)?

3 Can you write it (without making spelling mistakes)?

4 Can you use it in a sentence (if appropriate, in a different context to the one you've learned)?

If the answer is yes to all of these, then you know it!

⚠ Always learn the article (*der, die or das*) when learning a new noun.

5 👥 **Discuss your order of techniques with your partner.**

• Is his/hers the same? • Why (not)? • When can you say that you really know a new word?

The *ch* sound

6 🎧 **Listen carefully: how often do you hear *ch*?**

Vocabulary: practise describing the furniture in your room; use higher numbers
Grammar: practise using prepositions
Skills: develop accuracy in written work

1 **Match up the numbers and words.**

Beispiel: **a** *4*

a 36 **b** 91 **c** 82 **d** 44 **e** 75 **f** 53

1 fünfundsiebzig	4 sechsunddreißig
2 einundneunzig	5 vierundvierzig
3 dreiundfünfzig	6 zweiundachtzig

2 **Write down the jumbled-up words.**

Beispiel: **a** *ein Computer*

 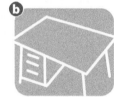    

a ein PUOMCERT **b** ein SCHETBRISICH **c** ein REHFESERN **d** eine PEMAL **e** ein STEROP **f** ein ERLAG

3 **Fill in the gaps with the noun and its article.**

NC 1–2

a Ich wohne in ___einem___ Einfamilienhaus .

b Ich wohne in ▬▬ ▬▬ .

c Ich wohne in ▬▬ ▬▬ .

d Ich wohne in ▬▬ ▬▬ .

e Ich wohne in ▬▬ ▬▬ .

f Ich wohne in ▬▬ ▬▬ .

4 **Choose the correct word.**

NC 2

Beispiel: **a** *neben*

a Die Lampe ist neben/hinter dem Bett.
b Die DVD ist auf/unter dem Bett.
c Der Computer ist auf/vor dem Schreibtisch.
d Das Buch ist unter/im Schreibtisch.
e Der Stuhl ist hinter/vor dem Schreibtisch.
f Das Skateboard ist neben/hinter der Lampe.

2B.7 / Extra Plus

Vocabulary: practise describing the furniture in your room; use higher numbers
Grammar: practise using prepositions
Skills: develop accuracy in written work

Schreib die Zahlen auf.

Beispiel: **a** *fünfundvierzig*

a 45   **b** 81   **c** 77   **d** 32   **e** 96   **f** 50

Schreib die richtigen Wörter für die Zimmer auf.

Beispiel: **a** *das Schlafzimmer*

Kathis Zimmer. Schreib die richtigen Wörter auf.

NC 2   *Beispiel:* **a** *im Kleiderschrank*

a Die Sporttasche ist ▬▬▬ ▬▬▬ .
b Die Stereoanlage ist ▬▬▬ ▬▬▬ ▬▬▬ .
c Die Lampe ist ▬▬▬ ▬▬▬ ▬▬▬ .
d Der Stuhl ist ▬▬▬ ▬▬▬ ▬▬▬ .

e Die Katze ist ▬▬▬ ▬▬▬ ▬▬▬ .
f Das Sofa ist ▬▬▬ ▬▬▬ Kleiderschrank und dem Bett.
h Die Gitarre ist ▬▬▬ ▬▬▬ ▬▬▬ .

In meinem Zimmer gibt es …
Schreib sechs Sätze für Kathi.

NC 3

Beispiel: *In meinem Zimmer gibt es ein Bett.*

Listen (1–6). Choose two pictures for each weather description. Tick (✓) or cross (✗) each one to show what the weather is and isn't doing! (See page 73.)

NC 2–3

Beispiel: **1** c✓, h✗

ⓐ ⓑ ⓒ ⓓ ⓔ ⓕ

ⓖ ⓗ ⓘ ⓙ **32°** ⓚ **22°** ⓛ

2 Where is everything? Write a sentence for each room. (See page 77.)

NC 3

Beispiel: Das Wohnzimmer ist im Erdgeschoss.

die Toilette *toilet*

3 Read Svenja's message and note a–e. (See pages 74–79.)

NC 3

a where she lives
b what her house is like
c what her room is like
d what there is in her room
e where everything is in her room

Ich wohne in einem Einfamilienhaus am Stadtrand. Unser Haus ist klein und modern. Wir haben einen Garten. Mein Zimmer ist im ersten Stock. Es ist groß und sehr schön, und es gibt einen Balkon. In meinem Zimmer gibt es auch ein Bett und einen Schreibtisch. Es gibt auch ein Sofa – das Bett ist neben dem Sofa. In meinem Zimmer gibt es auch ein Regal und einen Fernseher. Der Fernseher ist auf dem Regal.

4 Complete these sentences as part of a mini-presentation about yourself. (See pages 72–79.)

NC 3–4

Ich wohne in ... (*name of town/city*)
Das ist in ... (*region*)
Ich wohne in ... (*type of house and where*)
In meinem Zimmer gibt es ... (*description of furniture and its position in room*)
Mein Zimmer ist ... (*description/opinion*)
Das Wetter heute ist ... (*type of weather*)

Meine Region	My region
im Norden	in the north
im Nordosten	in the north-east
im Nordwesten	in the north-west
im Osten	in the east
im Süden	in the south
im Südosten	in the south-east
im Südwesten	in the south-west
im Westen	in the west

Das Wetter	The weather
Es ist heiß.	It is hot.
kalt	cold
neblig	foggy
schön	nice
sonnig	sunny
warm	warm
windig	windy
wolkig	cloudy
Es friert.	It's freezing/It freezes.
Es gewittert.	There's thunder and lightning.
Es regnet.	It's raining/It rains.
Es schneit.	It's snowing/It snows.
Es (regnet) nicht.	It isn't (raining)/It doesn't (rain).

Wo wohnst du?	Where do you live?
ich wohne	I live
du wohnst	you live
er/sie wohnt	he/she lives
wir wohnen	we live
ihr wohnt	you live (plural)
sie wohnen	they live
Sie wohnen	you live (formal)
am Stadtrand	on the edge of town
auf dem Land	in the countryside
in der Stadt	in town
in einem Bungalow	in a bungalow
in einem Doppelhaus	in a semi-detached house
in einem Dorf	in a village
in einem Einfamilienhaus	in a detached house
in einem Reihenhaus	in a terraced house
in einer Wohnsiedlung	on a housing estate
in einer Wohnung	in a flat

Wie ist es?	What is it like?
grün	green
interessant	interesting
langweilig	boring
laut	noisy, loud
praktisch	practical
schön	beautiful
toll	great

Mein Haus	My house
der Balkon	balcony
der Garten	garden
der Keller	cellar
die Dusche	shower
die Garage	garage
die Küche	kitchen
das Badezimmer	bathroom
das Esszimmer	dining room
das Schlafzimmer	bedroom
das Wohnzimmer	living room
im Erdgeschoss	on the ground floor
im ersten/zweiten Stock	on the first/second floor

Mein Zimmer	My room
In meinem Zimmer gibt es …	In my room there is …
einen Computer	a computer
einen Fernseher	a TV
einen Kleiderschrank	a wardrobe
einen Schreibtisch	a desk
einen Stuhl	a chair
eine Lampe	a lamp
eine Stereoanlage	a hi-fi system
ein Bett	a bed
ein Poster	a poster
ein Regal	a shelf
ein Sofa	a sofa
auf	on
hinter	behind
im	in the
neben	next to
unter	under
vor	in front of
zwischen	between

Zahlen	Numbers
vierzig	forty
fünfzig	fifty
sechzig	sixty
siebzig	seventy
achtzig	eighty
neunzig	ninety
hundert	a hundred

I can...

- say where I live and what the weather is like
- describe my house or flat
- say what's in my room
- count up to a hundred
- use *auf, in, hinter, neben, vor, zwischen, unter*

3A.1 Was isst du gern?

Vocabulary: say what you like and don't like to eat and drink
Grammar: write a sentence where the verb comes second
Skills: use familiar language in a new context

HÖREN 1 🎧 **Hör zu. Was ist die richtige Reihenfolge?**
Listen, look at the pictures and note the order of the items of food and drink as you hear them.

Beispiel: **i, …**

a Salat	b eine Banane	c Joghurt	d Reis	e ein Ei	f Milch	g Käse	h Kartoffeln
i Brot	j Orangensaft	k einen Apfel	l Nudeln	m Hähnchen	n Fisch	o Cola	

HÖREN 2 (NC 2–3) 🎧 **Hör zu. Was essen Kathi und Nina gern oder nicht gern?**
Listen, look at the pictures again and note what Kathi and Nina like (✓) and don't like (✗) to eat and drink.

Kathi	✓	
	✗	a

Nina	✓	
	✗	

? Think

In which other contexts have you come across *gern* and *nicht gern*? What else could you use them to say?

SCHREIBEN 3 **Und du – was isst/trinkst du gern oder nicht gern?**
Look again at the pictures. Then write two lists of what **you** like/don't like to eat and drink.

gern	nicht gern
Käse	Fisch

Ich esse (nicht) gern …

Äpfel	Salat	Käse
Bananen	Joghurt	Brot
Hähnchen	Nudeln	Reis
Kartoffeln	Fisch	Eier

Ich trinke (nicht) gern …

Orangensaft	Milch	Cola

SPRECHEN 4 (NC 2) 👥 **Macht Dialoge. A ↔ B.**
Take turns asking questions.

Beispiel: **A** *Was isst du gern?*
B *Ich esse gern Käse.*
A *Was isst du nicht gern?*

5 🎧 **Hör zu und lies.**

Nina: Zum Frühstück esse ich Cornflakes oder Müsli mit Milch oder Brot mit Marmelade. Ich trinke meistens Kaffee.

Nico: Zum Mittagessen esse ich Hähnchen mit Reis oder Kartoffeln. Ich esse auch eine Banane oder einen Apfel. Und ich trinke Wasser.

Ali: Zum Abendessen esse ich Brot mit Butter und Käse oder ein Ei mit Salat. Ich trinke normalerweise Tee.

6

Finde die passenden Bilder für Nina, Nico und Ali.
Find the matching pictures for each person.

NC 2–3

Beispiel: **Nina** *5, …*

❶

❷

❸

❹

❺

❻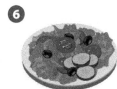

❼

❽

❾

❿

⓫

7 👥👥 **Was isst oder trinkst du? Macht Dialoge. A ⟷ B.**

NC 2–3

What do you eat or drink for breakfast/lunch/dinner?
Make up dialogues.

Beispiel: **A** *Was isst/trinkst du zum Frühstück/Mittagessen/ Abendessen?*
B *Meistens/Normalerweise esse/trinke ich …*

8 **Schreib einen Speiseplan.**

NC 3

Write a menu for yourself. Choose four items of food and one drink.

Beispiel: *Zum Frühstück esse ich Cornflakes/Müsli/Brötchen/ Marmelade. Ich trinke gern Kaffee/Tee/Wasser …*

Grammatik → p.167–8

⚠️ The verb should always come second:
Ich **esse** Müsli. →
Zum Frühstück **esse** ich Müsli.

🎯 **Challenge**
What are you eating today? Look up any unknown words in a dictionary. Write a description of your meal and include your opinions.

Beispiel: Zum Abendessen esse ich … Ich esse gern …   NC 4

3A.2 Ein Eis, bitte!

Vocabulary: learn how to order food
Grammar: use *ich möchte* to say what you would like
Skills: learn how to use polite language

HÖREN 1 🎧 **Hör zu. Was passt zusammen (1–4 und a–d)?**
Listen to Ali and Nico. Then match the photos with the menus below.

Beispiel: **a 2**

die Pizzeria

die Eisdiele

der Imbiss

die Bäckerei

a
Vanilleeis
Schokoladeneis
Erdbeereis
mit Sahne
ohne Sahne

b
Pizza mit Tomaten, Käse und:
Zwiebeln und Schinken
Pilzen und Oliven
Spinat und Thunfisch

c
Brötchen
Bio-Brot
Brötchen mit Käse oder Schinken
Schwarzwälder Kirschtorte
Apfelkuchen

d
Bratwurst
Currywurst
Hamburger
Cheeseburger
Pommes frites mit Ketchup oder Mayonnaise

SPRECHEN 2 👥 **Ratespiel: Wo isst du gern? A ↔ B.**
A chooses something to eat, **B** guesses which place it is.

Beispiel: **A** Ich esse Pizza mit Tomaten, Käse, Schinken und Zwiebeln.
B Das ist die Pizzeria!

? Think

Look at the menus: what do you think *mit* and *ohne* mean?

SCHREIBEN 3 **Schreib Sätze.**

NC 3

What do you like/not like eating in the restaurants pictured?
Write six sentences.

Beispiel: Ich esse gern Pizza mit Tomaten, Käse, Schinken und Zwiebeln. Ich esse nicht gern ...

VIDEO 4  **Sieh dir das Video an und lies.**

Verkäufer Ja bitte?

Ali Ich möchte eine Currywurst, bitte.

Verkäufer Mit Pommes?

Ali Ja, mit Pommes und mit Ketchup und Mayonnaise.

Verkäufer Und du? Was darf es sein?

Nico Ich nehme auch eine Currywurst – oder nein, ich nehme lieber einfach nur Pommes.

Verkäufer €5,40, bitte.

Nico Danke.

Verkäufer Bitte.

 HÖREN 5 **Hör zu und lies.**

Verkäufer Was möchtest du?

Kathi Ich möchte vier Brötchen, bitte.

Verkäufer Hier, bitte. Sonst noch etwas?

Kathi Ja, ich nehme ein Stück Apfelkuchen.

Verkäufer Bitte sehr. Ist das alles?

Kathi Und ein Stück Schwarzwälder Kirschtorte, bitte.

 LESEN 6 **Füll die Lücken aus.**

Now fill in the gaps.

a Ali would like a _curried sausage_ with fries, ▨▨▨ and ▨▨▨ .

b Nico would like ▨▨▨ .

c Kathi wants to buy ▨▨▨ .

d She also buys one ▨▨▨ and one ▨▨▨ .

 LESEN 7 **Wie sagt man das auf Deutsch?**

There is more than one way in German to say these phrases. Find them in activities 4 and 5.

Beispiel: **a** *Ja bitte?*

a What would you like? (3)

b I'd like … (2)

c Anything else? (2)

 SPRECHEN 8 NC 3 **Macht Dialoge. A ↔ B.**

Make up your own dialogues following the models above.

Beispiel: **A** *Was darf es sein?*

B *Ich möchte ein Erdbeereis, bitte.*

A *Mit Sahne?*

B *Nein, ohne Sahne.*

 ? **Think**

Compare this dialogue with the ones above:

A Ja? → **B** Ein Eis.

A Erdbeereis? → **B** Schoko.

A Ist das alles? → **B** Ja.

A Hier!

Do you think it is as polite as the ones above? Why (or why not)?

In what other situations would you use polite language?

Challenge

Invent your own funny menu for the week, combining as many items of food (and drink) as you can!

Beispiel: Am Montag esse ich Vanilleeis mit Mayonnaise und Käse. Ich trinke Orangensaft mit Sahne.

NC 4

Vocabulary: say what food you want to buy
Grammar: give quantities correctly
Skills: identify patterns in numbers

 SCHREIBEN 1

Füll die Lücken aus.
Write down the missing numbers.

 **Think**

Can you find the pattern for saying the numbers over 100? How would you say the missing numbers on the right?

100	hundert
200	zweihundert
300	dreihundert
400	vierhundert
576	fünfhundertsechsundsiebzig
600	▬
700	▬
800	▬
900	▬
1000	tausend

 HÖREN 2

🎧 **Hör zu. Ist alles richtig?**
Listen and check your answers.

 SPRECHEN 3

👥 **Was ist die richtige Antwort? A ↔ B.**
A says a sum and **B** gives the right answer.

Beispiel: **A** *a* – Fünfundachtzig plus fünfunddreißig.
   B Hundertzwanzig!

a	85 + 35
b	600 – 150
c	800 – 440
d	190 + 70
e	730 + 250

 VIDEO 4

NC 3

🎥 **Sieh dir das Video an. Füll die Lücken aus.**
Watch the video. Read the dialogue and fill in the gaps.

Gramm   300   Käse   Liter

Verkäufer Guten Morgen! Was darf es sein?
Ali Ich möchte ▬, bitte.
Verkäufer Wie viel?
Ali 250 ▬, bitte.
Verkäufer Außerdem?
Ali Und ich möchte ▬ Gramm Oliven und einen ▬ Olivenöl.
Verkäufer Sonst noch etwas?
Ali Nein, danke, das ist alles.
Verkäufer Bitte schön. Schönen Tag noch!

HÖREN 5 🎧 **Was passt zusammen? Ist alles richtig? Hör zu.**
Match the words (a–i) to the pictures (1–9). Then listen to check your answers.

Beispiel: **1 h**

Ich möchte …
a   einen Becher Joghurt
b   eine Packung Kaffee
c   eine Tüte Brötchen
d   eine Dose Cola
e   eine Flasche Wasser
f   ein Glas Marmelade
g   ein Stück Käse
h   eine Scheibe Schinken
i   einen Liter Milch

1
2
3
4

5
6
7
8
9

HÖREN 6 🎧 **Hör zu. Füll die Lücken aus.**
Listen and fill in the gaps.

NC 2–3

vier	Becher	Sahne			Brötchen
		Orangensaft			Joghurt
		Tee			Cola
		Milch			Marmelade
		Wurst			Butterkuchen

Was darf es sein?
Ich möchte …

250 Gramm …		
ein (halbes) Pfund …		
ein (halbes) Kilo …		

zwei	Becher …	Packungen …
drei	Dosen …	Flaschen …
vier	Tüten …	Scheiben …
…	Gläser …	Stücke …
	Liter …	

Sonst noch etwas?
Nein, danke, das ist alles.

SPRECHEN 7 👥 **Macht Einkaufsdialoge. A ⟷ B.**
Make up shopping dialogues for lists 1 and 2.

NC 3

Beispiel: **A** *Ja bitte? Was darf es sein?*
        B *Ich möchte 400 Gramm Schinken, bitte. Ich möchte auch …*

1
400 g ham
a packet of coffee
2 cans of cola
2 bags of bread rolls
2 pieces of cheese
1 lb apples

2
4 slices of sausage
1 kg bananas
1 bottle of orange juice
1 litre milk
2 pots of jam
$\frac{1}{2}$ lb olives

Challenge
You're planning a menu for a party or a dinner. Write a shopping list and then a shopping dialogue to buy all the ingredients you need.

Beispiel: *Chips, Cola, Eis, …*
            Ich möchte …   NC 3–4

Vocabulary: say what you like and dislike eating; talk about healthy eating

Grammar: use *Man soll ...* and *keinen/keine/kein* correctly

Skills: use different structures; build longer sentences

LESEN 1 Ist das gut (✓) oder schlecht (X)?

Are these foods healthy or not?

Beispiel: **1 X**

1 Fastfood **2** Milch **3** Gemüse **4** Chips **5** Schokolade

6 Fisch **7** Fleisch **8** Obst **9** Cola **10** Wasser

HÖREN 2 🎧 Hör zu und lies. Wer isst und trinkt gut (✓) und wer schlecht (X)?

NC 3–4 Listen and read. Whose diet is healthy – and whose isn't?

Ich esse gern Fastfood, und ich trinke sehr gern Kaffee. Ich esse keinen Fisch, denn ich finde Fisch doof. Ich trinke kein Wasser. Ich esse jeden Tag Hamburger und Pommes oder Pizza. Und ich esse jeden Tag ein Eis oder Kuchen.

Jan (13)

Ich esse gern Fisch – Fisch mit Reis oder Kartoffeln. Oder ich esse Nudeln mit Tomaten und Käse. Aber ich esse kein Fleisch, denn ich mag Fleisch nicht. Ich esse jeden Tag eine Banane und eine Orange. Und ich trinke jeden Tag Wasser.

Mona (14)

SPRECHEN 3 👥 Macht ein Interview. A ⟷ B.

NC 3–4 Interview each other about what you like/don't like to eat and drink. Give your opinion too.

Beispiel: **A** *Was isst du gern?*
B *Ich esse gern Pizza mit Pommes frites.*
A *Das ist schlecht! Und was isst du nicht gern?*
B *Ich esse nicht gern Obst, und ich esse kein Gemüse.*

⚙ Grammatik → p.162, 167

keinen/keine/kein

m	Ich esse keinen Fisch.
f	Ich trinke keine Cola.
n	Ich trinke kein Wasser.
pl	Ich esse keine Kartoffeln.

Essen und Trinken-Tipps

Ist das ein guter oder ein schlechter Tipp?

1	Man soll jeden Tag Fastfood essen.	6	Man soll jeden Tag Milch trinken.
2	Man soll keine Cola trinken.	7	Man soll jeden Tag Kuchen essen.
3	Man soll jeden Tag Obst essen.	8	Man soll keinen Fisch essen.
4	Man soll kein Wasser trinken.	9	Man soll keine Chips essen.
5	Man soll kein Gemüse essen.	10	Man soll jeden Tag Kaffee trinken.

 LESEN 4 **Lies die Tipps. Sind sie gut oder schlecht?**

Beispiel: **1** *schlecht*

 HÖREN 5 🎧 **Hör zu (1–10). Ist alles richtig?**

 SCHREIBEN 6 **Schreib die Sätze richtig auf.**

Beispiel: **a** *Man soll keine Chips essen.*

a Chips essen keine soll man
b keine soll man trinken Cola
c essen soll man Hamburger keine
d man keine Mayonnaise essen soll
e Kaffee man soll keinen trinken
f soll Schokolade keine essen man

Grammatik → p.166

sollen
To talk about what you should or shouldn't do, you use *sollen*. *Sollen* is a modal verb and sends the main verb to the end of the sentence in its infinitive form:

Man isst jeden Tag Obst.
→ Man **soll** jeden Tag Obst **essen**.

 SCHREIBEN 7 **Schreib Sätze mit *Man soll* ...**
Write sentences using the food in the pictures.

Beispiel: **1** *Man soll jeden Tag Salat essen.*

Challenge

Choose three items of food or drink that you like and three that you don't like or don't eat at all:

- Explain why you do or don't like each item, using *denn*.
- Are your choices good or bad? Explain using *Man soll* ...

NC 3–4

 SCHREIBEN 8 **Was soll man nicht essen? Schreib vier Sätze.**

Beispiel: *Man soll keine Hamburger essen.*

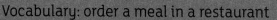

> Vocabulary: order a meal in a restaurant
> Grammar: 'verb second' word order; *ich möchte*
> Skills: use polite language; different strategies to work out meaning

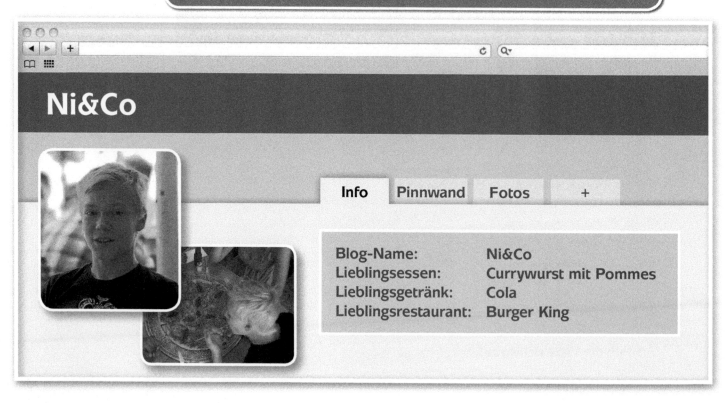

Ni&Co

Info | Pinnwand | Fotos | +

Blog-Name:	Ni&Co
Lieblingsessen:	Currywurst mit Pommes
Lieblingsgetränk:	Cola
Lieblingsrestaurant:	Burger King

VIDEO 1

Sieh dir das Video an. Beantworte die Fragen für Nico.

NC 4

a Was isst du gern?
Ich esse gern …

b Was isst du zum Frühstück?
Zum Frühstück esse ich …

c Was isst du zum Mittagessen?
Zum Mittagessen …

d Was isst du zum Abendessen/Abendbrot?
Zum Abendessen …

e Was isst du am Wochenende gern?
Am Wochenende esse ich gern … oder …

f Was isst du nicht gern?
Ich esse nicht gern … und …

g Was trinkst du gern?
Ich trinke gern … und …

h Was trinkst du nicht gern?
Ich trinke nicht gern …

HÖREN 2

Hör zu und lies die Speisekarte auf Seite 97.
Was bestellen Kathi und ihr Vater?

NC 3–4

Listen. What do Kathi and her father order for themselves?

Beispiel: **Vater:** *a, …*

SPRECHEN 3

Ist alles richtig?

NC 3

Check your answers to activity 2 by acting out the dialogues for Kathi and her father.

Beispiel: **A** *Ja bitte, was darf's sein?*
B *Als Vorspeise nehme ich …*

> Was darf's sein?
> Was möchtest du?
> Als Vorspeise nehme ich …, bitte.
> Und als Hauptgericht/Nachspeise?
> Ich möchte/nehme …
> Und zu trinken?

Speisekarte

Vorspeisen

a Suppe (Tomate oder Zwiebel)
b Salatteller
c Melone

Nachspeisen

g Eis mit Sahne
h Zitronentorte
i Kirschkuchen

✳

Hauptgerichte

d Schnitzel, Kartoffeln, Bohnen
e Kotelett, Pommes frites, Erbsen und Karotten
f Omelett mit Pilzen oder Käse, Salat

Getränke

j Limonade **k** Cola **l** Orangensaft
m Rotwein **n** Weißwein

SPRECHEN **4**

NC 3–4

👥 **Macht weitere Dialoge. A ↔ B.**
Make up other restaurant dialogues.

Beispiel: **A** *Was darf's sein?*
B *Als Vorspeise nehme ich Melone, bitte.*
A *Gern. Und als Hauptgericht?*
B ...

? *Think*

What do all the new words on the menu mean in English?

Use the pictures to help you to work them out. Look up any other words in the Glossary.

Challenge

Create your own restaurant menu. Illustrate it with drawings or photos. Then write a restaurant dialogue based on your menu.

NC 4

3A.6 Sprachlabor

Word order, *gern/nicht gern*, negatives, *man soll …*

Word order
Remember that in German sentences the verb is always the second piece of information – only one element can go in front of it:

1	2	3		1	2	3	4
Ich	**trinke**	Kaffee.	→ Zum	Frühstück	**trinke**	ich	Kaffee.

---

1 Write new sentences.

Beispiel: **a** *Zum Mittagessen esse ich Pommes frites.*

a Ich esse Pommes frites. (Zum Mittagessen)
b Ich trinke Milch. (Zum Frühstück)
c Ich esse Wurst. (Zum Abendessen)
d Ich trinke Wasser. (Zum Mittagessen)
e Ich esse Salat. (Zum Abendessen)
f Ich esse Cornflakes. (Zum Frühstück)

2 Write new sentences for the pictures.

Beispiel: **a** *Ich esse gern Kartoffeln.*

---

gern/nicht gern
Ich esse Käse.
Ich esse **gern** Käse. ☺
Ich esse **nicht gern** Käse. ☹

---

3 Fill in the gaps using *keinen/keine/kein*.

a Ich esse ___*keinen*___ Käse (m).
b Ich trinke ▒▒▒▒ Wasser (n).
c Ich esse ▒▒▒▒ Pommes frites (pl).
d Ich trinke ▒▒▒▒ Kaffee (m).
e Ich esse ▒▒▒▒ Gemüse (n).
f Ich esse ▒▒▒▒ Butter (f).

---

keinen/keine/kein
m   Ich esse keinen Salat.
f   Ich trinke keine Milch.
n   Ich esse kein Brot.
pl   Ich esse keine Tomaten.

Man soll ...
You use the verb *sollen* to talk about what you should or shouldn't do. Verbs like *sollen* are called modal verbs and send the main verb to the end of the sentence – in its infinitive form.

Man isst kein Fastfood. → Man **soll** kein Fastfood **essen.**

4 Write new sentences with *Man soll ...*

Beispiel: **a** *Man soll jeden Tag Wasser trinken.*

a Ich trinke jeden Tag Wasser.
b Ich esse keine Pommes frites.
c Ich esse Gemüse.

d Ich trinke keine Cola.
e Ich esse jeden Tag Obst.
f Ich trinke keinen Kaffee.

Linking words

Linking words are little words like 'and' which link sentences together.

5 Match the German and the English linking words.

Beispiel: **und** *and*

und   **aber**
   denn
      oder

because
but   and
   or

> **? Think**
> Why do you think it's useful to use linking words when you write or speak? Discuss this with a partner.

6 Link each pair of sentences with a different linking word to make sense.

Beispiel: **a** *Ich esse gern Pizza und ich trinke gern Cola.*

a Ich esse gern Pizza. Ich trinke gern Cola.
b Ich trinke Orangensaft. Ich trinke Wasser.
c Ich esse nicht gern Salat. Ich esse gern Obst.
d Ich esse kein Gemüse. Gemüse ist furchtbar.

Long *u* sound – short *u* sound

7 🎧 **Listen carefully: long *u* or short *u*? (1–8)**

8 🎧 **Listen again and practise pronouncing each word correctly.**

> Vocabulary: practise your knowledge of food
> Grammar: practise 'verb second' word order; *gern, nicht gern* and *kein*
> Skills: practise spelling

 1 **Write a shopping list for Nina.**

Beispiel: **a** *Nudeln*

 a N_ _ _ ln

b  H_ _ _ ch_ _

c K_ r_ _ _ _ _ _n

 d  B_ _ _ e_

e J_ _ _u_ _

f W_r_ _

 2 **Match the quantities with the items.**

Beispiel: **a 2**

a eine Packung
b 250 Gramm
c eine Dose
d ein Glas
e ein Becher
f eine Scheibe

1	Joghurt
2	Kaffee
3	Schinken
4	Käse
5	Cola
6	Marmelade

 3 **Unscramble the word order in these sentences.**

NC 1–2

Beispiel: **a** *Zum Abendessen esse ich Brötchen.*

a esse Abendessen ich Brötchen Zum
b ich Zum Müsli esse Frühstück
c Hähnchen ich Mittagessen Zum esse

d Frühstück trinke Kaffee ich Zum
e trinke Zum Wasser ich Mittagessen
f Tee ich Zum trinke Abendessen

 4 **Match the sentences with the pictures. Does each person like (✓) or dislike (✗) it?**

NC 2

Beispiel: **a 5 ✗**

a Ich esse kein Gemüse.
b Ich trinke nicht gern Milch.
c Ich esse gern Fastfood.
d Ich trinke keine Cola.
e Ich esse nicht gern Fisch.
f Ich trinke gern Orangensaft.

Vocabulary: practise your knowledge of food
Grammar: practise 'verb second' word order; *gern, nicht gern* and *kein*
Skills: identify detail in texts

SCHREIBEN 1

Schreib die Wörter auf.

Beispiel: **a** *Schinken*

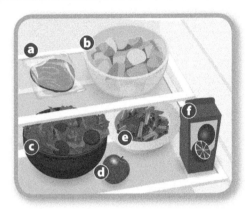

SCHREIBEN 2

Was isst und trinkst du gern/nicht gern/nicht? Schreib Sätze.

NC 2–3 *Beispiel:* **a** *Ich esse nicht gern Käse.*

SCHREIBEN 3

Und zum Frühstück/Mittagessen/Abendessen? Schreib Sätze.

NC 3 *Beispiel:* **a** *Zum Frühstück esse ich … Ich trinke …*

Frühstück   Mittagessen   Abendessen

Maja (15)

LESEN 4

Richtig, falsch oder nicht im Text?

NC 3–4 *Beispiel:* **a** *richtig*

- **a** Maja isst Brot, Butter und Marmelade.
- **b** Sie findet Cornflakes sehr gut.
- **c** Sie mag Kaffee.
- **d** Sie isst Nudeln.
- **e** Sie mag Fisch sehr gern.
- **f** Sie isst kein Obst.
- **g** Sie findet Gemüse nicht gut.
- **h** Sie mag keinen Tee.

Zum Frühstück esse ich Brot mit Butter und Marmelade. Ich esse nicht gern Müsli, denn Müsli ist langweilig. Und ich trinke nicht gern Milch, denn Milch ist nicht cool. Ich trinke gern Kaffee. Zum Mittagessen esse ich Nudeln mit Tomaten und Käse, und ich trinke Cola. Ich esse keinen Fisch, denn Fisch ist furchtbar!

Zum Abendessen esse ich Pizza oder Brötchen mit Schinken. Ich esse nicht gern Gemüse, denn Gemüse ist auch langweilig. Zum Abendessen trinke ich Tee.

HÖREN 1

NC 3

🎧 **Listen to Nico. True or false? (See pages 92 and 93.)**

Beispiel: **a** *true*

a Nico would like 500 grams of cheese.
b He would also like a pound of potatoes.
c He asks for a slice of sausage.
d He would like a bottle of milk.
e He also asks for four pots of yoghurt.
f His last purchase is half a dozen cans of cola.

 LESEN 2

NC 3

Read the sentences and match them to the pictures. (See pages 88–93.)

Beispiel: **a** *4, 5 …*

a Ich esse gern Fisch mit Kartoffeln und Spinat.
Ich trinke sehr gern Milch.
b Ich möchte eine Bratwurst mit Pommes frites und mit Ketchup,
bitte. Ich möchte auch eine Cola.
c Zum Mittagessen esse ich oft Hähnchen mit Reis und Salat.
Ich trinke normalerweise Orangensaft oder Kaffee.
d Ich möchte ein Stück Käse und 500 Gramm Tomaten. Ich
möchte auch eine Flasche Wasser.

 SPRECHEN 3

NC 3

Order the items of food below for two of you. (See pages 90 and 91.)

Beispiel: **a** *Ich möchte eine Currywurst mit …*

 SCHREIBEN 4

NC 3–4

Write at least one sentence for each of a–f. (See pages 88–89 and 94–95.)

Beispiel: **a** *Ich esse gern Pizza, denn Pizza ist super.*

a Food you like – and why.
b Food you don't like – and why not.
c What you don't eat at all – and why not.
d What you have for breakfast.
e What you have for lunch.
f What you have for your evening meal.

Essen und Trinken	Food and drink
Was isst du gern/nicht gern?	What do/don't you like eating?
Ich esse gern/nicht gern …	I like/don't like eating …
Brot	bread
ein Ei	an egg
eine Banane	a banana
einen Apfel	an apple
Fisch	fish
Hähnchen	chicken
Joghurt	yoghurt
Kartoffeln	potatoes
Käse	cheese
Nudeln	pasta
Reis	rice
Salat	salad, lettuce
Was trinkst du gern/ nicht gern?	What do/don't you like drinking?
Ich trinke gern/nicht gern …	I like/don't like drinking …
Cola	cola
Milch	milk
Orangensaft	orange juice

Mahlzeiten	Meals
Was isst/trinkst du …	What do you eat/drink …
zum Frühstück?	for breakfast?
zum Mittagessen?	for lunch?
zum Abendessen?	for dinner?
Zum Frühstück esse ich …	For breakfast I eat …
Zum Mittagessen trinke ich …	For lunch I drink …
Zum Abendessen …	For dinner …
Butter	butter
Cornflakes	cornflakes
Müsli	muesli
Marmelade	jam
Kaffee	coffee
Tee	tea
Wasser	water
meistens	mostly
normalerweise	usually

Etwas zu essen	Ordering food
Was darf es sein?	What would you like?
Was möchtest du?	What would you like?
Ja bitte?	Yes, please?
Ich möchte/nehme …, bitte.	I'd like …, please.
ein Erdbeereis	a strawberry ice cream
ein Schokoladeneis	a chocolate ice cream
ein Vanilleeis	a vanilla ice cream
mit/ohne Sahne	with/without cream
Pizza mit …	pizza with …
Oliven	olives
Pilzen	mushrooms
Spinat	spinach

Thunfisch	tuna
Tomaten	tomatoes
Zwiebeln	onions
Apfelkuchen	apple cake
Bio-Brot	organic bread
Bratwurst	fried sausage
Brötchen	bread rolls
Currywurst	curried sausage
Hamburger	hamburger
mit Mayonnaise	with mayonnaise
mit Ketchup	with ketchup
Pommes frites	fries
Schwarzwälder Kirschtorte	Black Forest gateau

Im Geschäft	In the shop
Sonst noch etwas?	Anything else?
Nein danke, das ist alles.	No thanks, that's all.
250 Gramm	250 grams
ein (halbes) Pfund	(half) a pound
ein (halbes) Kilo	(half) a kilo
ein Glas Marmelade	a jar of jam
ein Stück Käse	a piece of cheese
eine Dose Cola	a can of cola
eine Flasche Wasser	a bottle of water
eine Packung Kaffee	a packet of coffee
eine Scheibe Schinken	a slice of ham
eine Tüte Brötchen	a bag of bread rolls
einen Becher Joghurt	a pot of yoghurt
einen Liter Milch	a litre of milk

Ich esse kein Fleisch	I don't eat meat
Man soll … essen/trinken.	You should eat/drink …
Man soll keinen/keine/ kein … essen/trinken.	You shouldn't eat/drink …
Chips	crisps
Fastfood	fast food
Fleisch	meat
Gemüse	vegetables
Kuchen	cake
Obst	fruit
Schokolade	chocolate

I can…

- say what I like and don't like to eat and drink
- say what I eat at different mealtimes
- order food at a food stall
- buy food in a shop
- say how much I would like
- count up to 1000
- talk about healthy eating using *sollen*

3B.1 Berlin, Berlin!

Vocabulary: name the places in a town
Grammar: use *ein(e)(n)* and *kein(e)(n)* correctly
Skills: evaluate and improve your work

🎧 **Hör zu (1–16). Was passt zusammen?**
Listen and match each place to its picture and name (a–p).

Beispiel: **1** *i*

Es gibt …

 a einen Supermarkt
 b einen Zoo
 c einen Bahnhof
 d einen Park
 e einen Fernsehturm
f eine Post
 g eine Kirche
 h eine U-Bahn-Station

 i eine Skateboard-Bahn
 j ein Schloss
 k ein Schwimmbad
 l ein Stadion
 m ein Kaufhaus
 n ein Jugendzentrum
 o ein Museum
 p ein Kino

NC 2

👥👥 **Gedächtnisspiel.**
Memory game. Take turns to add another item each time.

Beispiel: **A** *In meiner Stadt gibt es einen Park.*
B *In meiner Stadt gibt es einen Park und eine Kirche.*
A *In meiner Stadt gibt es einen Park, eine Kirche und ein Schwimmbad.*

> ⚙️ *Grammatik* → p.162–3
>
> Es gibt …
> In meiner Stadt gibt es …
> **m** einen/keinen Park/Zoo/…
> **f** eine/keine Kirche/Post/…
> **n** ein/kein Kino/Schloss/…

NC 2

🎧 **Hör zu (1–6). Was gibt es (✓)? Was gibt es nicht (✗)?**
Listen. Look at the pictures in activity 1. What is/isn't there?

Beispiel: **1** c ✓ f ✗

NC 2

Schreib Sätze für diese Bilder. Was gibt es? Was gibt es nicht?
Write sentences for these pictures. What is/isn't there?

Beispiel: **a** *Es gibt ein Stadion, aber es gibt keinen Zoo.*

a
b
c
d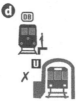
e
f

LESEN 5

NC 3–4

Lies. Richtig (R) oder falsch (F)?

Read Kathi's email to her cousin. Are the sentences true or false?

Beispiel: **a** *F*

a There is nothing to do for teenagers.
b Kathi finds the zoo boring.
c The department store is called KaDeWe.
d Kathi likes shopping.
e Kathi goes skateboarding every day.
f There is also a youth centre where she lives.

Hallo Rainer. Du kommst nach Berlin? Super! Es gibt hier viel für Teenager zu tun.

Ich wohne sehr zentral in Berlin-Mitte. Es gibt hier einen Zoo. Ich finde den Zoo toll, denn ich liebe Tiere. Es gibt auch ein Kaufhaus. Das Kaufhaus heißt KaDeWe. Es ist sehr groß. Ich gehe gern einkaufen.

Es gibt eine Skateboard-Bahn. Ich gehe nicht oft Skateboard fahren, denn ich bin nicht sehr sportlich. Es gibt aber kein Jugendzentrum in Berlin-Mitte. Ich finde das nicht gut.

Challenge

Write five to ten sentences about what there is (and what there isn't) where you live and what you think of it. Use the adjectives you have learned so far to give your opinions.

NC 3–4

? Think

After you have written a paragraph, evaluate it. How could it be improved? Use this checklist:

- Have I spelled all the words correctly?
- Have I used the correct word order?
- Have I used previously learned language from my memory, exercise book and textbook?
- Have I covered all the points I was supposed to write about?
- Have I given a variety of opinions?

HÖREN 6

NC 3–4

Hör zu. Was sagt Ali?

Ali's friend is coming to Berlin. What five places does Ali mention? What does he think of them?

Beispiel: **1** *Park – big*

Es gibt	in meiner Stadt in meiner Gegend in meinem Dorf	(k)einen (k)eine (k)ein	Bahnhof. Kirche. Stadion.
Ich finde	meine Stadt meine Gegend mein Dorf	gut/interessant/toll. nicht gut. langweilig/schlecht/schrecklich.	

3B.2 Was kann man machen?

- Vocabulary: say what you can do in a place
- Grammar: use *man kann*, and different forms of *können* and *wollen*
- Skills: work out language patterns

1 LESEN

Lies die Sätze. Wähle das richtige Wort.
Read the sentences and find the correct word in the box.

Beispiel: **a** *schwimmen*

essen	fahren	schwimmen
trinken	gehen	tanzen
spielen	treffen	

Man kann hier ▬▬ .

Man kann hier Pizza ▬▬ .

Man kann hier Kaffee
▬▬ .

Man kann hier
Mountainbike ▬▬ .

Man kann hier ins Kino
▬▬ .

Man kann hier Fußball
▬▬ .

Man kann hier Freunde
▬▬ .

Man kann hier ▬▬ .

2 HÖREN

🎧 **Hör zu (a–h). Ist alles richtig?**

3 SCHREIBEN
NC 2

Schreib Sätze. Was kann man hier machen?
Write sentences. What can one do here?

Beispiel: **a** *Man kann hier Skateboard fahren.*

- **a** Es gibt eine Skateboard-Bahn.
- **b** Es gibt eine Disco.
- **c** Es gibt ein Schwimmbad.
- **d** Es gibt ein Restaurant.
- **e** Es gibt einen Park.
- **f** Es gibt ein Café.

4 SPRECHEN
NC 2

👥 **Kann man das machen? A ↔ B.**
Take turns pointing at a picture in activity 1 and asking a question.

Beispiel: **A** *Kann man hier schwimmen?*
B *Ja (Nein), man kann hier (nicht) schwimmen.*

? Think

Can you work out the rule for how to say what there is to do?

To say that one **can** do something, you use *man* ▬▬ + a second verb. The second verb ends in ▬▬ and is at the ▬▬ of the sentence.

If 'one can swim' is *man kann schwimmen*, how would you say 'I can swim'?

 Hallo. Ich heiße Tatjana. Ich bin dreizehn Jahre alt und wohne in München. Das ist im Süden von Deutschland.

München ist super! Es gibt hier einen Park. Der Park heißt „Englischer Garten", aber er ist in Deutschland. Komisch, oder? Man kann im Park Rad fahren. Das finde ich toll. Man kann auch ins Kino gehen. Ich gehe gern ins Kino, denn ich liebe Filme.

Am Wochenende kann man ins Jugendzentrum gehen. Im Jugendzentrum kann man Tischtennis oder Billard spielen. Ich finde Tischtennis total gut, aber ich mag Billard nicht gern.

Ich kann hier leider nicht Skateboard fahren, denn es gibt keine Skateboard-Bahn – schade!

Billard *snooker*
schade! *what a shame!*

LESEN 5
NC 3–4

Lies die Nachricht von Tatjana und wähle die richtigen Antworten.

Beispiel: **a 2**

a Tatjana is **1** twelve **2** thirteen **3** fourteen years old.
b Munich is in the **1** North **2** West **3** South of Germany.
c The *Englischer Garten* is in **1** England **2** Germany **3** France.
d In the park, you can **1** go skateboarding **2** play table tennis **3** go cycling.
e Tatjana **1** likes going **2** doesn't like going **3** doesn't go to the cinema.
f Tatjana **1** really likes **2** can't play **3** doesn't really like snooker.

SCHREIBEN 6

Schreib die Fragen auf.

Beispiel: **a** *Willst du ins Kino gehen?*

VIDEO 7

Sieh dir das Video an. Beantworte die Fragen.
Watch the video and answer the questions.

Beispiel: **a** *a museum, …*

a Which four places does Nico suggest he and Kathi visit?
b What does she think about the final suggestion and why?

⚙ Grammatik → p.166

können – *to be able to*
ich kann — *I can*
du kannst — *you can*
man kann — *one can*

wollen – *to want to*
ich will — *I want to*
du willst — *you want to*
man will — *one wants to*

○ Challenge

Create a poster for your local tourist board, telling German-speaking visitors what there is to do and see in your area. Try to use the vocabulary you learned in Unit 2A.

For NC level 4, try to write paragraphs of three to four full sentences. Link your sentences with *und, oder* and *aber*. Give your opinions: *Das Schwimmbad ist fantastisch, denn es ist modern …*

NC 3–4

> Vocabulary: ask for and give directions
> Grammar: use *Geh/Gehen Sie* and *Nimm/Nehmen Sie* to give instructions
> Skills: deal with unfamiliar words

 Hör zu (1–11). Was passt zusammen?

Beispiel: **1 b**

 **a**

 b

 c

d

e

f

Geh links.	**Geh rechts.**	**Geh geradeaus.**

Nimm die erste Straße links.	**Nimm die zweite Straße links.**	**Nimm die dritte Straße links.**

g

h

i

j

k

Nimm die erste Straße rechts.	**Nimm die zweite Straße rechts.**	**Nimm die dritte Straße rechts.**	**Es ist auf der linken Seite.**	**Es ist auf der rechten Seite.**

 Hör zu (1–7). Wohin gehen sie?

NC 2–3

Listen. Which place (in the box on the right) does each person want to go to? Where is it on the map (a–g)?

Beispiel: **1** *Supermarkt* **c**

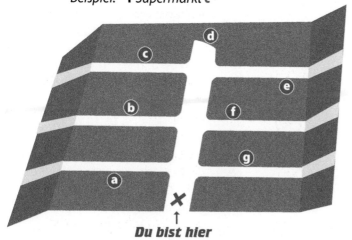

Du bist hier

    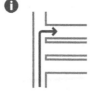 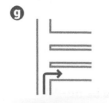

Grammatik → p.167

There are two different ways of giving instructions:

- *Nehmen Sie/Gehen Sie* is used when you speak to an adult you don't know well.
- *Nimm/Geh* is used when you talk to a friend, another young person or someone older who you do know well.

SCHREIBEN 3

NC 2–3

Wo ist das Schwimmbad? Schreib Sätze für a–c in Übung 2.
Give directions to go to a–c on the map in activity 2. Start from X.

Beispiel: **a** *Nimm die erste Straße links. Das Schwimmbad ist auf der linken Seite.*

SPRECHEN 4

NC 2–3

Wo ist das Schloss, bitte? Macht Dialoge für d–g in Übung 2. A ←→ B.

Beispiel: **A** *Wo ist das Schloss, bitte?*
B   *Geh geradeaus.*
A   *Danke.*
B   *Bitte. Tschüs.*

Wo ist	der Supermarkt? die Kirche? das Schwimmbad? der Zoo? das Stadion? der Bahnhof? das Schloss?
Geh Gehen Sie	links/rechts/geradeaus.
Nimm Nehmen Sie	die erste/zweite/dritte Straße links/rechts.
Der/Die/Das … ist auf der linken/rechten Seite.	

über die Kreuzung

über die Ampel

über die Brücke

VIDEO 5

NC 3–4

Sieh dir das Video an. Beantworte die Fragen.
Watch the video and answer the questions.

Beispiel: **a** *department store*

a Where does Frau Winter want to go?
b What directions does Nico give her?
c Where does Bernd want to go?
d What directions does Kathi give him?

? Think

You will hear some unfamiliar words and expressions in the video for activity 5. Use the following tips to work out what's going on.

- Listen for any words and phrases you already know.
- See if the context gives you any clues.
- See what you can work out from the body language of the characters.

Challenge

Using the map in activity 2, write a tour of the town. Give an opinion about each place you get to.

Beispiel: Nimm die erste Straße links. Hier ist das Schwimmbad. Das Schwimmbad ist auf der linken Seite. Das Schwimmbad ist fantastisch. Geh dann …

NC 3–4

Vocabulary: learn to buy tickets and presents
Grammar: use verbs to ask questions
Skills: ask and answer questions

HÖREN 1 🎧 **Hör zu und lies. Beantworte die Fragen.**

Beispiel: **a** *three*

a How many tickets does the customer want?
b For how many adults and how many children?
c What question does the customer ask in picture 2?
d What do you think the words *bitte schön* mean in picture 3?
e What does the ticket vendor say in picture 4?

1

A: Guten Tag. Kann ich Ihnen helfen?

B: Ich möchte **drei Karten**, bitte.

2

Preisliste
Erwachsene 12€
Kinder 8€
Gruppen ab 10 Personen
6€ pro Person

A: Für Erwachsene oder Kinder?

B: **Zwei Erwachsene** und **ein Kind**. Was kostet das?

3

Preisliste
Erwachsene 12€
Kinder 8€
Gruppen ab 10 Personen
6€ pro Person

A: Das kostet **32 Euro**.

B: Bitte schön. **32 Euro**.

4

ab 10 Personen
rson

A: Danke. Viel Spaß!

SPRECHEN 2 👥 **Macht Dialoge. A ↔ B.**

NC 2–3 *Beispiel*: **A** *Guten Tag. Kann ich Ihnen helfen?*
B *Ich möchte vier Karten, bitte.*
A *Für Erwachsene oder Kinder? ...*

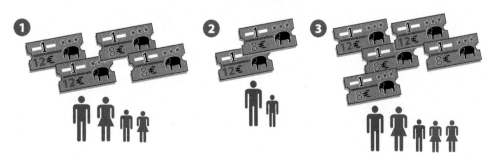

Kann ich Ihnen helfen?
Ich möchte eine Karte …
zwei Karten …
für einen Erwachsenen. 👨
für ein Kind. 🧒
für zwei Erwachsene. 👨👩
für zwei Kinder. 🧒🧒
Was kostet das?
Das kostet zehn Euro.

HÖREN 3

NC 3–4

🎧 **Hör zu. Füll die Tabelle aus.**

	Tickets?	Adults/children?	Price?
a	3	2 adults + 1 child	€19
b			
c			
d			
e			

HÖREN 4

🎧 **Hör zu (1–6). Was passt zusammen?**

Beispiel: **1** *c*

a der Schlüsselanhänger
b die Schneekugel
c der Lolli
d die Plastikschlange
e das Notizbuch
f die Schachtel Schokolade

SPRECHEN 5

 👥 **Was möchtest du? A ⟷ B.**
Take turns asking each other questions, using the pictures in activity 4.

Beispiel: **A** *Was möchtest du? (pointing at picture c)*
B *Ich möchte einen Lolli.*

LESEN 6

NC 3

Lies die Dialoge und finde die Sätze im Text.

Beispiel: **a** *Ich suche ein Geschenk.*

a I am looking for a present.
b Does she like writing?
c Would she like …
d Does he like eating …?
e I'll take …

Ich suche ein Geschenk für Britta.
Schreibt sie gern?
Ja, sie schreibt gern.
Möchte sie ein Notizbuch?
Gute Idee. Ich nehme ein Notizbuch.

Ich suche ein Geschenk für Heinz.
Isst er gern Schokolade?
Ja, er isst sehr gern Schokolade.
Möchte er eine Schachtel Schokolade?
Prima Idee. Ich nehme eine Schachtel Schokolade.

⚙️ **Grammatik → p.162**

Ich möchte einen/eine/ein …
der words → einen
die words → eine
das words → ein

❓ **Think**

Can you work out the rule for forming questions in German?

'When you ask a question in German, you move the verb to the ▭▭▭▭ of the sentence.'

Challenge

Write two dialogues – one buying tickets and one buying a present. Each dialogue should include at least four sentences. Use *denn* to explain your choice of present.

NC 3–4

3B.5 Besuchen Sie Zoomsdorf!

Vocabulary: understand tourist information
Grammar: learn the format of instructions
Skills: identify formality of language (*du* and *Sie*)

 LESEN 1

(NC 2)

Was passt zusammen? Schreib Sätze.

Beispiel: **a** *Komm nach Berlin!*

a
Komm	mit dem Boot auf der Spree!
Iss	den Zoo!
Besuch	nach Berlin!
Fahr	Berliner Spezialitäten!

die Spree
the river in Berlin

b
Kommen Sie	mit dem Rad im Park!
Besuchen Sie	frischen Fisch!
Fahren Sie	nach Hamburg!
Essen Sie	die Galerien!

 HÖREN 2

(NC 3–4)

🎧 Hör zu. Was ist die richtige Reihenfolge für die Bilder?

Look at the advert for Zoomsdorf below. Listen and note the order in which the places are mentioned.

Beispiel: **e**, …

 Think

Which of the two jigsaws is aimed at adults and which at young people? How can you tell?

 SPRECHEN 3

(NC 2)

👥👥 Was kann man in Zoomsdorf besuchen? A ↔ B.

Take turns choosing something to do in Zoomsdorf. Your partner points to the matching picture.

Beispiel: **A** *Besuch den Zoo!*
B *Das ist Bild* **e.**

 SCHREIBEN 4

(NC 3–4)

Mach ein Poster für deinen Wohnort.

Adapt the sentences from activity 1 to make a leaflet about your own home town.

Kommen Sie nach Zoomsdorf
Attraktionen für Jung und Alt!

5 **Sieh dir Ninas Videoblog an. Beantworte die Fragen auf Englisch.**
NC 4

Watch Nina's video blog and answer the questions.

Beispiel: **a** *TV tower*

a What should you visit first in Berlin?
b What should you do if it rains?

c Where should you go when it is sunny?
d Why does Nina like Berlin? Give two reasons.

6 **Lies den Text. Beantworte die Fragen.**
NC 4

Beispiel: **a** *in the centre*

a Where in Munich is the pedestrian zone?
b What can you find in the pedestrian zone?
c What sort of food can you eat in Munich?

d What two things can you do at the *Oktoberfest*?
e What can you do in winter?

Kommen Sie nach München!

Es gibt hier viel für Jung und Alt zu tun. <u>Es gibt</u> viele Attraktionen.
<u>Im Zentrum gibt es</u> eine fantastische Fußgängerzone mit Geschäften.
<u>Kaufen Sie bei</u> Kaufhof <u>ein</u>. Das ist ein großes Kaufhaus in der Mitte
der Stadt. Sie wollen nicht einkaufen? <u>Gehen Sie</u> in ein Restaurant.
<u>Man kann</u> internationale und deutsche Spezialitäten essen.
<u>Besuchen Sie</u> ein Café.

<u>Gehen Sie</u> im Herbst auf das Oktoberfest. <u>Man kann</u> mit dem Riesenrad
fahren und Freunde aus der ganzen Welt treffen.

Und im Winter? Es gibt hier einen wunderbaren Park, den Englischen
Garten. <u>Machen Sie</u> einen Spaziergang durch den Park im Schnee.
München hat für alle eine Attraktion.

7 **Stell Fragen. A ↔ B.**

Take turns to ask and answer questions about Munich.
Use the questions from the box below.

Beispiel: **A** *Wo kann man einkaufen?*
　　　　　 B *Man kann bei Kaufhof einkaufen.*

die Fußgängerzone *pedestrian zone*
das Geschäft *shop*
das Oktoberfest *festival in Munich*
das Riesenrad *Ferris wheel*
einen Spaziergang machen *to go
for a walk*

Wo kann man einkaufen?
Wohin kann man gehen?
Was kann man essen?/trinken?/
machen?

Challenge

Give a presentation about where you live. Imagine you're inviting
someone to your home town, and suggest at least five things he or
she can do there.

Use the underlined phrases in activity 6 as a framework. Either
write down your presentation or make a video blog like Nina.

Beispiel: Kommen Sie nach London! Es gibt …

NC 3–4

Modal verbs, giving instructions

können, wollen

The modal verbs *können* (to be able to) and *wollen* (to want to) are always followed by a second verb. The second verb ends in *-en* and is at the end of the sentence.

If you want to say that you cannot or don't want to do something, add the word *nicht* after the modal verb: *Ich will (nicht) in die Stadt gehen.*

		können	**wollen**
I	ich	kann	will
you	du	kannst	willst
he/she/one	er/sie/man	kann	will
we	wir	können	wollen
you (informal plural)	ihr	könnt	wollt
they/you (formal)	sie/Sie	können	wollen

1 **Put the words into the correct order.**

Beispiel: **a** *Ich will in den Zoo gehen.*

a Ich will gehen in den Zoo.
b Großeltern Ich meine kann besuchen.
c Er das will sehen Fußballspiel.
d im Restaurant Wir können essen.
e finden kann Sie das Stadion nicht.
f Sie mit der U-Bahn fahren können.

2 **Make sentences using the correct forms of *können* and *wollen*.**

Beispiel: **a** *Er kann schwimmen.*

a Er + können + [swimming]	**b** Du + wollen + [plate]	**c** Man + können + [running]
d Wir + wollen + [KINO]	**e** Sie (pl) + können + [bicycle]	

Giving instructions to a friend, you use the *du* form of the verb and take off the *-st*.

> Du nimm**st** → Nimm!
> Du geh**st** → Geh!
> Du mach**st** → Mach!

Giving instructions to an adult stranger, you use the *Sie* form but put the verb first.

> Sie nehmen → Nehmen Sie!
> Sie gehen → Gehen Sie!
> Sie machen → Machen Sie!

3 Change the following statements into instructions.

Beispiel: **a** *Geh die zweite Straße rechts!*

a Du gehst die zweite Straße rechts.
b Sie gehen die erste Straße links.
c Du nimmst die dritte Straße rechts.
d Sie nehmen die dritte Straße links.
e Du trinkst Orangensaft.
f Sie essen Obst.
g Du hörst Musik.
h Sie gehen über die Kreuzung.

Asking questions

When you ask a question in German you need to move the verb to the beginning of the sentence and make sure that the verb ending is correct.

> Spiel**st** du Fußball? *Do you play football?*
> Spiel**t** er Fußball? *Does he play football?*

4 Turn each statement into a question.

Beispiel: **a** *Gehst du ins Kino?*

a Du gehst ins Kino.
b Er macht Hausaufgaben.
c Wir fahren Rad.
d Sie sehen fern.
e Sie tanzt gern.
f Sie essen gern Schokolade.

5 🎧 **Listen (a–d). Is it a statement or a question?**

Beispiel: **a** *question*

v and w

The *v* and *w* sounds are different in German and in English. The German *w* sounds like the English *v*, and normally the German *v* is pronounced like an English *f*.

Remember the word *Volkswagen* – pronounced in the German way, of course!

6 🎧 **First try to pronounce these words. Then listen and repeat.**

a wollen **b** wohnen **c** Erwachsene **d** schwimmen **e** Wien
f Wein **g** Wort **h** vier **i** viel **j** voll

7 🎧 **Listen. Do you hear v or w?**

Beispiel: **a** *schwarz*

a sch_arz **b** _ilhelm **c** _erstehen **d** Kur_e
e Ki_i **f** _ie **g** _or **h** Kra_atte

3B.7 Extra Star

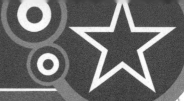

- Vocabulary: practise the names of places in a town and what you can do
- Grammar: practise using *ein(e)(n)* and *kein(e)(n)* correctly and giving directions
- Skills: read for gist and detail

LESEN **1** **Look at the picture. Are the sentences true or false?**

NC 2 *Beispiel*: **a** *true*

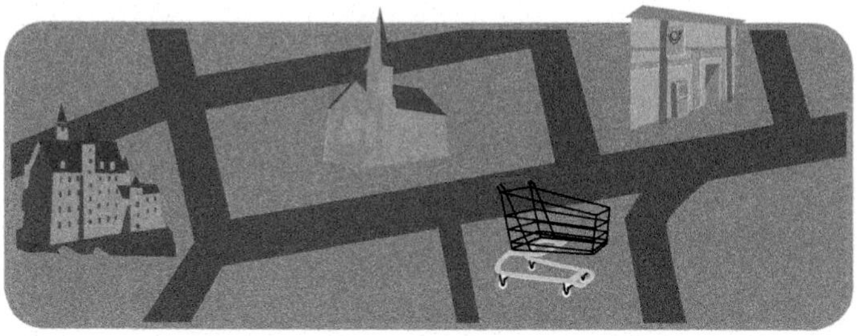

- **a** Es gibt einen Supermarkt.
- **b** Es gibt ein Schloss.
- **c** Es gibt eine Skateboard-Bahn.
- **d** Es gibt eine Post.
- **e** Es gibt ein Kaufhaus.
- **f** Es gibt eine Kirche.

SCHREIBEN **2** **Fill the gaps with the words from the box on the right.**

tanzen fahren essen gehen trinken

Beispiel: **a** *Man kann eine Pizza essen.*

a 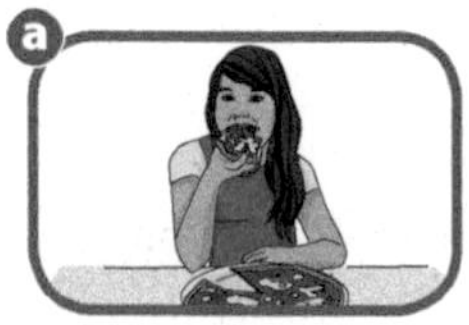
Man kann eine Pizza ___ .

b 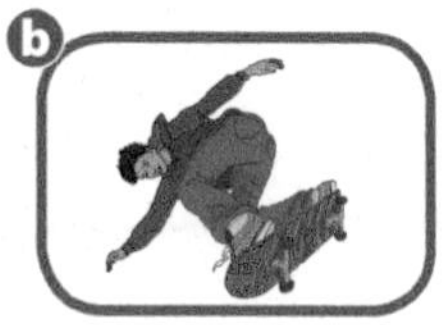
Man kann Skateboard ___ .

c 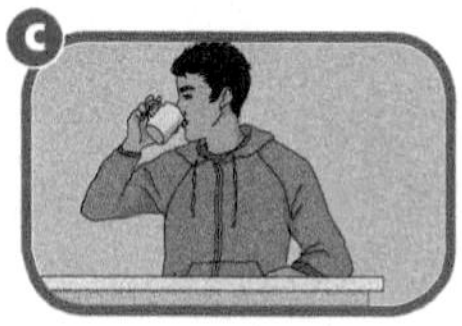
Man kann einen Smoothie ___ .

d 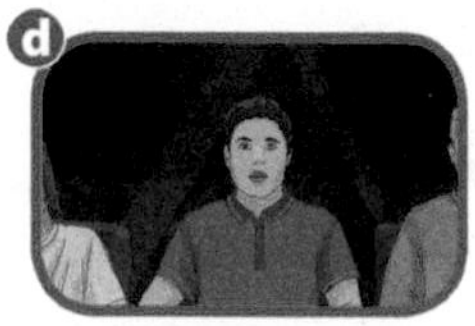
Man kann ins Kino ___ .

e 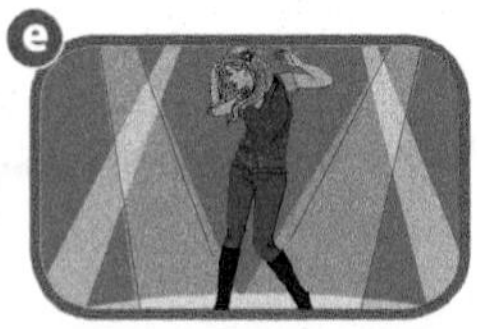
Man kann in der Disco ___ .

LESEN **3** **Read Britta's email and answer the questions.**

NC 3 *Beispiel*: **a** *it's great*

- **a** What does Britta think of her city?
- **b** Which three places does she mention first?
- **c** What is Britta's favourite place?
- **d** Give two reasons why it is her favourite place.
- **e** What isn't there in Britta's town?
- **f** Where does Britta go instead to play football?

> Hallo!
>
> Ich heiße Britta. Ich wohne in Augsburg. Ich finde Augsburg toll. Es gibt hier einen Park, ein Schwimmbad und ein super Museum. Ich gehe am liebsten ins Schwimmbad. Das Schwimmbad ist groß und ich kann dort meine Freunde treffen. Aber es gibt kein Jugendzentrum. Das finde ich nicht gut, aber ich kann im Park Fußball spielen.
>
> Deine Britta

SCHREIBEN **4** **Write down which directions you would give.**

NC 1–2 *Beispiel*: **a** *Gehen Sie links.*

a 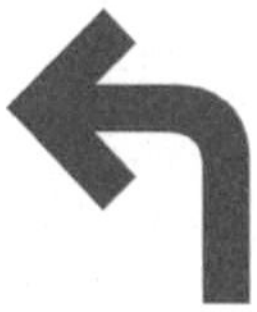
G_h_n S_ _ l_nks.

b 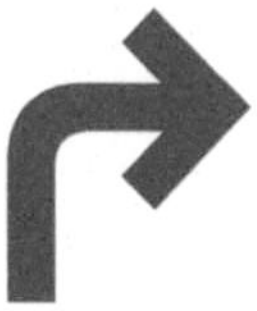
G_h r_chts.

c 
G_h g_r_d_ _ _s.

d 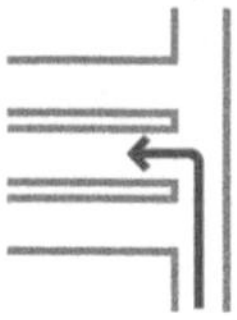
N_mm die zw_ _ _ _ Str_ß_ l_ _ _ _.

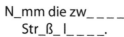

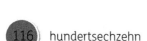

Vocabulary: practise places in a town and what you can do there
Grammar: *es gibt* + *(k)ein(e)(n)* ...; *man kann* + infinitive
Skills: practise dealing with unfamiliar words

LESEN 1

NC 4

Was gibt es zu tun?

Read. Note what there is to do in each city.

Beispiel: **a** *mountain biking*

a

Axel

Ich wohne in Rüdesheim im Westen von Deutschland. Ich finde es hier langweilig. Es gibt in Rüdesheim viele Touristen und viele Souvenirgeschäfte. Im Sommer kann man Mountainbike fahren und wandern, aber im Winter gibt es für Teenager nicht viel zu tun. Es gibt kein Jugendzentrum und kein Fußballstadion.

b

Evi

Ich wohne in Germering. Das ist bei München im Süden von Deutschland. Ich finde das total klasse! Im Sommer kann man hier schwimmen, denn es gibt ein sehr großes Schwimmbad. Im Winter kann man im Eislaufstadion Schlittschuh laufen. Ich fahre auch oft nach München. Dort kann man gut einkaufen und es gibt auch viel Kultur dort – Museen, Galerien usw.

LESEN 2

NC 4

Lies den Text noch einmal. Wer ist das?

Beispiel: **a** *Evi*

Who ...
a likes the place where they live?
b has an ice-skating rink in their town?
c has a lot of facilities for tourists?
d mentions that you can do things all year round?
e says that there isn't a youth centre or stadium?
f lives in the South of Germany?

Willkommen in Mittelstadt!

SCHREIBEN 3

NC 3–4

Willkommen in Mittelstadt! Was gibt es hier (nicht)? Was kann man (nicht) machen? Schreib Sätze.

Beispiel: *In Mittelstadt gibt es ...*
Man kann hier ...
In Mittelstadt gibt es kein(e/en) ...
Man kann nicht ...

LESEN 1

NC 3–4

Read the email and choose the correct answer. (See pages 104–107.)

Beispiel: **a 2**

a Saarbrücken is in the **1** East **2** West **3** North of Germany.

b Carola finds Saarbrücken **1** not good **2** very good **3** quite good.

c Carola is in a **1** dance team **2** skiing team **3** football team.

d France is **1** 10 kilometres **2** 1 kilometre **3** 20 kilometres **away.**

e Carola mentions **1** a swimming pool and a castle **2** many churches and a TV tower **3** a castle and many churches.

f Carola mentions that in Saarbrücken you can **1** shop, eat and drink **2** only shop **3** only eat and drink.

> Hallo. Ich heiße Carola. Ich komme aus Saarbrücken im Westen von Deutschland. Ich finde Saarbrücken ziemlich gut. Ich kann hier Sport machen und ich gehe auch oft tanzen, denn ich bin in einer Tanzgruppe. Wir machen Streetdance. Ski fahren kann ich aber nicht, denn es gibt hier keine Berge.
>
> Frankreich ist nur einen Kilometer von Saarbrücken entfernt. Es gibt auch viel für Touristen zu sehen, zum Beispiel ein Schloss und viele alte Kirchen. Man kann hier sehr gut einkaufen, essen und trinken.
>
> Komm doch mal nach Saarbrücken!

HÖREN 2

NC 3–4

🎧 **Listen (1–6). Which places are mentioned? What do people think about them (positive ✓ or negative X)?** (See pages 104 and 105.)

Beispiel: **1** zoo ✓

SPRECHEN 3

NC 3

👥 **Make dialogues.** (See pages 108 and 109.)

Beispiel: **a** A *Wo ist das Schloss?*
          B *Geh links.*
          A *Wie findest du das Schloss?*
          B *Ich finde es toll.*

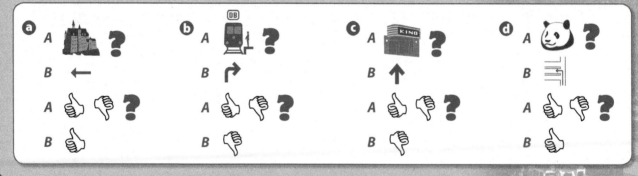

SCHREIBEN 4

NC 3–4

Write a report on your own town using the bullet points. (See pages 104–107.)

Beispiel: *In meiner Stadt gibt es einen/eine/ein … Man kann hier (nicht) … Ich finde meine Stadt gut/schlecht/langweilig.*

- Was gibt es in deiner Stadt zu sehen und zu tun?
- Was kann man machen?
- Was kann man nicht machen?
- Wie findest du deine Stadt?

Was gibt es?	What is there?
Es gibt (keinen/keine/kein)…	There is (no)…/There are (no)…
Gibt es …?	Is there …?
einen Bahnhof	a railway station
einen Fernsehturm	a TV tower
ein Geschäft	a shop
ein Jugendzentrum	a youth centre
ein Kaufhaus	a department store
ein Kino	a cinema
eine Kirche	a church
ein Museum	a museum
einen Park	a park
ein Schloss	a castle
ein Schwimmbad	a swimming pool
ein Stadion	a stadium
einen Supermarkt	a supermarket
eine Post	a post office
eine Skateboard-Bahn	a skatepark
eine U-Bahn-Station	an underground station
einen Zoo	a zoo

Was kann man machen?	What can one do?
Man kann (nicht) …	One can (not) …
Ich kann …	I can …
Kannst du …?	Can you …?
Freunde treffen	meet friends
Fußball spielen	play football
in der Disco tanzen	dance in the disco
ins Kino gehen	go to the cinema
ins Theater gehen	go to the theatre
Kaffee trinken	drink coffee
Pizza essen	eat pizza
Rad fahren	cycle
schwimmen	swim

Wo ist …?	Where is …?
der Bahnhof	the railway station
der Park	the park
die Post	the post office
das Schloss	the castle
das Schwimmbad	the swimming pool
die Skateboard-Bahn	the skatepark
das Stadion	the stadium
der Supermarkt	the supermarket

Richtungen	Directions
Geh …	Go … (informal)
Gehen Sie …	Go … (formal)
Nimm …	Take … (informal)
Nehmen Sie …	Take … (formal)
links	left
rechts	right
geradeaus	straight on

die erste Straße	the first road
die zweite Straße	the second road
die dritte Straße	the third road
über die Ampel	over the traffic lights
über die Kreuzung	over the crossing
über die Brücke	over the bridge
auf der linken Seite	on the left-hand side
auf der rechten Seite	on the right-hand side

Im Zoo	At the zoo
Ich möchte …	I'd like …
eine Karte	a ticket
zwei Karten	two tickets
für ein Kind	for a child
für zwei Kinder	for two children
für einen Erwachsenen	for an adult
für zwei Erwachsene	for two adults
Was kostet das?	How much does it cost?
Das kostet …	That costs …
Danke (schön).	Thank you.
Bitte (schön).	You're welcome.

Im Souvenirladen	In the souvenir shop
der Lolli	lollipop
das Notizbuch	notebook
die Plastikschlange	plastic snake
der Schlüsselanhänger	key ring
die Schneekugel	snow globe
die Schachtel Schokolade	box of chocolates
Ich suche …	I am looking for …
ein Geschenk	a present
Ich kaufe einen/eine/ein …	I (will) buy a …
Ich nehme einen/eine/ein …	I (will) take a …
Ich möchte einen/eine/ein …	I would like a …

I can...

- say what there is and isn't in a town using *ein(e)(n)* and *kein(e)(n)*
- say what you can do in a town, using *man kann*
- give opinions about places using adjectives
- ask for and give directions
- buy tickets for adults and children
- buy presents in a souvenir shop using *einen/eine/ein* correctly
- ask questions using verbs

4A.1 Die Jeans ist cool!

Vocabulary: talk about clothes and say what you think of them
Grammar: use *ist* after a singular noun and *sind* after a plural noun
Skills: recycle adjectives you already know; learn about true and false friends

Die Kleidung

a der Rock
b der Pullover
c die Jeans
d das Kleid
e der Kapuzenpullover
f die Ballerinas
g das Hemd
h die Lederjacke
i das T-Shirt
j die Sportschuhe
k die Stiefel
l die Shorts

HÖREN 1 🎧 **Hör zu (1–12). Was ist die richtige Reihenfolge?**
Listen. What is the correct order?

Beispiel: **1 e**

LESEN 2 **Was passt zusammen?**

Beispiel: **1 g**

1 hässlich	2 schick	3 alt	4 neu	5 modisch
6 altmodisch	7 bequem	8 unbequem	9 teuer	10 billig

a cheap	b new	c fashionable
d comfortable	e old	f expensive
g ugly	h uncomfortable	i chic, smart
j old-fashioned		

? Think

Many words in German and English look very similar and have the same meaning: *die Jeans* means 'jeans'.

But beware of 'false friends' – words which look the same but mean something different. *Die Hose* doesn't mean 'hose' – it means 'trousers'!

Grammatik → p.162,166

der/die/das + singular noun + ist
Der Rock **ist** … *The skirt is* …

die + plural noun + sind
Die Sportschuhe **sind** … *The trainers are* …

⚠️ In German, *die Hose* and usually also *die Jeans* are singular:
Die Jeans/Die Hose **ist** blau. *The jeans/trousers are blue.*

But *die Shorts* are usually plural, like in English:
Die Shorts **sind** blau. *The shorts are blue.*

Der Rock/Mantel/Pullover/ Kapuzenpullover Die Hose/Bluse/Jeans/ Lederjacke Das Hemd/Kleid/T-Shirt	ist	schwarz	rot	weiß
		bequem	unbequem	lässig
		schön	schick	hässlich
Die Shorts/Sportschuhe/ Stiefel/Ballerinas	sind	billig	teuer	neu
		modisch	altmodisch	alt

lässig *casual*
der Mantel *coat*

 ? Think

Express your opinions about items of clothing by:

- using adjectives and words like *sehr* (very), *ziemlich* (quite) and *total* (totally)
- using *ich finde* … + adjective
- using *ich mag (nicht)*

Add extra detail to your opinions using *denn* and *aber*:

Ich mag das Hemd nicht, denn es ist total unbequem. *I don't like the shirt, because it is totally uncomfortable.*

Ich mag die Sportschuhe, aber sie sind teuer. *I like the trainers, but they are expensive.*

⚠️ Don't forget to put a comma before *denn* and *aber*.

 3 Wähle das richtige Verb – *ist* oder *sind*?

a Ich mag die Jeans nicht. Sie _ist_ total unbequem.
b Das Hemd ▨▨▨ langweilig.
c Die Stiefel ▨▨▨ teuer.
d Die Ballerinas ▨▨▨ neu.
e Mein Kapuzenpullover ▨▨▨ warm.
f Die Shorts ▨▨▨ altmodisch.

 4 👥 Macht Sätze. Richtig oder falsch? A ↔ B.
NC 2–3
Take turns describing the clothing on these two pages. Is your partner's description true or false?

Beispiel: **A** *Das Kleid ist rot und ziemlich altmodisch.*
B *Falsch! Das Kleid ist schwarz und sehr modisch.*

5 Was ist die richtige Reihenfolge?
Put the words in the right order.

Beispiel: **a** *Ich finde die Lederjacke blöd, aber* …

a Ich finde blöd die Lederjacke, aber cool ist der Rock
b mag nicht Ich die Stiefel, denn unbequem sind sie
c Jeans schick Die ist, teuer aber
d unbequem ist Die Bluse, denn altmodisch ist sie

die Hose

die Bluse

 Challenge

Imagine you are a fashion journalist. Create a fashion scrapbook containing pictures of at least 10 items of clothing. Write a brief description of each one and give your opinion of it.

Beispiel: Ich mag die Ballerinas, denn sie sind rot und sehr schick! …

NC 3–4

> Vocabulary: say what you wear and what you would like to wear
> Grammar: learn about adjective endings
> Skills: use language you already know in a new context

LESEN 1

NC 3–4

Sieh dir die Bilder an und lies die Texte. In jedem Text gibt es zwei Fehler.
Look at the pictures and read the texts. Find two mistakes in each text.

Beispiel: **a** *blaue Jeans*

? Think

- Did you notice the different forms of *ein* in these texts? What forms are there and in which contexts have you come across them before?
- Look at the adjectives that come after *einen/eine/ein*, e.g. *ein **rotes** Top*. What is different about them?

Was tragen die Stars?

a Hi Fans. Wir tragen sehr lässige Kleidung. Wir tragen blaue Jeans oder gelbe Hosen, schwarze oder bunte T-Shirts und schwarze Sportschuhe. Wir finden die Kleidung bequem, schick und modisch.
Tokio Hotel

b Hi, ich bin Profi-Fußballspieler und ich trage ein grünes T-Shirt und grüne Shorts. Das die Farbe für Deutschland.
Michael Ballack

c Hallo, wir sind eine Band aus Deutschland. Ich heiße Stefanie und ich trage ein schwarzes Top, eine schwarz-weiße Jacke und eine schwarze Jeans. Meine Bandkollegen tragen alle schwarze Jacke. Sie tragen auch ein schwarzes Hemd und ein blaues T-Shirt.
Silbermond

d Hallo, ich bin Heidi Klum und ich bin Fotomodell. Mein Outfit ist teuer, aber sehr modern. Ich trage ein rot-weißes Top und eine gelbe Jacke. Schick, oder?
Heidi Klum

bunt *multicoloured*

ich trage du trägst er/sie trägt wir tragen ihr tragt sie tragen Sie tragen	einen	gelb**en** schwarz-weiß**en** lässig**en**	Rock/Kapuzenpullover.
	eine	modisch**e** bun**te**	Jeans/Hose/Jacke/Bluse.
	ein	teur**es** schick**es**	T-Shirt/Kleid/Top/Hemd.
	—	modern**e** hässlich**e**	Schuhe/Sportschuhe/ Shorts.

SPRECHEN 2

NC 3

A beschreibt ein Bild. B gibt einen Punkt für jeden richtigen Satz. A ↔ B.

A describes a picture. **B** gives one mark for each correct sentence. Use the language box on page 122.

Beispiel: **A**   *Bild **a**. Er trägt einen gelben Kapuzenpullover.*
B   *Falsch! Er trägt ein**en bunten** Kapuzenpullover.*
A   *Ach ja, richtig! Und er trägt ein bunt**es** T-Shirt.*
B   *Richtig! Ein Punkt!*

SCHREIBEN 3

NC 3–4

Schreib Sätze.

Choose one of the pictures from activity 2 and write a detailed description of the person's clothing. Try to use as many adjectives as possible, and give your opinion.

Beispiel: Er/sie trägt …

HÖREN 4

NC 4–5

🎧 **Hör zu. Was tragen Lena, Jimi und Heidi? Was möchten sie kaufen?**

Listen. What do Lena, Jimi and Heidi wear? What would they like to buy?

	Lena	Jimi	Heidi
wears	*comfortable jeans, …*		
would like to buy			

? Think

- In sentences with the auxiliary verb *möchten*, what do you notice about the verb in the infinitive, e.g. *kaufen* and *tragen*?
- What other verbs have this effect on word order?

Ich trage normalerweise (eine bequeme Jeans/…).
Ich **möchte** (neue Sportschuhe/…) **kaufen/tragen/haben**.
Ich **möchte** einkaufen **gehen**.
Ich **möchte** (modisch/cool/schick/lässig/…) **aussehen**.

Challenge

Describe what three people usually wear, and what they would like to wear in the future or for a special occasion. Use activities 3, 4 and the language box to help you. Draw pictures, showing the people in their everyday clothing and in the clothing they would like to buy.

Beispiel: **1** *Michael trägt normalerweise … Er möchte … kaufen.*

NC 4–5

4A.3 Wir gehen einkaufen!

Vocabulary: give your opinion of clothes; go shopping for clothes
Grammar: learn how to say 'it' (*ihn/sie/es*) and 'them' (*sie*)
Skills: identify grammar patterns

VIDEO 1

NC 4

Sieh dir das Video an und lies den Dialog. Beantworte die Fragen.
Watch the video and read the dialogue. Answer a–e below.

Ali Wie findest du das karierte Hemd? Ich finde es schick.

Kathi Ich mag es nicht. Ich denke, es steht dir nicht.

Ali Und das gestreifte T-Shirt? Wie findest du es?

Kathi Ich finde es hässlich.

Ali Wie findest du den grauen Pullover? Ich mag ihn.

Kathi Ja, du kannst ihn ja mal anprobieren. Ich passe auf deine Jacke auf.

Ali Schau mal! Der Pullover ist sehr bequem. Ich mag ihn.

Kathi Ja, es geht.

Ali Und gar nicht teuer.

Kathi Bequem, aber nicht cool.

Ali Nicos Bruder, Ralf, sieht cool aus …

kariert *checked*
es steht dir nicht *it doesn't suit you*
gestreift *stripy*
du kannst ihn … anprobieren
 you can try it on
gar nicht teuer *not at all expensive*

a What does Ali think of the checked shirt?
b What is Kathi's opinion of the shirt?
c What does Kathi think of the striped T-shirt?
d Which item of clothing is comfortable?
e What is Kathi's opinion of the jumper?

SCHREIBEN 2

Füll die Lücken aus: *ihn/sie/es* oder *sie*?
Fill in the gaps with *ihn/sie/es* (it) or *sie* (them).

Beispiel: **a** *Der Rock ist modisch. Ich möchte ihn kaufen.*

a Der Rock ist modisch. Ich möchte ▨▨▨ kaufen.
b Ich mag die Jeans. Ich möchte ▨▨▨ kaufen.
c Ich trage ein schickes Hemd. Ich finde ▨▨▨ modisch.
d Die Lederjacke ist bequem. Mein Freund findet ▨▨▨ lässig.
e Magst du meinen Pullover? Ich finde ▨▨▨ altmodisch.
f Ich möchte neue Sportschuhe haben, aber ich finde ▨▨▨ zu teuer.

? Think

Why do you think the word for 'it' (*ihn/sie/es*) changes? Compare these sentences:

Ich trage **den** Rock (m).
→ Ich trage **ihn**.
Ich finde **die** Bluse (f) klasse.
→ Ich finde **sie** klasse.
Ich möchte **das** Hemd (n) kaufen.
→ Ich möchte **es** kaufen.
The word for 'them' (*sie*) doesn't change:
Ich trage **die** Shorts (pl).
→ Ich trage **sie**.

 Grammatik → p.162, 165

When the object of the sentence is masculine, the word for 'the' changes from *der* to *den*:
Ich trage **den** Rock. *I wear the skirt.*
And the word for 'it' changes to *ihn*:
Ich trage **ihn**. *I wear it.*
We say that the object of the sentence is in the **accusative case**.

3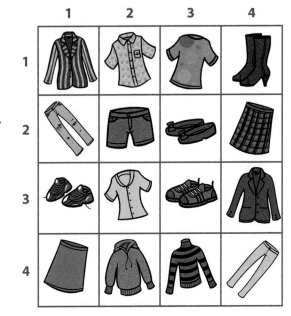

Ein Spiel. Vier gewinnt! A ↔ B.

Play Four-in-a-Row!

NC 4–5
- You need eight counters each.
- **A** chooses some grid coordinates.
- **B** finds this clothing item in the grid and gives an opinion.
- If **A** is happy with **B**'s answer, **B** places a counter on the grid.
- To win, you need four counters in a row!

Beispiel: **A** *Wie findest du (4, 2) den karierten Rock?*
B   *Ich finde ihn hässlich/schön.*
                Ich möchte ihn (nicht) kaufen.

Wie findest du …	den karierten Rock? die gestreifte Jacke? das bunte T-Shirt? die grünen Shorts?
Ich finde ihn/sie/es/sie …	hässlich/schön. zu altmodisch. zu groß/klein.
Ich möchte ihn/sie/es/sie …	(nicht) kaufen. anprobieren.

zu	*too*
zu groß/klein	*too big/small*
zu altmodisch	*too old-fashioned*

4 🎧 **Hör zu. Wer kauft was? Warum (nicht)?**

What are these people interested in buying? Why do they decide

NC 4–5
(not) to buy it? Make notes in English.

a Julia   **b** Jürgen   **c** Michi   **d** Doro

5 ### Was ist die richtige Reihenfolge?

Put the sentences in the correct order to make a dialogue.

NC 3

Beispiel: **c**, …

a Wie gefällt dir die Jeans?
b Ich möchte die blaue Jeans anprobieren, bitte.
c Wie kann ich dir helfen?
d Ich möchte sie nicht kaufen.
e Ich finde die Jeans cool, aber sie ist zu groß.
f Natürlich. Die Kabine ist um die Ecke.

Wie kann ich dir helfen?
How can I help you?
die Kabine *cubicle*
um die Ecke *round the corner*

6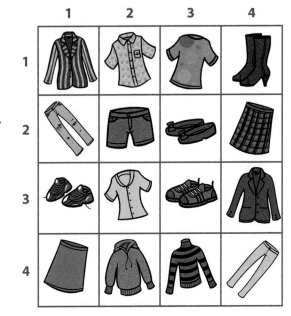

Macht Einkaufsdialoge mit den Bildern. A ↔ B.

Make up shopping dialogues using the pictures. **A** is the shop

NC 3–4
assistant and **B** is the customer.

Challenge

Choose an outfit in one of the pictures from this unit. Write a description of the items of clothing, and say whether you like them or not, giving reasons. Say whether you would like to buy them.

Beispiel: Der Rock ist kariert und altmodisch. Ich finde ihn schrecklich. Ich möchte ihn nicht kaufen, denn er ist zu hässlich.

NC 4–5

4A.4 Die Hose ist zu klein!

Vocabulary: talk about problems with clothes

Grammar: talk about the future using *werden*; use the comparative with *als*

Skills: prepare for and evaluate language tasks

NC 4–5

 HÖREN 1

🎧 **Hör zu und lies. Wer sagt was?**

Listen and read. Who says what?

Beispiel: **a** *Nico*

a Our favourite game is Super Mario Galaxy.
b My new skirt is too big.
c I am not interested in fashion.
d I will change my skirt.
e My outfit is too old.
f I would like to look good.
g I will get a size smaller.

Nina

Ich habe am Samstag eine Party, aber es gibt ein Problem: mein Outfit ist zu alt. Am besten werde ich am Freitag in die Stadt fahren und ein neues Outfit kaufen. Vielleicht werde ich eine modische Hose und eine lässige Bluse kaufen.

Kathi

Mein neuer Rock von Esprit ist zu groß. Ali und ich werden ihn umtauschen. Er ist total schick, aber ich werde ihn eine Größe kleiner kaufen.

Ich interessiere mich nicht für Mode, aber ich möchte gut aussehen. Deshalb werde ich einkaufen gehen. Dann werde ich Ali besuchen und wir werden Wii spielen. Super Mario Galaxy ist unser Lieblingsspiel.

Nico

⚙️ Grammatik → p.167

To form the future tense, use the correct form of *werden* (will) as the second idea in the sentence. Put the infinitive of the second verb at the end of the sentence.

1	2	3	4	5
Ich	**werde**	am Wochenende	meine Jeans	**tragen**.
Am Wochenende	**werde**	ich	meine Jeans	**tragen**.
Du	**wirst**	ein T-Shirt		**kaufen**.
Wir	**werden**	Wii		**spielen**.

umtauschen *exchange*
die Größe *size*
deshalb *therefore*

 SPRECHEN 2

NC 4

👥 **Macht Dialoge. Was wirst du machen? A ↔ B.**

What will you do? Take turns making up dialogues talking about the future.

Beispiel:

A *Was wirst du am Wochenende kaufen?*
B *Am Wochenende werde ich einen lässigen Kapuzenpulli kaufen.*
A *Und was wirst du zu Ninas Party tragen?*
B *Ich werde ein cooles T-Shirt tragen.*

 **? Think**

Why is Level 4 the highest you can get for activity 2?
What would you have to do to achieve Level 5?

Grammatik → p.164

- Use the comparative when you want to say something is smaller, bigger, nicer, etc. As in English, you usually add **-er** to the adjective in German.
  klein → klein**er** *smaller*
  schön → schön**er** *more beautiful*

- For some short adjectives you also have to add an umlaut to the first vowel.
  alt → **ä**lt**er** *older*
  groß → gr**öß**er *bigger*

- And some comparatives are irregular, just like in English.
  gut → besser *better*

- You use *als* to mean 'than' in German.
  Das Hemd ist schicker **als** das T-Shirt.
  *The shirt is smarter **than** the T-shirt.*

3 LESEN Was passt zusammen?
Which words match?

Beispiel: **1 d**

1 klein	2 groß	3 schön	4 cool
5 lässig	6 billig	7 hässlich	

a cooler	b billiger	c hässlicher	d kleiner
e lässiger	f größer	g schöner	

4 SCHREIBEN Was ist der richtige Komparativ?
What is the correct comparative?

Beispiel: **a** *bequemer*

a bequem **b** langweilig **c** schick **d** toll **e** nett **f** laut

5 SCHREIBEN Schreib Sätze.

NC 3–4

Make sentences comparing the different items of clothing.

Beispiel: **c + d** *Die Sportschuhe sind billiger als die Stiefel.*

Challenge

You are invited to a party but you have nothing to wear! A rich relative gives you €100 to buy yourself an outfit. Write a text of at least 80 words:

- Who is having the party and when?
- Where will you go shopping?
- What will you buy?
- Compare the new item to one of your old items of clothing and give an opinion.

Beispiel: Am Samstag macht Nina eine große Party! Ich werde zu H&M gehen …

NC 4–5

Vocabulary: talk about designer clothing and school uniform

Grammar: use verbs in the first, second and third person (*ich, du* and *er/sie*)

Skills: adapt and build texts

Ali der Große

| Info | Pinnwand | Fotos | + |

Blog-Name: Ali der Große
Lieblingsklamotten: Jeans + weißes T-Shirt
Lieblingsschuhe: Pumas
Lieblingsfarbe: blau

VIDEO 1
NC 4

Sieh dir Alis Videoblog an. Was ist die richtige Antwort?
Watch Ali's video blog. What is the correct answer?

Beispiel: **a** *many*

a In Berlin there are no/many fashion designers.
b Ali thinks/doesn't think he's very fashionable.
c Ali's leather jacket is by Wolfgang Joop/Karl Lagerfeld.
d Ali shops at Karl Lagerfeld/H&M.
e Ali wears a boring school uniform/his own clothes to school.

SPRECHEN 2
NC 3–4

Macht eine Klassenumfrage mit Alis Fragen.
Fragt drei Personen und macht Notizen.

	Person 1	Person 2	Person 3
a Was trägst du gern?	*Jeans, …*		
b Wo kaufst du ein?			
c Was trägst du in der Schule?			

Was trägst du gern?
Ich trage gern …
Wo kaufst du ein?
Ich kaufe meine Kleidung bei …
Was trägst du in der Schule?
In der Schule trage ich …

SCHREIBEN 3
NC 4

Schreib die Antworten aus Übung 2 auf.
Write down the answers to your questions in activity 2.

Beispiel: **a** *Person 1: Er trägt gern bequeme Kleidung, zum Beispiel eine modische Jeans. Er findet Sportschuhe total gut.*

Paula aus England

In der Schule trage ich eine Schuluniform. Ich finde das total blöd und unbequem. Ich mag meinen Rock nicht, denn er ist hässlich. Jeden Tag trage ich einen grauen Rock, ein weißes Hemd und eine Krawatte, eine Jacke und schwarze Schuhe. Langweilig!

Meine Mutter und mein Freund Jan aus Deutschland finden die Uniform gut. Meine Mutter sagt, es ist besser, denn keiner trägt Designerkleidung. Ich möchte aber Designerkleidung in der Schule tragen! Mein Lieblingsoutfit ist Jeans und T-Shirt.

In meiner Schule gibt es keine Schuluniform. Normalerweise trage ich meine Jeans und einen Pulli. Das ist praktisch, aber eine Schuluniform ist besser. Ich möchte gern eine Schuluniform tragen. Meine Freundin Paula aus England trägt eine Schuluniform und sie ist total schick. Ich mag modische und schicke Kleidung. Sie ist besser als langweilige Straßenkleidung.

Paula findet die Schuluniform aber hässlich.

Meine Lieblingsuniform ist eine schwarze Hose, ein hellblaues Hemd, eine Krawatte, eine Jacke und schwarze, schicke Schuhe.

Jan aus Deutschland

LESEN 4 NC 4–5

Lies die Texte von Paula und Jan und beantworte die Fragen.
Read the texts and answer the questions.

Beispiel: **a** *Paula trägt eine Schuluniform.*

a Wer trägt eine Schuluniform?
b Was trägt Paula in der Schule?
c Wie findet Paula die Schuluniform?
d Was sagt Paulas Mutter über die Schuluniform?
e Was trägt Jan in der Schule?
f Was möchte er tragen?
g Wie sieht seine Lieblingsuniform aus?

SPRECHEN 5 NC 4–5

Macht ein Interview. A ↔ B.
Interview each other about school uniform. Use the questions on the notepad.

1 Trägst du eine Schuluniform?
2 Was trägst du in der Schule?
3 Wie findest du die Schuluniform?
4 Was möchtest du tragen?

Ich trage einen/eine/ein …
Ich finde die Schuluniform …
Ich möchte … tragen.

die Krawatte *tie*
die Straßenkleidung *street wear*
hellblau *light blue*

? Think

The *Challenge* task gives you a chance to talk about the future. In this unit you have learned two ways of doing this: what are they?

Challenge

You have been asked by your head teacher to describe your school uniform, give your opinion of it and then design your school uniform of the future.

Beispiel: In der Schule trage ich … Ich finde das … Jeden Tag trage ich … Ich möchte … tragen. Meine ideale Schuluniform ist …

NC 5

4A.6 Sprachlabor

The accusative case, forming the future tense with *werden*

The accusative case

The object of a sentence is the person or thing at the receiving end of the verb. In the following sentence, *einen gelben Pulli* is the object of the sentence because it is the thing being worn:
Paul trägt **einen gelben Pulli**. *Paul wears a yellow jumper.*
We say that the object of the sentence is in the **accusative case**.
Verbs like *tragen* and *haben* and phrases like *es gibt* are always followed by the accusative case.

1 Underline the objects in the accusative case.

Beispiel: **a** *Ich finde <u>das Outfit</u> langweilig. Ich mag <u>es</u> nicht.*

a   Ich finde das Outfit langweilig. Ich mag es nicht.
b   Sie möchte den Blazer kaufen. Sie findet ihn toll.
c   Er trägt das T-Shirt. Er mag es gern.
d   Wir finden die Schuluniform doof. Wir mögen sie nicht.
e   Ich mag den Pulli nicht. Ich trage ihn nicht.
f   Er mag die Hose. Er möchte sie kaufen.
g   Er trägt neue Schuhe. Er findet sie modisch.

ihn/sie/es (*it*), sie (*them*)

The German word for 'it' changes, depending on the gender of the noun it replaces:

Ich trage den Rock (m).   → Ich trage **ihn**.
Ich finde die Bluse () cool. → Ich finde **sie** cool.
Ich kaufe das Hemd (n).   → Ich kaufe **es**.
Er mag die Stiefel (pl).   → Er mag **sie**.

The words 'it' (*ihn/sie/es*) and 'them' (*sie*) are called object pronouns. They are in the accusative case.

2 Fill in the gaps with *ihn*, *sie*, *es* and *sie* (plural).

a Der Rock ist doof. Ich mag <u>ihn</u> nicht.

b Ich mag die Krawatte. Ich möchte ____ kaufen.

c Ich möchte ein neues Skateboard haben, aber ich finde ____ zu teuer.

d Meine Mutter findet den Kapuzenpulli hässlich, aber ich finde ____ gut, denn er ist cool.

werden

To form the future tense, use the correct form of *werden* (will) as the second idea in the sentence. Put the infinitive of the second verb at the end of the sentence.

1	2	3	4	5
Ich	**werde**	am Wochenende	meine Jeans	**tragen.**
Am Wochenende	**werde**	ich	meine Jeans	**tragen.**
Wir	**werden**	Wii		**spielen.**

ich werde
du wirst
er/sie/es wird
wir werden
ihr werdet
sie/Sie werden

3 **Fill in the gaps with the correct form of *werden* and underline the infinitive of the second verb.**

Beispiel: **a** Er __wird__ ein neues Outfit <u>kaufen</u>.

a Er ▉▉▉ ein neues Outfit kaufen.
b Wir ▉▉▉ Wii spielen.
c Ich ▉▉▉ ins Kino gehen.
d Er ▉▉▉ seine karierte Jacke zur Party tragen.
e Ihr ▉▉▉ bei McDonalds essen.
f ▉▉▉ du bei H&M einkaufen?

Evaluating and improving your written work

To get a high mark for your writing, you need to be accurate. Check that you have used the correct:

* **verb forms** * **plural forms** * **word order**

4 **The text on the right has one mistake in every sentence. Write each sentence correctly, saying what type of mistake it is.**

Beispiel: tragen: Ich <u>trage</u> (verb form) eine weiße Jeans und Sportschuhe.

Ich <u>tragen</u> eine weiße Jeans und Sportschuhe. Ich finde nicht gut Ballerinas. Ich finde Sportschuhen besser als Ballerinas. Gibt es in meiner Stadt ein Einkaufszentrum. Mag ich es gern. Am Wochenende wird ich im Einkaufszentrum einkaufen.

ich, ig, isch

5 🎧 **Listen to the words and repeat them.**

ich   dich   hässlich   modisch   freundlich
altmodisch   launisch (*moody*)   fantastisch   billig
nervig (*annoying*)   traurig (*sad*)

The sounds *ich* and *ig* sound very similar in standard German. The *ch* and *g* sounds both make the soft *ch* sound at the end of the Scottish word 'loch'. *Sch* sounds like the *sh* sound in English.

6 👥 **Now make sentences using the words in activity 5 and practise them with your partner.**

Beispiel: **Ich** finde die Jacke **altmodisch**.

> Vocabulary: practise clothing vocabulary
> Grammar: practise using adjectives
> Skills: use knowledge of grammar and other strategies to understand texts

Find the six comparatives in the word snake.

NC 2   *Beispiel:* besser, ...

schönbesserqutneubilligerteuermodernermodernlangweiligerinteressanterlaunischerkleinklasse

Fill in the gaps using the words in the box below.

NC 3–4   Ich bin Jimi Blue Ochsenknecht und ich __komme__ aus Deutschland. Ich mache Filme und Musik. Ich ▭ sehr lässige Kleidung. Ich trage gern eine ▭ Jeans, einen ▭ Kapuzenpulli und schicke Sportschuhe. Mein Bruder Wilson Gonzalez trägt schickere Kleidung als ich. Seine Kleidung ist teuer, modisch und er kauft sie bei ▭ in Berlin. Er mag H&M nicht, denn die Kleidung ist zu billig.

Auf der Party am Samstag ▭ ich mein neues Outfit tragen. Ich werde eine Jeans, ein ▭ T-Shirt und einen schwarzen Blazer tragen. Ich finde das Outfit ▭ .

| trage | bequemen | toll | rotes |
| Adidas | werde | coole | komme |

Read the speech bubbles. True or false?

NC 4   *Beispiel:* **a** *true*

a Paul Pauli likes his outfit.
b The jeans are not suitable for skateboarding.
c His hoodie is his favourite jumper.
d His dad likes his jumper.
e Trainers are very fashionable at the moment.

f Tanja likes wearing trousers.
g Her hobby is cycling.
h She wears a red helmet.
i She doesn't like trainers.

Ich mag mein Outfit. Die Jeans ist total super, denn sie ist sehr bequem. Total toll zum Skateboard fahren. Der Pullover ist mein Lieblingspulli. Mein Vater sagt, es ist ein Gangsterpulli, aber ich finde ihn cool und ich bin nett – kein Gangster. Sportschuhe sind bequem und supermodisch.

Paul Pauli

Ich trage gern eine Jacke und einen Rock, denn beides ist schick. Ich fahre gern Motorrad und habe einen roten Motorradhelm. Sportschuhe finde ich hässlich, aber die Ballerinas sind total modisch.

beides ist schick *both are chic*

Tanja Kurzrock

4A.7 / Extra Plus

Vocabulary: practise clothing and shopping vocabulary
Grammar: identify the words for 'it' (*ihn/sie/es*) and 'them' (*sie*)
Skills: use knowledge of grammar and other strategies to understand texts

Lies den Dialog. Sind die Sätze unten richtig oder falsch?

NC 4–5

Beispiel: **a** *falsch*

Tanja	Ich möchte ein neues Outfit für meine Party kaufen.
Paul	Kein Problem! Ich komme mit. Wir kaufen es zusammen.
Tanja	Toll! Vielleicht kaufe ich die neue Jeans von H&M. Ich mag sie sehr. Sie hat einen super Schnitt.
Paul	Ach nein, die Jeans ist doch doof. Aber es gibt einen total modischen Rock bei Esprit. Meine Schwester trägt ihn und sie findet ihn großartig.
Tanja	Hm, gut. Wie viel kostet der Rock? Ich kaufe ihn nur, wenn er nicht zu teuer ist.
Paul	Der Rock kostet 45 Euro. Superbillig, finde ich. Und was kaufe ich?
Tanja	Vielleicht ein schickes Hemd von Lagerfeld? Es gibt ein graues Hemd mit schwarzen Streifen. Ich mag es sehr gern. Du kannst es anprobieren, wenn wir in die Stadt fahren.
Paul	Okay, wann möchtest du einkaufen gehen?
Tanja	Jetzt?
Paul	Prima!

a Tanja Kurzrock wants to buy a new school uniform.
b Paul Pauli finds the new jeans, designed by H&M, cool.
c Paul's sister bought a skirt from Esprit.
d The skirt was a disaster.
e The skirt costs fifty-four euros.
f Tanja suggests Paul buys a black and grey striped shirt.

zusammen *together*
vielleicht *maybe*
der Schnitt *cut (design)*
großartig *great*
die Streifen *stripes*
anprobieren *to try on*
einkaufen *to go shopping*
jetzt *now*

Mach aus den falschen Sätzen oben richtige Sätze.
Write the wrong sentences above correctly.

NC 4–5

Beispiel: **a** *Tanja wants to buy a new outfit for her party.*

Lies den Dialog noch einmal. Was passt zusammen?

Beispiel: **1** *b*

1 Pauls Schwester findet ihn großartig.
2 Tanja möchte es für die Party kaufen.
3 Tanja findet, sie hat einen super Schnitt.
4 Paul wird es bei Lagerfeld anprobieren.

a das Hemd
b den Rock
c das Outfit
d die Jeans

HÖREN 1
NC 3

🎧 **Listen (a–k) and look at the pictures. Who is speaking?**
(See pages 120–123.)

Beispiel: **a** *3*

① Herr von Essen

② Paul Pauli

③ Tanja Kurzrock

LESEN 2
NC 4–5

Read the email and answer the questions.
(See pages 124–127.)

Beispiel: **a** *on Saturday*

a When does Oliver want to go into town?
b Why does he want to buy a new outfit?
c What exactly does he want to buy?
d How often does he go shopping?
e Where does he buy his clothes and why?

Hallo Tim!

Am Samstag werde ich in die Stadt fahren. Ich möchte ein neues Outfit für die Schule kaufen, denn meine Kleidung ist altmodisch und hässlich. Vielleicht werde ich eine modische Jeans und ein lässiges Hemd kaufen.

Ich interessiere mich sehr für Mode. Normalerweise kaufe ich zweimal im Monat ein. Ich mag Geschäfte wie H&M, denn die Kleidung ist toll, aber billiger als in Designergeschäften.

Was trägst du in der Schule und was kaufst du gern ein?

Dein Oliver

SPRECHEN 3
NC 3–5

👥 **Discuss your clothing style with a partner. (See pages 120–127.)**

- Was trägst du normalerweise? *Normalerweise trage ich …*
- Was ist dein Lieblingsoutfit?
- Wie findest du Kapuzenpullover?
- Was möchtest du zu deiner Geburtstagsparty tragen?
- Was wirst du am Wochenende tragen?

SCHREIBEN 4
NC 4–5

Imagine you are Paul Pauli and you have to describe your clothing style. (See pages 120–127.)

Beispiel: *Ich trage … Ich finde … Ich möchte/werde …*

- What do you wear?
- What do you think of your outfit and why?
- What would you like to wear?

? **Think**

Use the following grammatical structures to give you access to a high mark and NC level: adjectives, opinions, *denn* clauses, comparatives, *Ich möchte/Ich werde … tragen.*

Die Jeans ist cool!	Jeans are cool!
die Ballerinas	pumps/ballerina shoes
die Bluse	blouse
das Hemd	shirt
die Hose	trousers
die Jeans	jeans
der Kapuzenpullover	hoodie
das Kleid	dress
die Lederjacke	leather jacket
der Mantel	coat
der Pullover	jumper
der Rock	skirt
die Shorts	shorts
die Sportschuhe	trainers
die Stiefel	boots
das T-Shirt	T-shirt

alt	old
altmodisch	old-fashioned
bequem	comfortable
billig	cheap
bunt	multicoloured
gestreift	stripy
hässlich	ugly
kariert	checked
kurz	short
lässig	casual
modisch	fashionable
neu	new
schick	chic/smart
schön	beautiful
teuer	expensive
unbequem	uncomfortable
sehr	very
total	totally
ziemlich	quite

Coole Outfits	Cool outfits
Ich trage …	I wear …
Er/sie trägt …	He/she wears …
… einen gelben Rock	… a yellow skirt
… ein teures Kleid	… an expensive dress
… eine schwarze Jacke	… a black jacket
… lässige Shorts	… casual shorts
normalerweise	normally/usually
Ich möchte … tragen.	I'd like to wear …
Ich möchte … kaufen.	I'd like to buy …
Ich möchte einkaufen gehen.	I'd like to go shopping.
Ich möchte schick aussehen.	I'd like to look smart.

Wir gehen einkaufen!	We're going shopping!
Wie findest du …?	What do you think of …?
Ich finde ihn/sie/es …	I find it …
Ich finde sie (pl) …	I find them …
zu groß/klein	too big/small
zu teuer	too expensive
Es steht dir gut.	It suits you.
Es steht dir nicht.	It doesn't suit you.
Wie kann ich dir helfen?	How can I help you?
Ich möchte (ihn) anprobieren.	I'd like to try it on.
Ich möchte (sie) kaufen.	I'd like to buy it/them.
Ich möchte (es) nicht kaufen.	I wouldn't like to buy it.

Die Hose ist zu klein!	The trousers are too small!
Mein Outfit ist zu alt.	My outfit is too old.
Ich werde einkaufen gehen.	I'll go shopping.
Ich werde … kaufen.	I'll buy …
Ich werde (ihn) umtauschen.	I'll exchange it.
Ich werde … tragen.	I'll wear …
eine Größe kleiner	a size smaller
eine Größe größer	a size bigger
besser (als)	better (than)

Das trage ich!	That's what I wear!
Was trägst du gern?	What do you like wearing?
Ich trage (am liebsten) …	My favourite clothes are …
Wo kaufst du ein?	Where do you go shopping?
Ich kaufe meine Kleidung bei …	I buy my clothes at …
Was trägst du in der Schule?	What do you wear at school?
In der Schule trage ich …	At school I wear …
die Schuluniform	school uniform
die Designerkleidung	designer clothing
die Krawatte	tie
hellblau	light blue

I can...

- talk about items of clothing and say what I think of them
- use the singular and plural forms of nouns followed by *ist* and *sind*
- say what I usually wear and what I would like to wear in the future, using *ich möchte*
- use adjective endings in the accusative case
- go shopping for clothes
- use the words for 'it' (*ihn/sie/es*) and 'them' (*sie*)
- use the future tense
- compare clothes using the comparative

Vocabulary: talk about your holidays
Grammar: use the prepositions *in* and *auf* followed by the dative case
(*einem/einer...*)
Skills: use compound nouns; identify language patterns

1 **Wo wohnst du in den Ferien? Was passt zusammen?**
Where will you stay on your holidays? Find the matching
pictures (1–6) for a–f below.

Beispiel: **a**2

Ich wohne .../Wir wohnen ...
a in einer Ferienwohnung
b in einem Hotel
c in einem Wohnwagen
d auf einem Campingplatz
e in einer Jugendherberge
f in einem Ferienhaus

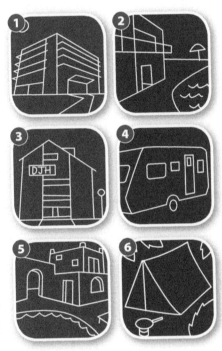

2 🎧 **Hör zu (1–6). Ist alles richtig?**
Listen. Is everything correct?

3 👥 **Macht Dialoge. A ↔ B.**
Roll a dice to choose a picture. Then make up a
dialogue about it.

NC 2

Beispiel: **A** *Wo wohnst du in den Ferien? Bild 1!*
B *Wir wohnen in einem Hotel.*

Ich wohne/Wir wohnen ...
auf einem Campingplatz
in einem Wohnwagen
in einem Ferienhaus/Hotel/Wohnmobil/Zelt
in einer Ferienwohnung/Jugendherberge

? *Think*

- Look again at the sentences in activity 1. Which
one is the odd one out? Why?
- What do you notice about the endings after each
preposition (*in*, *auf*)? Can you identify the pattern?

⚙️ *Grammatik* → p.163

in/auf + einem/einer

m der/ein Wohnwagen →
Wir wohnen in ein**em** Wohnwagen. (in + dem)

f die/eine Ferienwohnung →
Ich wohne in ein**er** Ferienwohnung. (in + der)

n das/ein Hotel → Wir wohnen in ein**em** Hotel.

VIDEO 4

NC 3–4

Sieh dir das Video an. Lies a–c. Wer ist das – Ali, Nico oder Nina?
Watch the video. Which text (a–c) is Ali, Nico and Nina?

a
Wir fahren mit dem Auto und dem Wohnwagen nach Italien – nach Südtirol. Wir bleiben drei Wochen dort. Ich freue mich darauf!

b
Wir fahren mit dem Zug an die Nordsee. Wir bleiben zwei Wochen dort. Das ist langweilig, finde ich.

c
Wir fliegen in die Türkei. Meine Oma hat ein Haus am Meer – man kann den ganzen Tag schwimmen. Wir bleiben jeden Sommer dort. Ich fahre gern in die Türkei.

① Ali
② Nico
③ Nina

LESEN 5

Lies den Text in Übung 4 noch einmal. Was passt zusammen?
Read the texts in activity 4 again. Which pictures (1–10) go with each text (a–c)?

Beispiel: **a 1, …**

❶
❷
❸
❹
❺
❻
❼
❽ Türkei
❾
❿ Italien

SPRECHEN 6

NC 3–4

Macht Dialoge. A ←→ B.
Take turns to make up dialogues.

Beispiel: **A** *Wohin fährst du in den Ferien?*
B *Ich fahre nach Spanien.*
A *Wie fährst du …?*

❶  Spanien Hotel
❷  Irland
❸  Schottland

- Wohin fährst du in den Ferien?
- Ich fahre nach Italien/in die Türkei.
- Wie fährst du?
- Ich fahre mit dem Auto/Zug. Ich fliege.
- Wo wohnst du?
- Ich wohne in/auf …
- Wie lange bleibst du dort?
- Ich bleibe zwei Wochen/eine Woche dort. Ich freue mich darauf! Das finde ich langweilig.

Challenge

Imagine you're going on your dream holiday. Write sentences to say where you're going, how you're travelling and how long you're going for. Remember to give your opinion!

Beispiel: *Ich fahre nach … Wir fahren mit … Wir wohnen in … Ich bleibe … Ich freue mich darauf!*

NC 4

4B.2 Wir fahren nach Wien!

1 🎧 **Hör zu. Was ist die richtige Reihenfolge?**
Meinung: gut (✓) oder schlecht (✗)?
Listen and give the order of the attractions that Kathi, Ali, Nina and Nico mention, and also their opinions: good (✓) or bad (✗).

Beispiel: **b** ✓, …

Wir können …

a   einen Ausflug machen

b   in einen Freizeitpark gehen

c   den Stephansdom besuchen

d   eine Stadtrundfahrt machen

e   ein Wiener Schnitzel essen

f   ins Museum gehen

2 👥 **Macht Dialoge. Was können wir in Wien machen? A ↔ B.**

NC 3–4

Take turns making dialogues with the pictures from activity 1.

Beispiel: **A**   *Was können wir in Wien machen?*
B   *Wir können einen Ausflug machen.*
A   *Nein, das ist langweilig.*
B   *Wir können …*

3 **Lies den Text und füll die Lücken aus.**
Read the text and fill in the gaps with the words on the right.

Hallo Jan! Ich freue mich auf deinen Besuch! Es __gibt__ viel zu machen für Teenager in Wien. Wir ▓▓▓ im Markt-Café Kaffee ▓▓▓. Wir können auch in den Zoo ▓▓▓. Und man ▓▓▓ in den Park gehen – wir können dort Rad ▓▓▓. Willst du auch Tennis ▓▓▓? Oder ▓▓▓ du ins Kino gehen?

> fahren   können   trinken   willst
> gehen   gibt   spielen   kann

4 **Was kann man in Bremen machen? Schreib einen Text.**

NC 3

What can one do in Bremen? Write a text to go with these pictures.

Beispiel: *Man kann ein Eis essen und einen Kaffee trinken …*

Was passt zusammen?

What will Kathi, Nico, Nina and Ali do in Vienna? Find the correct pictures.

Beispiel: **a** *3*

a Wir werden Souvenirs kaufen.
b Wir werden ins Theater gehen.
c Wir werden Pizza essen.
d Wir werden schwimmen.
e Wir werden das Schloss Schönbrunn besuchen.
f Wir werden meine Freunde treffen.

 Hör zu (1–6). Ist alles richtig?

Listen. Is everything correct?

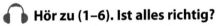 **Macht Dialoge. A ⟷ B.**

Take turns suggesting a new activity for each day of the week.

`NC 3–4`

Beispiel: **A** *Was werden wir am Montag machen?*
B *Wir werden Pizza essen.*

 Schreib die Sätze im Futur auf.

Rewrite these sentences in the future tense.

Beispiel: **a** *Wir werden eine Stadtrundfahrt machen.*

a Wir machen eine Stadtrundfahrt.
b Ich esse ein Eis.
c Wir gehen ins Museum.
d Ich tanze in der Disco.
e Ich besuche meine Oma.
f Ich gehe ins Schwimmbad.

> Es gibt viel zu machen.
> Man kann/Wir können … einen Ausflug machen/in einen Freizeitpark gehen/eine Stadtrundfahrt machen.
> Das ist toll/super/schön/langweilig.
> Das gefällt mir nicht.
> Willst du Rad fahren/Tennis spielen/ins Kino gehen?
> Ich werde/Wir werden Souvenirs kaufen/ins Theater gehen/ schwimmen/Pizza essen.

 Grammatik → p.167

Talking about the future
Remember that you use the verb *werden* to talk about the future. *Werden* sends the main verb to the end of the sentence in its infinitive form:

Ich gehe ins Kino.
→ Ich **werde** ins Kino **gehen**.
I will go to the cinema.

Wir fahren nach Wien.
→ Wir **werden** nach Wien **fahren**.
We will go/travel to Vienna.

Challenge

Kathi, Nico, Nina and Ali are coming to visit your town next week. Write them a plan for each day and give your opinion of each activity.

Beispiel: *Am Montag können wir einen Ausflug machen. Das gefällt mir. Am Dienstag werden wir …*

`NC 4–5`

4B.3 Was hast du gemacht?

Vocabulary: say what you did on holiday
Grammar: recognise and use the perfect tense
Skills: recycle familiar language in the perfect tense

 HÖREN 1

🎧 **Was passt zusammen? Ist alles richtig? Hör zu.**
Match each activity (a–e) to a photo (1–5). Then listen to check.

Beispiel: **1 c**, …

Wir haben	a	in der Disco getanzt.
	b	Frisbee gespielt.
	c	einen Ausflug gemacht.
	d	Musik im Park gehört.
	e	Souvenirs gekauft.

Grammatik → p.166

To say what happened in the past, use the perfect tense (*das Perfekt*):

Wir haben gespielt.
We played/We have played.

Ich habe gehört.
I listened/I have listened.

 SPRECHEN 2

👥 **Welcher Satz passt? A ↔ B.**
A says the number of a photo in activity 1. **B** says the correct sentence.

Beispiel: **A** *Foto 1!* **B** *Wir haben einen Ausflug gemacht.*

 SCHREIBEN 3

Schreib Sätze im Perfekt mit *Ich habe* … .
Write a sentence in the perfect tense for each picture below. Use one word from the box in each sentence.

Beispiel: **a** *Ich habe einen Hamburger gekauft.*

gespielt	gekauft	gespielt
gekauft	gehört	gemacht

❓ Think

You can use familiar language to make new sentences in the perfect tense. How would you say these in German?

- *We played football.*
  → Wir haben …
- *What did you do?*
  → Was habt ihr … ?

 a
 b
 c
 d
 e
 f

HÖREN 4 NC 2–3

🎧 **Was passt zusammen? Hör zu und lies.**

Listen and read. Where did they go on holiday last year – and how did they get there? Find the correct pictures.

Beispiel: **Nina** *2 d*

Nina: Wir sind mit dem Zug nach Griechenland gefahren. Wir haben in einem Ferienhaus gewohnt.

Kathi: Wir sind nach Spanien geflogen. Wir haben in einem Hotel gewohnt.

Ali: Wir sind mit dem Auto nach Istanbul gefahren. Wir haben in einer Wohnung gewohnt.

Nico: Wir sind mit dem Wohnwagen nach Frankreich gefahren. Wir haben auf einem Campingplatz gewohnt.

Grammatik → p.166

A few verbs form their perfect tense with *sein* instead of *haben*:

fahren → Ich bin gefahren.
I went/travelled.
fliegen → Wir sind geflogen.
We flew.

 a
 b

 c
 d

 ❶
 ❷
 ❸
 ❹

LESEN 5

Lies den Brief und füll die Lücken aus.

Read the letter and fill in the gaps using words from the box.

Hallo Martin!
Wir <u>sind</u> im Sommer nach Österreich gefahren. Wir sind mit dem Auto ▭, und wir ▭ in einer Ferienwohnung gewohnt. Wir haben ein Picknick im Park ▭. Ich ▭ auch Souvenirs ▭. Und ich habe in der Disco ▭!

getanzt gemacht haben
gefahren sind gekauft habe

SCHREIBEN 6 NC 2–3

Schreib Sätze.

Write sentences.

Beispiel: **a** *Ich bin mit dem Auto nach Italien gefahren. Ich habe in einem Hotel gewohnt.*

Challenge

Write a similar letter to the one in activity 5, describing a holiday (real or imaginary!). Answer these questions:

• Wohin?
• Wie?
• Wo hast du gewohnt?
• Was hast du gemacht?

Beispiel: Ich bin im August nach Italien geflogen …

NC 4

Vocabulary: talk about going to an amusement park

Grammar: recognise and use the present, past and future tenses

Skills: recycle familiar language in the present, past and future tenses

HÖREN 1

NC 5–6

🎧 **Hör zu und lies. Welche Sätze sind im Präsens (Pr), im Perfekt (Pe) und im Futur (F) – und welche enthalten Modalverben (M)?**

Which sentences are in the present tense, the perfect tense or the future tense – and which contain a modal verb?

Beispiel: Wohin bist du gestern gefahren, Kathi? (Pe)

Susi	Wohin bist du gestern gefahren, Kathi?
Kathi	Wir sind mit dem Bus zum Prater gefahren. Der Prater liegt in einem großen Park in der Stadtmitte.
Susi	Und was habt ihr dort gemacht?
Kathi	Im Prater gibt es viel zu machen: Wir sind Achterbahn und mit dem Riesenrad gefahren, und wir haben im Wasserpark gespielt. Wir haben auch in der Open-Air-Disco getanzt!
Susi	Und was macht ihr heute?
Kathi	Wir machen heute eine Stadtrundfahrt, und wir besichtigen den Stephansdom. Und wir wollen ins Mozart-Museum gehen. Und heute Abend können wir in ein Konzert gehen – an der Donau.
Susi	Was werdet ihr morgen machen?
Kathi	Wir werden einen Ausflug in den Wienerwald machen – man kann dort gut ein Picknick machen. Das macht Spaß! Meine Oma hat Salat gemacht, und Nina und ich werden Pizza machen.

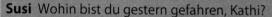

die Achterbahn *rollercoaster*

? Think

Which of these phrases do you use to describe events in the past, the present and the future?

- letztes Wochenende
- zweimal in der Woche
- heute
- jeden Tag
- gestern
- morgen

Can you think of other phrases that go with each tense?

LESEN 2

NC 5–6

Richtig (R) oder falsch (F)?

Are the sentences true or false?

Beispiel: a F

a Kathi and her friends took the metro to the Prater.
b They went on the Ferris wheel and to the waterpark.
c They are doing lots of sightseeing today.
d There is nothing for them to do this evening.
e They are going on an excursion tomorrow.
f Kathi's grandmother's cook has prepared a picnic for them.

Wohin bist du gefahren?
Was habt ihr gemacht?
Was macht ihr heute?
Was werdet ihr morgen machen?
Ich bin/Wir sind zum Prater gefahren/
   Achterbahn gefahren.
Ich habe/Wir haben Karten gekauft/
   einen Ausflug gemacht.
Wir kaufen Souvenirs. Wir können im
Wasserpark spielen. Wir wollen mit dem
Riesenrad fahren.
Wir werden ein Picknick machen. Ich werde
ein Eis kaufen.

3 Hör zu und lies. Was passt zusammen?
Listen and read. Find the pictures that match the sentences.

Beispiel: **a 7**

a	**9 Uhr:** Wir machen einen Ausflug zum Prater!
b	**10 Uhr:** Wir fahren mit der U-Bahn.
c	**11 Uhr:** Wir kaufen ein Programm für den Prater.
d	**12 Uhr:** Wir machen eine Fahrt mit dem Karussell.
e	**13 Uhr:** Wir spielen im Wasserpark.
f	**14 Uhr:** Wir hören tolle Musik.
g	**15 Uhr:** Wir tanzen in der Open-Air-Disco.

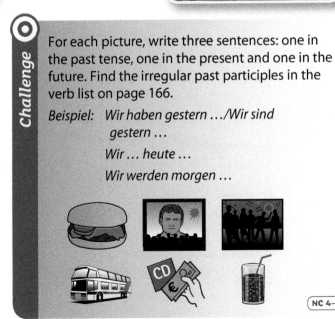

4 Schreib die Sätze von Übung 3 im Perfekt auf.
What did they do yesterday? Write down the sentences in activity 3 in the perfect tense.

Beispiel: **a** *Wir haben um neun Uhr einen Ausflug zum Prater gemacht.*

5 Was werden sie morgen machen? Jetzt schreib die Sätze im Futur auf!
Now write the sentences from activity 3 in the future tense.

Beispiel: **a** *Wir werden morgen einen Ausflug zum Prater machen.*

Challenge

For each picture, write three sentences: one in the past tense, one in the present and one in the future. Find the irregular past participles in the verb list on page 166.

Beispiel: *Wir haben gestern …/Wir sind gestern …*

Wir … heute …

Wir werden morgen …

NC 4–5

Vocabulary: talk about holiday experiences and plans
Grammar: use verbs in the past, present and future; use modal verbs
Skills: use different structures; apply previously learned language
in new contexts

Ni&Co

Info	Pinnwand	Fotos	+

Blog-Name:	Ni&Co
Land:	Deutschland
Alter:	14
Geburtstag:	13. September
Lieblingsort:	Wien

 VIDEO 1

NC 4–5

 Sieh dir das Video an. Wähle die passenden Antworten.
Watch Nico's video diary. Choose the right answers for him.

a Nico fährt am Wochenende nach
 1 Wien **2** Berlin

b Wien ist **1** klein **2** groß

c Das Wetter in Wien ist im Sommer
 1 schön **2** schlecht

d Im Winter ist es **1** kalt **2** warm

e Das Schloss in Wien heißt
 1 Donau **2** Schönbrunn

f Nico möchte gern
 1 Kaffee trinken und Kuchen essen
 2 Wiener Schnitzel mit Pommes essen

g Er will **1** einen Ausflug machen
  2 eine Stadtrundfahrt machen

h Nico will auch **1** Souvenirs kaufen
  2 den Prater besuchen

Am Wochenende fahren wir nach Wien! Das wird bestimmt super! Wir fahren mit dem Zug von Berlin aus.

Wien ist sehr groß – dort leben fast 2 Millionen Menschen. Und im Sommer ist es dort sehr sehr heiß und sonnig, natürlich auch. Aber im Winter ist es dort kalt und es schneit oft, sagt Kathi.

In Wien ist auch ein Fluss: die Donau. Da kann man Schiffsfahrten darauf machen. Und es gibt auch ein Schloss: Schloss Schönbrunn. Das ist sehr alt und ziemlich berühmt.

Und was kann man dann noch in Wien machen? Wir können auch in ein Kaffeehaus gehen, denn die Wiener essen gern Kuchen und trinken viel Kaffee. Das wollen wir natürlich auch machen!

Und wir wollen auch eine Stadtrundfahrt machen, und Souvenirs für meine Eltern kaufen. Das wird bestimmt total toll!

LESEN 2

NC 4–5

Lies den Text und beantworte die Fragen.
Read the text and answer the questions.

Beispiel: **a** *Bernd is going to Edinburgh for two weeks.*

Ich werde in den Sommerferien für zwei Wochen nach Schottland fahren – nach Edinburgh.

Ich fahre mit dem Bus, der Fähre und dem Zug. Die Fahrt ist sehr lang – 12 Stunden. Das ist bestimmt langweilig! Aber ich werde meinen Nintendo und meinen iPod mitnehmen.

Ich werde bei meinem Brieffreund Joseph und seiner Familie wohnen. Er hat eine Schwester, Sandra – sie ist elf – und einen Bruder. Er heißt William und er ist 16 Jahre alt. Josephs Eltern heißen Penny und Angus.

In Edinburgh werde ich den ganzen Tag Englisch sprechen, denn Josephs Familie spricht kein Deutsch. Das ist ganz schön anstrengend, glaube ich!

Aber es gibt in Edinburgh viel für Jugendliche: es gibt ein Jugendzentrum, viele Kinos und Discos. Es gibt auch ein Fußballstadion und viele Schwimmbäder. Und wir können Skateboard fahren – das gefällt mir!

Bernd (14)

die Fähre	ferry
lang	long
bestimmt	surely
mitnehmen	to take along
der Brieffreund	penfriend

a Where is Bernd going – and for how long?
b How is he travelling?
c What does he say about the journey?
d Who is he staying with?
e What does he think will be quite exhausting – and why?
f Name six things that Bernd can do in Edinburgh.

SCHREIBEN 3

NC 4–5

Schreib einen neuen Brief – im Perfekt oder im Futur.
Write your own letter (like Bernd) about a holiday. Choose either the perfect or the future tense. Say:

● where you went/where you will go
● how you went there/how you will go
● where you stayed/where you will stay
● what you did/what you will do.

Beispiel: *Ich bin nach Spanien gefahren …/*
Ich werde nach Spanien fahren …

Challenge

Write a letter to your German penfriend inviting him/her to visit you. Include:

● an invitation:
Willst du/Kannst du nach … kommen?

● details of when and for how long:
in den Sommerferien/zwei Wochen (lang)/…

● how to travel:
Du kannst (mit dem Zug) fahren.

● what there is to do:
Es gibt …

● ideas for activities:
Man kann … Wir können … Wir werden …

For Level 6, use different tenses and modals, and give opinions!

NC 5–6

4B.6 Sprachlabor

The perfect tense with *haben* and *sein*

The perfect tense with *haben*

To say what happened in the past, you use the perfect tense (*das Perfekt*). The perfect tense is usually formed from:
- the present tense of *haben* (see page 166)
- the past participle of the main verb

To form the past participle:
- take the infinitive: *wohnen*
- remove the -en ending: *wohnen*
- add **ge-** and **-t**: **ge**wohn**t**

The past participle goes to the end of the sentence:

Ich wohne in einem Hotel. → Ich **habe** in einem Hotel **gewohnt**.
I lived/have lived in a hotel.

Wir machen einen Ausflug. → Wir **haben** einen Ausflug **gemacht**.
We went on an excursion.

1 Unscramble the word order in these sentences.

Beispiel: **a** *Wir haben in einem Ferienhaus gewohnt.*

a gewohnt Wir einem haben Ferienhaus in.
b Kuchen habe gekauft Ich.
c ein Ich gemacht Poster habe.
d in Wohnwagen habe Ich einem gewohnt.
e Wir Stadtrundfahrt gemacht eine haben.
f gekauft viele Ich Souvenirs habe.

The perfect tense with *sein*

A small number of verbs form their perfect tense with *sein* instead of *haben*. They are usually verbs of motion (to go, to travel). Their past participles are different too – they add **ge-** and **-en** (instead of **-t**):

Ich fahre nach Wien. → Ich **bin** nach Wien **gefahren**.
I travelled/went to Vienna.

Wir fliegen in die Türkei. → Wir **sind** in die Türkei **geflogen**.
We flew/have flown to Turkey.

See page 166 for a list of some of these past participles.

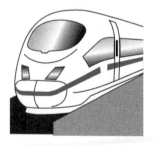

2 Fill in the gaps with the correct form of *sein* or *haben*.

a Ich __bin__ nach Amerika geflogen.
b Wir ▆▆▆ Pommes frites gegessen.
c Wir ▆▆▆ ein Geschenk gekauft.
d Ich ▆▆▆ ins Kino gegangen.
e Wir ▆▆▆ ein Picknick gemacht.
f Wir ▆▆▆ mit dem Auto nach Italien gefahren.

3 Fill in the missing past participles.

a Wir haben in einem Zelt gewohnt.
b Wir sind mit dem Bus _____ .
c Wir haben Karten _____ .
d Ich habe Musik _____ .
e Ich bin Achterbahn _____ .

4 Write the sentences in the perfect tense.

Beispiel: **a** *Wir sind nach Spanien geflogen.*

a Wir fliegen nach Spanien.
b Ich kaufe Souvenirs.
c Wir essen Schokoladeneis.
d Ich fahre nach Berlin.
e Ich tanze in der Disco.
f Ich mache eine Stadtrundfahrt.

Improving your listening skills

When listening to German, it's important that you get a rough idea of what the recording is about first – then you can listen for details. These techniques can help you:

- Look at the pictures, titles and introductions – these often help to show the context and the kind of content to expect.
- Read the questions carefully and try to anticipate or guess what the answers are likely to be. Then listen to see if you were right.
- Listen to the tone of voice: does the speaker sound happy, unhappy, surprised, angry …? Is he/she asking a question?

Also try to work out which bits you can ignore because they don't provide any of the information you need.

Word endings

It is important to pronounce word endings clearly – and to focus closely on them when you're listening. Word endings such as *einen*, *einer* and *einem* tell you the gender of the noun and what case it is in.

5 Listen carefully: *einen, einer* or *einem*? (a–h)

Beispiel: **a** *einem*

6 Listen again to check your answers.

7 Now practise pronouncing a–h. Be careful to say the word endings clearly!

Vocabulary: practise words describing holidays
Grammar: practise prepositions with the dative (*mit, in*);
verbs in the past and the future tense
Skills: identify language patterns; use knowledge of grammar to
work out meaning

 SCHREIBEN 1 **Fill in the gaps.**

NC 2

  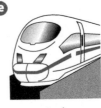  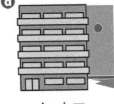

a mit d<u>em</u> Wohnwagen   **b** in ein___   **c** mit d___   **d** in ein___   **e** mit d___   **f** in ein___

 LESEN 2 **Find the correct pictures.**

NC 2

Beispiel: **a** 3

a Wir werden eine Stadtrundfahrt machen.
b Wir werden Pizza essen und Cola trinken.
c Wir werden Souvenirs kaufen.
d Wir werden in der Disco tanzen.
e Wir werden das Schloss besichtigen.
f Wir werden mit der U-Bahn fahren.

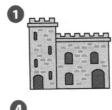 

1 **2** **3**
4 **5** **6**

 LESEN 3 **Match up the sentences.**

NC 2

Beispiel: **a** 3

a Ich habe eine Karte gekauft.
b Wir können ins Museum gehen.
c Wir fahren nach Österreich.
d Ich werde einen Ausflug machen.
e Wir sind in die Türkei geflogen.
f Man kann ins Theater gehen.

1 We're going to Austria.
2 You can go to the theatre.
3 I bought a ticket.
4 We flew to Turkey.
5 We can go to the museum.
6 I will go on an excursion.

 LESEN 4 **Fill in the gaps using the words below.**

a Ich __*bin*__ am Sonntag nach Paris gefahren.
b Ich habe in einem Hotel _____ .
c Wir _____ heute einen Ausflug.
d Ich _____ auch ins Kino.
e Wir _____ morgen nach Versailles fahren.
f Ich werde dort Souvenirs _____ .

gehe   bin   kaufen   gewohnt   werden   machen

4B.7 / Extra Plus

Vocabulary: practise words describing holidays
Grammar: practise verbs in the present, past and future; practise modal verbs (*können*)
Skills: identify language patterns; use knowledge of grammar to work out meaning

LESEN 1

Was ist die richtige Reihenfolge?

Beispiel: **a** *Wir haben in einem Zelt gewohnt.*

a in Wir gewohnt einem haben Zelt.
b können Eis essen Wir ein.
c fahre am Wochenende Ich Berlin nach.

d den besichtigen Wir werden Stephansdom.
e einen Man in Ausflug kann Wien machen.
f nach bin geflogen Spanien Ich.

SCHREIBEN 2

Beantworte diese Fragen.

NC 4–6

a	b	c	d	e	f

Wohin bist du in den Ferien gefahren? *Ich bin …*	Wo hast du gewohnt? *Ich habe …*	Was hast du gemacht? *Ich bin …*	Was kann man in deiner Stadt machen? *Man kann …*	Was machst du heute? *Ich …*	Was wirst du morgen machen? *Ich werde …*

LESEN 3

Richtig (R) oder falsch (F)?

NC 5–6

Beispiel: **a** *R*

a Thomas went to Switzerland by train.
b He is going to do a sightseeing tour.
c He bought some chocolates.
d They are going to an amusement park today.
e There are no restaurants at the amusement park.
f They will go on an excursion into the mountains.
g He doesn't want to dance in the disco.
h They will be going back on Sunday.

> Ich bin gestern nach St. Gallen gefahren – mit dem Zug. St. Gallen ist in der Schweiz.
> Man kann dort viel machen. Wir haben eine Stadtrundfahrt gemacht, und ich habe eine Uhr gekauft.
> Wir gehen heute in die Stadt und wir besuchen Conny-Land – das ist ein Freizeitpark. Wir können dort im Restaurant Hamburger oder Bratwurst essen.
> Und morgen? Wir werden einen Ausflug in die Berge machen, und abends werde ich in der Disco tanzen! Wir werden am Sonntag wieder zurück nach Berlin fahren.
>
> Thomas (13)

LESEN 4

Füll die Lücken aus.

Ich ___bin___ am Sonntag nach Paris ▦▦▦.
Ich ▦▦▦ in einem Hotel ▦▦▦. Wir ▦▦▦ heute den Eiffelturm. Wir können auch den Louvre ▦▦▦.
Wir ▦▦▦ morgen nach Versailles fahren, und ich werde dort Souvenirs ▦▦▦.

> werden   gefahren   kaufen   gewohnt   bin
> besichtigen   habe   besuchen

HÖREN 1

NC 4–5

🎧 **Listen and answer the questions. (See pages 140 and 141.)**

Beispiel: **a** *Greece*

a Where did Jan go?
b How did he get there?
c Where did he stay?
d Which three activities did Jan do?
e What did he eat and drink?
f What did he do in the evenings?

LESEN 2

NC 4–5

Read Maja's message and answer the questions below in English. (See pages 138–143.)

Beispiel: **a** *Maja went to Spain.*

a Where did Maja go in the summer?
b How did she get there and where did they stay?
c Where is she going next weekend?
d How will they get there and who are they staying with?
e Where will she go in the winter?
f What will she do there?

> Ich bin in den Sommerferien mit meiner Mutter nach Spanien gefahren. Wir sind mit dem Zug gefahren und wir haben in einer Ferienwohnung gewohnt.
>
> Am Wochenende fahre ich mit meinem Vater nach München. Wir fahren mit dem Auto. Wir besuchen dort meine Großeltern. Man kann dort viel machen, denn München ist sehr groß.
>
> Und was werde ich im Winter machen? Ich werde mit der Schule nach Zürich reisen. Wir werden mit dem Bus fahren, und wir werden eine Woche dort bleiben. In Zürich schneit es im Winter oft, und wir können Ski fahren.

SPRECHEN 3

NC 3–5

Describe your holiday plans. Make a mini-presentation if you can, using the following points. (See pages 136–143.)

- Where you're going: *Ich fahre nach/fliege in die/den …*
- With whom: *mit meinen Eltern/meinem Vater …*
- For how long: *eine Woche/zwei Wochen/zehn Tage …*
- Where you'll stay: *in einem Hotel/einer Ferienwohnung/einem Zelt/einem Wohnwagen …*
- What there is to do: *man kann …/es gibt …/wir können …*

⚠️ If you want to aim for Level 5, include a sentence about another holiday in the past or the future tense.

SCHREIBEN 4

NC 4–6

Write at least five sentences about a recent holiday. Include the details below. (See pages 140–143.)

- Where you went.
- Where you stayed.
- What there is for teenagers to do.
- What you did.
- Your opinion of it.

Beispiel: *Ich bin nach … geflogen …*

⚠️ To aim for Level 6, include a sentence in the future tense about your holiday plans.

Wohin fährst du in den Ferien?	*Where are you going on holiday?*
Ich fahre/Wir fahren …	*I am/We are going …*
nach Frankreich	*to France*
nach Italien	*to Italy*
an die Nordsee	*to the North Sea*
in die Türkei	*to Turkey*

Wie fährst du?	*How are you travelling/ going?*
Ich fahre/Wir fahren mit …	*I am/We are going by …*
dem Auto	*car*
dem Wohnmobil	*camper van*
dem Wohnwagen	*caravan*
dem Zug	*train*
Ich fliege/Wir fliegen.	*I am/We are going by plane. I am/We are flying.*

Wo wohnst du?	*Where are you staying?*
Ich wohne/Wir wohnen …	*I am/We are staying …*
auf einem Campingplatz	*on a campsite*
in einem Ferienhaus	*in a holiday home*
in einer Ferienwohnung	*in a holiday apartment*
in einem Hotel	*in a hotel*
in einer Jugendherberge	*in a youth hostel*
in einem Wohnmobil	*in a camper van*
in einem Wohnwagen	*in a caravan*
in einem Zelt	*in a tent*
Wie lange bleibst du/bleibt ihr dort?	*How long are you staying there?*
Ich bleibe/Wir bleiben (eine Woche) dort.	*I am/We are staying there (a week).*
zwei Wochen (lang)	*two weeks*
eine Woche	*one week*
zehn Tage	*ten days*

Was können wir machen?	*What can we do?*
Wir können/wollen …	*We can/want to …*
Ich kann/will …	*I can/want to …*
in einen Freizeitpark gehen	*go to an amusement park*
ins Museum gehen	*go to the museum*
mit dem Riesenrad fahren	*go on the Ferris wheel*
den Stephansdom besuchen	*visit St Stephan's Cathedral*
eine Stadtrundfahrt machen	*go on a tour of the town*
im Wasserpark spielen	*play in the waterpark*
ein Wiener Schnitzel essen	*eat a veal escalope*

Was werdet ihr machen?	*What will you do?*
Wir werden …	*We will …*
(meine) Freunde treffen	*meet up with (my) friends*
ein Eis kaufen	*buy an ice cream*
ein Picknick machen	*go on a picnic*
Pizza essen	*eat pizza*
das Schloss Schönbrunn besuchen	*visit Schönbrunn Palace*
schwimmen	*go swimming*
Souvenirs kaufen	*buy souvenirs*
ins Theater gehen	*go to the theatre*

Was hast du gemacht?	*What did you do?*
Wir haben/Ich habe …	*We/I …*
einen Ausflug gemacht	*went on an excursion*
in der Disco getanzt	*danced in the disco*
Frisbee gespielt	*played frisbee*
Karten gekauft	*bought tickets*
Musik im Park gehört	*listened to music in the park*
Souvenirs gekauft	*bought souvenirs*

Wohin bist du gefahren?	*Where did you go?*
Ich bin/Wir sind …	*I/We …*
nach Italien gefahren	*went to Italy*
in die Türkei geflogen	*flew to Turkey*
Wo hast du gewohnt?	*Where did you stay?*
Ich habe/Wir haben in … gewohnt.	*I/We stayed in …*

I can...

- say where I'm going on holiday
- say where I'm staying and for how long
- say how I get there
- say what I can do on holiday, using modal verbs such as *können* and *wollen*
- say what I can do on a future holiday, using the future tense (*werden* + infinitive)
- describe a past holiday, saying where I went, how I travelled and where I stayed
- use the perfect tense with *haben, sein* and the past participle

Deutschsprachige Länder

Northern Germany has two coastlines: one with the *Nordsee* (North Sea) and one with the *Ostsee* (Baltic Sea). In southern Germany are the *Alpen* (Alps). The highest mountain is the *Zugspitze*. It is 2962 m high.

The Austrian mountains are excellent for skiing as it frequently snows in winter. Austria is famous for different types of coffee: a *Schwarzer* is a small cup of black coffee, a *Brauner* is coffee with cream and a *Melange* is half coffee and half milk.
It's best to have one of these with a slice of *Apfelstrudel*, an apple pastry.

There are 32 mountain peaks over 4000 m high in Switzerland. 64% of the population speak German as their first language. Most people in Switzerland speak at least one other of the official languages fluently (French, Italian or Romansh). Switzerland is famous for its chocolate.

Hallo. Wie geht's? Ich heiße Richard. Ich bin vierzehn Jahre alt. Ich habe im Mai Geburtstag. Ich wohne in Österreich, in der Hauptstadt Wien. Wien ist super.

Richard

Guten Tag. Ich heiße Tanja. Ich bin dreizehn Jahre alt und ich habe im Juli Geburtstag. Ich wohne in Zürich. Zürich ist in der Schweiz. Ich spreche drei Sprachen: Deutsch, Französisch und Italienisch. Das finde ich toll.

Tanja

Hallo. Ich heiße Thomas. Ich wohne in Deutschland, in Bremen, aber ich komme aus England. Ich spreche Deutsch und Englisch. Ich bin zwölf Jahre alt und ich habe im Januar Geburtstag. Ich finde Bremen sehr gut.

Thomas

LESEN 1

Answer the questions in English about Richard, Tanja and Thomas.

A 1 Who speaks three languages?
2 Who was not born in a German-speaking country?
3 Who is the oldest person?

B 1 What are Wien, Zürich and Bremen?
2 What is the more formal greeting used in one of the paragraphs?
3 *Super* is a positive expression. Find two more in the texts.

LESEN 2

What do the words *Sprachen* and *Hauptstadt* mean?

Top-Ten-Haustiere

More than 30% of all German households own at least one pet – that's 23.3 million pets altogether!

Die Top Ten der Haustiere in Deutschland

1 Katze
2 Hund
3 Fisch
4 Vogel
5 Meerschweinchen
6 Kaninchen
7 Hamster
8 Pferd
9 Maus
10 Schlange

Die Top Ten der Katzen- und Hundenamen in Deutschland

Katzen

1 Mieke	6 Micki
2 Janosch	7 Gizmo
3 Minka	8 Lilly
4 Garfield	9 Zorro
5 Max	10 Pauli

Hunde

1 Hasso	6 Diego
2 Bentley	7 Aldo
3 Benno	8 Luna
4 Anton	9 Johna
5 Abby	10 Rex

 LESEN 1 Which is the most common name for a cat in Germany – and which for a dog?

 **LESEN 2** Read the text about 'Tokio Hotel' and answer the questions in English.

a Where do 'Tokio Hotel' come from?
b How old are Bill and Tom?
c When is their birthday?
d What does *Zwillinge* mean?
e What languages do they speak and sing in?

Hallo! Wir sind die Band „Tokio Hotel" aus Deutschland. Ich heiße Bill Kaulitz und ich bin 21 Jahre alt – ich habe im September Geburtstag. Das ist mein Bruder Tom. Er ist auch 21 Jahre alt und er hat auch im September Geburtstag – wir sind Zwillinge! Ich spreche – und singe – auf Deutsch und Englisch, und Tom auch.

Lieblingsfächer in Deutschland

	Mädchen	Jungen
1	Kunst 27%	Mathe 41%
2	Deutsch 16,8%	Sport 17%
3	Sport/Musik 11,4%	Deutsch 7%

$$a^2 + b^2 = c^2$$

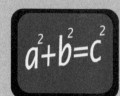

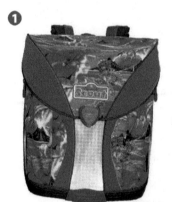

a Mein Lieblingsfach ist Musik – ich bin sehr musikalisch. Ich liebe auch Popmusik.

b Ich bin sehr romantisch, und mein Lieblingsfach ist Französisch.

c Mein Lieblingsfach? Sport – Sport ist super! Ich bin sehr sportlich – ich bin Fußballer.

d Ich bin ziemlich intelligent, und mein Lieblingsfach ist Biologie – ich mag Tiere!

LESEN 1 Look at the survey results above. Are these sentences true or false?

a Art is the least favourite subject for girls.
b Girls like German more than sports.
c Boys' favourite subject is maths.
d Boys also like German more than sports.

LESEN 2 Match speech bubbles a–d to the school bags 1–4.

Im Internet!

Carsten

Ich bin täglich im Internet. Ich mache meine Hausaufgaben oder ich chatte mit Freunden auf Facebook. Ich interessiere mich für soziale Netzwerke.

Katharina

Ich bin nicht so oft im Internet, aber ich lade Musik runter und ich sehe mir Musikclips auf YouTube an. Hausaufgaben mache ich nicht im Internet – das ist zu unpraktisch.

 LESEN 1

Read the texts for Carsten, Katharina and Heiko. Can you guess what a and b mean?

a soziale Netzwerke
b ich lade Musik runter

 LESEN 2

Read the texts and answer the questions.

a Which two teenagers use the internet every day?
b Which two teenagers download music?
c Which two teenagers talk to friends using the internet?
d Who does not use the internet very often?
e Who uses the internet for homework?
f Who shops on the internet?

 LESEN 3

Read the text on the right and answer the questions in English.

a What do you think *Hannover* is?
b What sort of dance does Lena do?
c What is Lena's favourite hobby?
d What does she mention about Europe?
e What language does she sing in?
f What does she say about Jack Johnson and Adele?
g How does she use the internet? (2)
h Why is the internet practical for her?

Heiko

Ich bin jeden Tag im Internet. Ich kaufe nie CDs. Ich lade Musik im Internet runter. Das finde ich praktisch. Ich kaufe auch im Internet ein, zum Beispiel Bücher oder Computerspiele. Und ich chatte mit Freunden über MSN.

Ich heiße Lena. Mein Nachname ist Meyer-Landrut. Ich tanze sehr gern und mache Ballett. Am liebsten singe ich und ich habe schon einen Nummer-1-Hit in Europa. Ich spreche Deutsch, aber ich singe auf Englisch. Ich höre auch gern Musik. Meine Lieblingssänger sind Jack Johnson und Adele. Ich lade Musik im Internet runter. Ich chatte auch mit meinen Freunden im Internet. Das ist gut, denn ich bin nicht immer in Hannover. Ich singe oft in anderen Ländern und Städten und auf Facebook zu chatten ist praktisch.

Deutschland!

Wer wohnt wo in Deutschland?

in der Stadt: 86%
auf dem Land: 14%

Großstädte in Deutschland

Berlin: 3,5 Millionen Einwohner

Hamburg: 1,7 Millionen Einwohner

München: 1,2 Millionen Einwohner

Berge, Berge, Berge – die Top 3

Dufourspitze (Schweiz) 4634 m

Großglockner (Österreich) 3798 m

Zugspitze (Deutschland) 2962 m

Die meisten Deutschen mieten Häuser und Wohnungen (61%) – in Großbritannien sind es nur 40% und in Frankreich nur 45%.

Willkommen auf Hallig Hooge!

Hallo! Ich heiße Annika und ich wohne auf einer Insel – Hallig Hooge. Hallig Hooge ist im Meer im Nordwesten von Deutschland – das ist die Nordsee. Hallig Hooge ist sehr klein, und hier wohnen nur 80 Menschen. Wir haben eine Schule. Sie ist auch sehr klein: es gibt nur vier Schüler und Schülerinnen!

Wie ist das Wetter? Es ist immer windig! Im Winter ist es kalt und es schneit manchmal. Im Herbst und im Frühling ist es sehr, sehr windig, und es gewittert oft. Im Sommer ist es manchmal heiß – und es regnet manchmal …

Was gibt es für Kinder auf Hallig Hooge? Also, wir haben einen Sportplatz und einen Spielplatz. Im Winter ist es manchmal langweilig, aber wir haben Fernsehen und Internet.

LESEN 1 **Read the notes above. Are these sentences true or false?**

a Most Germans live in the countryside.
b Berlin is the largest city in Germany.
c Austria has the highest mountain.
d Most Germans rent (mieten) their homes.

LESEN 2 **Read the text on the left and answer the questions in English.**

a What is Hallig Hooge – and where is it?
b How many people live on Hallig Hooge?
c What's unusual about Annika's school?
d What's the weather like?
e What is there for children to do on Hallig Hooge?
f What does Annika say about living there in the winter?

Lieblingsessen in Deutschland

1	Döner Kebab	6	Steak
2	Currywurst	7	Gemüsesuppe
3	Pasta Bolognese	8	Lasagne
4	Wiener Schnitzel	9	Gulasch
5	Pizza	10	Braten

 LESEN 1

Match each picture to one of the dishes above.

Beispiel: **1 f**

a  **b**  **c**  **d**  **e**

f  **g**  **h**  **i** 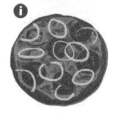 **j**

 LESEN 2

Look at the Top Ten German dishes (1–10) above. Are these sentences true or false?

a In Deutschland isst man am liebsten Döner.
b In Deutschland isst man sehr gern Fleisch.
c In Deutschland isst man kein Essen aus Italien.

 LESEN 3

Read Ali's text and answer the questions in English.

a What is Ali's favourite fast food?
b What does his uncle own?
c Where do doners come from?
d What do they consist of?
e How many doner stalls are there in Germany – and how many in Berlin?
f How often do Ali and his family eat doners?

Was ist mein Lieblingsfastfood? Ich esse am liebsten Döner Kebabs! Mein Onkel hat hier in Berlin eine Dönerbude – das ist super! Da gibt es Pommes frites, Hamburger – und natürlich Döner Kebabs. Döner kommen aus der Türkei. Und was ist ein Döner? Das ist Grillfleisch in Scheiben mit Fladen- oder Pittabrot, Salat, Zwiebeln und Joghurtsoße mit viel Knoblauch. Total lecker! Döner sind das Fastfood Nummer eins in Deutschland: es gibt 15 000 Dönerbuden in Deutschland – 1400 sind in Berlin! Meine Familie und ich – wir essen viermal pro Woche Döner.

Ali

Eine Reise durch Berlin

a Berlin ist die Hauptstadt von Deutschland und liegt im Nordosten des Landes. Berlin hat 3,5 Millionen Einwohner. Es gibt viele Sehenswürdigkeiten in Berlin. Der Alexanderplatz ist zum Beispiel ein beliebter Treffpunkt. Hier gibt es viele Geschäfte und hier steht auch der **Fernsehturm**. Er ist 368 Meter hoch.

b Gehst du gern ins Museum? Es gibt viele Museen in Berlin, zum Beispiel das **Pergamonmuseum**. Im Pergamonmuseum kann man Kunst aus der Antike sehen. Ein anderes Museum ist das Museum am Checkpoint Charlie. Das ist ein Museum über die Geschichte von Berlin von 1961 bis 1990.

c Viele Berliner fahren im Sommer in den **Grunewald**. Das ist ein großer Wald im Westen von Berlin. Man kann dort super Rad fahren, schwimmen oder spazieren gehen.

d Einkaufen kann man auch toll in Berlin. Das berühmte Kaufhaus KaDeWe ist am **Kurfürstendamm**. Nach dem Einkaufen kann man im Café ein Eis essen. Das Café Kranzler ist sehr berühmt.

e Wenn man in Berlin ist, muss man auch das **Brandenburger Tor** sehen. Es ist ein nationales Symbol Deutschlands. Nur 100 Meter vom Brandenburger Tor entfernt ist das deutsche Parlament – der Reichstag.

LESEN 1 **Find the correct photo for each paragraph above.**

LESEN 2 **Find the German words for a–g in the texts above.**

Beispiel: **a** *Hauptstadt*

a capital city
b inhabitants
c a popular meeting point
d a museum about the history
e a big forest
f is very famous
g a national symbol

Did you know that Berlin was a divided city from 1961 until 1989?

The eastern half of the city was part of the communist DDR (*Deutsche Demokratische Republik*) and the western half was part of federal West Germany, the BRD (*Bundesrepublik Deutschland*).

A wall divided the East and the West. Travelling from East to West was very difficult, and in most cases impossible. Friends and families were divided until the Berlin Wall came down in 1989 and Germany was reunified.

Today, Berlin is one big city in which people can move around freely.

Deutsche Designer sind cool!

Deutsche Designer sind weltweit sehr berühmt. Karl Lagerfeld, Hugo Boss, Wolfgang Joop, Wunderkind oder Jil Sander: Jeder möchte ihre Kleidung kaufen. Lagerfeld und Sander sind die bekanntesten Modedesigner in Deutschland. Ihre Mode ist schick, modisch, hip – und sehr, sehr teuer! Es gibt sie in allen großen deutschen Städten, zum Beispiel in Köln, München, Hamburg und Berlin. Sie repräsentieren Luxus und Schönheit.

Magst du sportliche Kleidung und trägst du Mode von Esprit, Adidas und Puma? Sie kommen alle aus Deutschland! Esprit-Mode ist nicht so teuer und es gibt über 14 000 Esprit-Geschäfte in 44 Ländern. Das größte englische Geschäft ist in Regent Street in London. Adidas und Puma machen Sportmode – vor allem Sportschuhe. Stars wie David Beckham und Snoop Dogg sind große Fans von Adidas. Es gibt Adidas seit 1949 und es ist die Sportmarke Nummer 1 auf der Welt.

 LESEN 1 **Read the text. Choose the correct answer.**

a Karl Lagerfeld is
  1 a famous German fashion designer.
  2 a German department store.

b Clothes by Jil Sander are
  1 quite cheap.
  2 very expensive.

c Esprit shops can be found
  1 only in Germany.
  2 in many countries.

d Adidas is a sports brand from
  1 Germany.
  2 England.

e Puma sells
  1 only trainers.
  2 lots of sports fashion.

f Adidas is
  1 over 60 years old.
  2 49 years old.

 LESEN 2 **Find the German words in the text above.**

a worldwide
b famous
c fashion designer
d they represent
e luxury
f beauty
g huge fans
h sports brand

 LESEN 3 **Answer the questions in English.**

a Where can you find German designer shops?
b Describe the clothes made by Karl Lagerfeld and Jil Sander.
c How do you say Cologne and Munich in German?
d Where in England can you find a branch of the German shop Esprit?
e Which German designers are producing sports clothes?
f Who wears Adidas?

 LESEN 4 **Research a German fashion designer and write a paragraph about him or her in German. Illustrate your work with the type of fashion he or she designs.**

Ferienländer: die Top 10 der Deutschen!

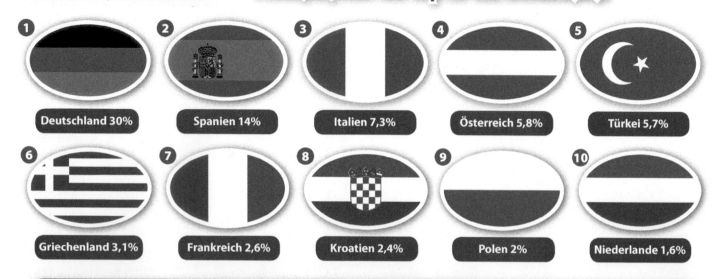

❶ Deutschland 30%	❷ Spanien 14%	❸ Italien 7,3%	❹ Österreich 5,8%	❺ Türkei 5,7%
❻ Griechenland 3,1%	❼ Frankreich 2,6%	❽ Kroatien 2,4%	❾ Polen 2%	❿ Niederlande 1,6%

Willkommen in meiner Stadt – Zürich!

Zürich ist im Nordosten der Schweiz und hat 1,1 Millionen Einwohner. Und in Zürich gibt es viel zu sehen – und zu besuchen! Letztes Jahr haben über 9 Millionen Touristen Zürich besucht. Warum? Also, Zürich ist toll, interessant, schön, alt … Es gibt eine Oper, viele Theater – und über 50 Museen. Mein Lieblingsmuseum ist das Puppenmuseum.

Du willst lieber einkaufen gehen? Die Bahnhofstraße ist sehr berühmt. Dort gibt es große Kaufhäuser, teure Modegeschäfte, moderne Boutiquen, viele Uhrengeschäfte – und dort kann man auch die berühmte Schweizer Schokolade kaufen.

In Zürich gibt es auch einen Fluss – die Limmat – und einen See: das ist der Zürichsee. Er ist sehr groß und man kann dort eine Schiffsrundfahrt machen, schwimmen, segeln oder einen Spaziergang machen. Ich bin im Sommer dort jede Woche gesegelt!

Zürich hat auch viele Parks und viel Natur – und viele Berge! Im Winter schneit es in Zürich viel, und ich werde dann viel Ski fahren.

LESEN 1

Look at the list of German holiday destinations at the top of the page. True or false?

a Die Deutschen bleiben im Urlaub am liebsten zu Hause.
b Italien ist beliebter als Spanien.
c Im Ferienland Nummer vier spricht man Deutsch.
d Die Niederlande sind auch sehr beliebt.

LESEN 2

Answer the questions in English.

a Where is Zurich?
b How many people live there – and how many visit each year?
c What is there to do for culture lovers?
d Where can you go if you want to go shopping – and why?
e What can you do at the lake?
f What can you do in winter?

Grammatik

Introduction

In order to speak or write correctly in a language, we need to know the grammar basics behind the construction of sentences. The ability to identify patterns and to understand and apply grammar rules in German allows you to use the language to say what you want to say.

In this section you will find a summary of the main grammar points covered by this book with some activities to check that you have understood and can use the language accurately.

Grammar index

1	Nouns	page 162
2	Cases	page 162
3	Prepositions	page 163
4	Adjectives	page 163
5	Possessive adjectives	page 164
6	Pronouns	page 164
7	Verbs	page 165
8	Negatives	page 167
9	Gern, lieber, am liebsten	page 167
10	Word order	page 167
11	Asking questions	page 168
	Answers to grammar activities	page 168
	Useful expressions	page 169

Glossary of terms

noun *das Nomen* = a person, animal, place or thing

Maja und ihre **Katze** spielen im **Garten**. *Maja and her cat are playing in the garden.*

article *der Artikel* = the word in front of a noun such as 'the', 'a' or 'my'

der Hund, **eine** Tasche, **mein** Haustier *the dog, a bag, my pet*

singular *der Singular* = one of something

Der Hund isst **eine Wurst**. *The dog is eating a sausage.*

plural *der Plural* = more than one of something

Die Kinder gehen in die Schule. *The children are going to school.*

pronoun *das Pronomen* = a word used instead of a noun or a name

Er isst eine Wurst. *He (It, The dog) is eating a sausage.*
Sie gehen in die Schule. *They are going to school.*

subject *das Subjekt* = a person or thing 'doing' the action or verb

Tom geht ins Kino. *Tom is going to the cinema.*
Ich mag Mathe. *I like maths.*

object *das Objekt* = a person or thing affected by the action or verb

Jana kauft **eine CD**. *Jana is buying a CD.*
Ich trage **einen Pullover**. *I'm wearing a jumper.*

nominative case *der Nominativ* = the subject of the sentence

Der Hund heißt Bello. *The dog is called Bello.*
Eine Banane kostet 50 Cent. *A banana costs 50 cents.*

accusative case *der Akkusativ* = used for the object of a sentence

Ich habe **einen Bruder**. *I have a brother.*
Jan kauft **eine Tasche**. *Jan is buying a bag.*

dative case *der Dativ* = used after some prepositions

Ich wohne in **einem Reihenhaus**. *I live in a terraced house.*
Sie fahren mit **dem Zug**. *They are going by train.*

adjective *das Adjektiv* = a word which describes a noun

Meine Schwester ist **nett**. *My sister is nice.*
Berlin ist eine **schöne** Stadt. *Berlin is a beautiful city.*

preposition *die Präposition* = describes position: where something is

Wir gehen **in** die Disco. *We are going to the disco.*
Meine Tasche ist **auf** dem Bett. *My bag is on the bed.*

Grammatik

1 Nouns and articles
Nomen und Artikel

1.1 Masculine, feminine or neuter?

All German nouns are either masculine, feminine or neuter. Nouns always start with a capital letter and their articles have different endings:

	masculine	feminine	neuter
the	der	die	das
a/an	ein	eine	ein

 Every time you learn a new noun, make sure you learn its gender (masculine, feminine or neuter) too.

Don't learn:	*Hund*	✗
Learn:	*der Hund*	✓

1.2 Singular or plural?

In English, you usually add -s to a noun to make it plural when you are talking about more than one thing (one cat → two cats). In German, there are several different ways of forming the plural, but the plural word for 'the' is always *die*:

der Bleistift (*pencil*)	→	**die** Bleistift**e**
die Schwester (*sister*)	→	**die** Schwester**n**
der Opa (*grandfather*)	→	**die** Opa**s**
der Bruder (*brother*)	→	**die** Br**ü**der

 Each time you learn a new noun, try to learn its plural too.

2 Cases
Fälle

2.1 Subject and object

The subject of a sentence is the person or thing 'doing' the verb. The object of a sentence is the thing or person affected by the verb. We say that the subject and the object are in different cases.

subject	verb	object
Der Hund	isst	eine Wurst.
Sven	kauft	ein Buch.

2.2 The nominative and accusative case

The endings for *der/die/das* and *ein/eine/ein* never change when they come before the subject of a sentence. We say that the subject is in the nominative case:

	masculine	feminine	neuter	plural
the	der	die	das	die
a	ein	eine	ein	–

The endings for *der* and *ein* change slightly when they come before the object of a sentence – but only for masculine nouns. We say that the object of the sentence is in the accusative case:

subject	verb	object
Er	hat liebt	**einen** Computer. **den** Hund.
Sie	kauft liest	eine CD. die Zeitung.
Uwe Ich	trägt habe	ein T-Shirt. das Buch.

2.3 The dative case

The endings for *der/die/das* and *ein/eine/ein* change after certain prepositions (words like 'in', 'on', 'at'). We say that the nouns that come after these prepositions are in the dative case:

> Ich wohne in **einem Dorf**. *I live in a village.*
> Tom tanzt in **der Disco**. *Tom is dancing in the disco.*

2.4 *mein*, *dein* and *kein*

The words for 'my' (*mein*), 'your' (*dein*) and 'no/none' (*kein*) also change their endings when used before a masculine object in the accusative case:

> Tanja hat **meinen** CD-Spieler. *Tanja has my CD player.*
> Ich mag **deine** Bluse. *I like your blouse.*
> Ich habe **kein** Haustier. *I haven't got a pet.*

Summary

Here are all the case endings used in *Zoom Deutsch 1*:

der/die/das				
	masculine	feminine	neuter	plural
nominative	der	die	das	die
accusative	den	die	das	die
dative	dem	der	dem	den

ein/eine/ein

	masculine	feminine	neuter	plural
nominative	ein	eine	ein	–
accusative	einen	eine	ein	–
dative	einem	einer	einem	–

mein/dein/kein
These all follow these endings:

	masculine	feminine	neuter	plural
nominative	mein	meine	mein	meine
accusative	meinen	meine	mein	meine
dative	meinem	meiner	meinem	meinen

A You're going shopping. Write sentences with *Ich kaufe einen/eine/ein...*

a die Tasche b der Pullover c das Eis

d der Füller e das Computerspiel f die CD

3 Prepositions

Präpositionen

Prepositions are words like 'in' and 'on' which tell you where someone or something is. They always change the endings of the articles *der/die/das* and *ein/eine/ein*:

m der Schreibtisch → Das Buch ist **im** Schreibtisch.
                          (in + dem)
f die Lampe → Die CD ist **neben** der Lampe.
n das Regal → Der Fußball ist **auf** dem Regal.

Here is a list of all the prepositions you will learn in *Zoom Deutsch 1*:

auf	*on*	neben	*next to*
aus	*from*	über	*above*
hinter	*behind*	unter	*under*
in	*in/into*	vor	*in front of*
mit	*with, by (+ transport)*	zu	*to*
nach	*after*	zwischen	*between*

3.1 Accusative or dative case?

Prepositions take either the accusative or the dative case:

- *aus, mit, nach* and *zu* always take the dative case
- *auf, hinter, in, neben, über, unter, vor* and *zwischen* either take the dative or the accusative case.

When followed by the accusative case, the preposition indicates movement or a direction (for example where someone or something is going or moving to):

Tom fährt **in** die Stadt. *Tom drives into town.*
Ich gehe **hinter** den Tisch. *I go behind the table.*

But when followed by the dative, the preposition tells you where someone or something is already:

Tom wohnt **in** der Stadt. *Tom lives in the city.*
Der Test ist **auf** dem Tisch. *The test is on the table.*

B Where is everything? Write six sentences in German using *unter, auf, über, neben, in* and *hinter*, e.g.
Der Fußball ist unter dem Bett.
Die Katze…; Das Regal…; Der Kleiderschrank…;
Die Tasche…; Die Schuhe…

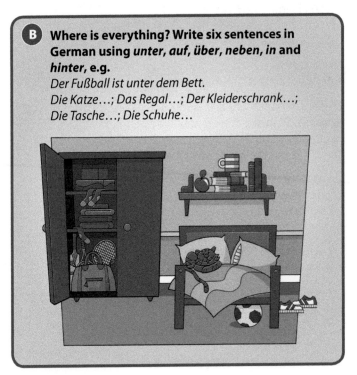

4 Adjectives

Adjektive

Adjectives are the words we use to describe nouns. When an adjective follows a noun, you can use the form in which it appears in the dictionary, with no additional ending:

Das T-Shirt ist **schön**.
Meine Mutter ist **nett**.

But when the adjective is placed directly before a noun, it adds an extra ending according to the gender of the noun and the case used:

Grammatik

Das ist ein schön**er** Pullover.
Ich trage einen rot**en** Pullover.

Frau Klar ist eine gut**e** Lehrerin.
Susi hat eine neu**e** Lehrerin.

Berne ist ein alt**es** Dorf.
Ich wohne in einem alt**en** Dorf.

4.1 Comparatives

When you want to say something is smaller, bigger, nicer, etc., you use the comparative form. As in English, you add **-er** to the adjective to form the comparative in German:

klein → klein**er**
schön → schön**er**
billig → billig**er**

For some short adjectives you also have to add an umlaut to the first vowel:

alt → **ä**lt**er**
groß → gr**öß**er

And some comparatives are irregular:

gut → **besser**

To say 'than' use *als*:

Die Bluse ist schicker **als** das T-Shirt. *The blouse is smarter than the T-shirt.*

> **C** Give the comparative form of the adjective in brackets.
>
> **a** Dieses T-Shirt ist (billig).
> **b** Der rote Rock ist (schön).
> **c** Der Film mit Lena ist (gut).
> **d** Jakob ist (frech).
> **e** Berlin ist (alt).
> **f** Dein Haus ist (modern).

5 Possessive adjectives

Possessivpronomen

Possessive adjectives show who or what something belongs to ('my dog', 'your brother'):

Das ist **meine** Mutter. *That is my mother.*
Ist das **dein** Pullover? *Is that your jumper?*

They come before the noun they describe and they take the same endings as *ein/eine/ein*:

	masculine	feminine	neuter	plural
my	mein Füller	meine Tasche	mein Buch	meine Schuhe
your	dein Füller	deine Tasche	dein Buch	deine Schuhe

6 Pronouns

Pronomen

Pronouns are used instead of a noun or a name:

Ich heiße Lola. *I am called Lola.*
Er ist sehr frech. *He is very naughty.*
Sie wohnt in Berlin. *She lives in Berlin.*

Here is a list of all the German pronouns used in *Zoom Deutsch 1*:

ich	*I*	wir	*we*
du	*you*	ihr	*you (informal, plural)*
er/sie/es	*he/she/it*	sie	*they*
man	*one*	Sie	*you (formal)*

> **D** Replace the noun in brackets with the correct pronoun.
>
> **a** (Mein Bruder) ist sehr frech!
> **b** (Meine Freundin) wohnt in einem Dorf.
> **c** (Die CDs) kosten 30 Euro.
> **d** (Das Pferd) heißt Luna.
> **e** (Deine Eltern) sind sehr nett.
> **f** (Ich + Mila) gehen ins Kino.

6.1 *sie, Sie, du* and *man*

- *sie* (with a small 's') can mean 'she' (singular) or 'they' (plural):

    Wo wohnt **sie**? *Where does she live?*
    Wo wohnen **sie**? *Where do they live?*

- *Sie* (with a capital 'S') is the polite form of 'you' used when talking to adults, strangers and in formal situations:

    Haben **Sie** Apfelsaft? *Do you have apple juice?*

- *du* is the informal form of 'you' used when talking to family, friends, children or animals:

    Wie alt bist **du**? *How old are you?*
    Hast **du** einen Hund? *Do you have a dog?*

- *man* is often used in German and can mean 'one', 'you', 'they' or 'we':

    Wie kommt **man** zum Schwimmbad? *How does **one**/ How do **you** get to the pool?*
    Man spricht Deutsch in der Schweiz. ***They** speak German in Switzerland.*
    Man kann ins Kino gehen. ***You** can go to the cinema.*

6.2 Object pronouns

The words 'it' and 'them' in these sentences are called object pronouns:

> I like the skirt – I'll buy **it**.
> The trainers are expensive – I won't buy **them**.

In the following sentences, notice how in German the word for 'it' changes (*ihn/sie/es*), depending on the gender of the noun it replaces. Remember that the object of the sentence is in the accusative case (see Section 2.2):

> Ich mag den Rock. Ich kaufe **ihn**. *I like the skirt. I'll buy it.*
> Die Bluse ist schick. Ich trage **sie**.
> *The blouse is smart. I'll wear it.*
> Ich mag das Hemd. Ich nehme **es**. *I like the shirt. I'll take it.*

The word for 'them' is *sie*:

> Die Shorts sind cool. Ich kaufe **sie**.
> *The shorts are cool. I'll buy them.*

7 Verbs

Verben

Verbs are words which describe an action. If you can put 'to' in front of a word or '-ing' at the end, it is probably a verb:

go	to go ✓	going ✓	= a verb
listen	to listen ✓	listening ✓	= a verb
desk	to desk ✗	desking ✗	= not a verb
happy	to happy ✗	happying ✗	= not a verb

7.1 The infinitive

A verb takes many different forms:

> I **have** a cat.
> Tom **has** a dog.
> They **haven't** any pets.

Not all verb forms are listed in a dictionary. For example, you won't find 'has' or 'haven't'. You will have to look up the infinitive 'to have'.

In German, infinitives are easy to recognise as they always end in **-en** or **-n**:

> spiel**en** *to play*
> wohn**en** *to live*
> sammel**n** *to collect*

7.2 The present tense

A verb in the present tense describes an action which is taking place now or takes place regularly.

There are two present tenses in English:

> I am playing tennis. (now)
> I play tennis. (every day)

There is only one present tense in German:

> Ich spiele Tennis. (jetzt – *now*)
> Ich spiele Tennis. (jeden Tag – *every day*)

To describe an action, you need a subject (the person or thing doing the action) and a verb. The ending of the verb changes according to who or what the subject of the sentence is:

> **Ich** les**e**. *I read.*
> **Sie** lies**t**. *She reads*.
> **Wir** geh**en**. *We go*.
> **Er** geh**t**. *He goes*.

7.3 Regular verb endings

Most German verbs follow the same pattern. They have regular endings which are always added to the verb stem, which is the infinitive without its -(**e)n** ending (e.g. *spielen →* *spiel, schwimmen → schwimm*):

spielen	*to play*
ich spiel**e**	*I play*
du spiel**st**	*you play*
er/sie/es/man spiel**t**	*he/she/it/one plays*
wir spiel**en**	*we play*
ihr spiel**t**	*you play (plural)*
sie spiel**en**	*they play*
Sie spiel**en**	*you play (formal)*

7.4 Irregular verb endings

Some common verbs do not follow this regular pattern. They are irregular, and they change their endings, as well as their stem, in the *du* and the *er/sie/es* forms.

 You'll need to learn them by heart.

Here are some examples of common irregular verbs:

fahren *to go*	lesen *to read*	essen *to eat*
a → ä	**e → ie**	**e → i**
ich **fah**re	ich **le**se	ich **es**se
du **fähr**st	du **lie**st	du **iss**t
er/sie/es **fähr**t	er/sie/es **lie**st	er/sie/es **iss**t

tragen *to wear*	sehen *to see*	nehmen *to take*
a → ä	**e → ie**	**e → i**
ich **trag**e	ich **seh**e	ich **nehm**e
du **träg**st	du **sieh**st	du **nimm**st
er/sie/es **träg**t	er/sie/es **sieh**t	er/sie/es **nimm**t

Grammatik

7.5 haben and sein

The verbs haben (to have) and sein (to be) don't follow the pattern of any other verbs, so you need to learn them:

haben	sein
ich **habe**	ich **bin**
du **hast**	du **bist**
er/sie/es **hat**	er/sie/es **ist**
wir **haben**	wir **sind**
ihr **habt**	ihr **seid**
sie **haben**	sie **sind**
Sie **haben**	Sie **sind**

E Fill in the correct form of *haben* or *sein*.

a Ich ▨▨▨ keine Geschwister.
b Tina ▨▨▨ 15 Jahre alt.
c Wann ▨▨▨ du Geburtstag?
d Ich ▨▨▨ im Wohnzimmer.
e Meine Eltern ▨▨▨ sehr nett.
f ▨▨▨ Sie einen Bleistift, bitte?

7.6 Modal verbs

Modal verbs (*können*, *wollen* and *sollen*) are used to say what you 'can', 'want to' and 'should' do. When you use a modal verb in a sentence, the main verb goes to the end in its infinitive form:

Wir **können** ein Picknick **machen**. *We can have a picnic.*
Ich **will** ins Kino **gehen**. *I want to go to the cinema.*
Man **soll** viel Obst **essen**. *One should eat lots of fruit.*

können	wollen	sollen
ich **kann**	ich **will**	ich **soll**
du **kannst**	du **willst**	du **sollst**
er/sie/man **kann**	er/sie/man **will**	er/sie/man **soll**
wir **können**	wir **wollen**	wir **sollen**
ihr **könnt**	ihr **wollt**	ihr **sollt**
sie/Sie **können**	sie/Sie **wollen**	sie/Sie **sollen**

F Write new sentences using the modal verbs.

Beispiel: **a** *Ich will ins Museum gehen.*

a Ich gehe ins Museum. (wollen)
b Wir machen eine Stadtrundfahrt. (können)
c Man trinkt viel Wasser. (sollen)
d Man macht hier viel. (können)
e Wir fahren nach Berlin. (wollen)
f Hörst du Musik? (wollen)

7.7 The perfect tense with haben

If you want to talk about an action in the past, you use the perfect tense (*das Perfekt*).

The perfect tense is normally formed with:

- the present tense of *haben* (see 7.5)
- the past participle of the main verb

To form the past participle:

- take the infinitive: *spielen*
- remove the -*en* ending: *spiel~~en~~*
- add *ge*- and -*t*: **ge**spiel**t**

The past participle goes to the end of the sentence:

Ich kaufe Souvenirs. → Ich **habe** Souvenirs **gekauft**.
Wir wohnen in einem Wohnwagen. → Wir **haben** in einem Wohnwagen **gewohnt**.

7.8 The perfect tense with sein

A small number of verbs form their perfect tense with *sein* instead of *haben*. They are usually verbs of motion (to go, to travel) and their past participles are formed with *ge*- and -*en* (instead of *ge*- and -*t*)

Ich fahre nach Spanien. → Ich **bin** nach Spanien **gefahren**.
Wir fliegen nach Schottland. → Wir **sind** nach Schottland **geflogen**.

7.9 Irregular past participles

Here are some common verbs that form their past participle with *ge*- and -*en*. The ones marked with * use *sein* instead of *haben* in the perfect tense.

infinitive		past participle
essen	*to eat*	gegessen
fahren*	*to go/travel*	gefahren
fliegen*	*to fly*	geflogen
gehen*	*to go*	gegangen
schlafen	*to sleep*	geschlafen
sehen	*to see*	gesehen
trinken	*to drink*	getrunken

G Rewrite the sentences in the perfect tense.

Beispiel: **a** *Ich habe einen Ausflug gemacht.*

a Ich mache einen Ausflug.
b Maike kauft ein Eis.
c Wir essen Pizza.
d Ich fahre Rad.
e Wir wohnen in einem Reihenhaus.
f Tom spielt Tennis.

7.10 Talking about the future

You can use the future tense to talk about things in the future. It is formed with the present tense of the verb *werden* and the infinitive of the main verb, which is sent to the end of the sentence:

Ich **werde** nach Italien **fahren**. *I will go to Italy.*
Wir **werden** Souvenirs **kaufen**. *We will buy souvenirs.*

The present tense of *werden* is as follows:

werden	
ich **werde**	wir **werden**
du **wirst**	ihr **werdet**
er/sie/es **wird**	sie/Sie **werden**

7.11 The imperative (giving instructions)

The imperative form of the verb is used to give instructions or advice.

If you are talking to a friend, use the *du* form of the verb without the word *du*, and remove the -*st* ending:

Du gehst links. → **Geh** links!
You go left. → *Go left!*

If you are talking to an adult stranger, use the *Sie* form but put the verb first:

Sie gehen rechts. → **Gehen Sie** rechts!
You go right. → *Go right!*

8 Negatives
Negationen

8.1 *nicht*

nicht means 'not' and usually comes directly after the verb:

Ich bin **nicht** groß. *I'm not tall.*
Jan geht **nicht** ins Kino. *Jan is not going to the cinema.*
Katja isst **nicht** gern Fisch. *Katja does not like eating fish.*

H Write new sentences with *nicht*.

a Das ist interessant!
b Susi geht in die Schule.
c Meine Stadt ist groß.
d Wir fahren mit dem Zug.
e Mein Bruder ist frech.
f Ich bin schüchtern.

8.2 *kein/keine/kein*

Use *kein/keine/kein* to say 'no', 'not a(ny)'. It is always followed by a noun and follows the pattern of *ein/eine/ein* (see the Summary table in Section 2.4):

Ich habe **keinen** Füller. *I do not have a fountain pen.*
Rudi trinkt **keine** Milch. *Rudi doesn't drink milk.*
Ich esse **kein** Fleisch. *I do not eat meat.*
Ich habe **keine** Haustiere. *I do not have any pets.*

I Fill the gaps with the correct form of *keinen/keine/kein*.

a Ich habe heute ▇▇▇ Schule.
b Berne hat ▇▇▇ Jugendzentrum.
c Ich esse ▇▇▇ Käse.
d Ich habe ▇▇▇ Hund.
e Wir trinken ▇▇▇ Milch.
f Ich habe ▇▇▇ Geschwister.

9 Gern, lieber, am liebsten

To say what you like or don't like doing, use *gern* or *nicht gern* with a verb. The words *gern* and *nicht gern* follow the verb:

Ich spiele **gern** Gitarre. *I like playing guitar.*
Ich spiele **nicht gern** Tennis. *I don't like playing tennis.*

To say what you prefer doing, use *lieber*:

Ich gehe **lieber** ins Kino. *I prefer going to the cinema.*

To say what you like doing most of all, use *am liebsten*:

Ich fahre **am liebsten** Rad. *Most of all I like cycling.*

10 Word order
Wortstellung

9.1 Subject–verb

Sentences usually start with the subject (the person or thing

Grammatik

doing the action). The verb is always the second piece of information:

1	2	3	
Ich	**gehe**	ins Kino.	*I'm going to the cinema.*
Mein Bruder	**spielt**	Fußball.	*My brother plays football.*

9.2 Time–manner–place

When a sentence contains several pieces of information, the order of the different parts is time–manner–place:

	time	**manner**	**place**
Ich fahre	am Nachmittag	mit dem Bus	nach Hamburg.

9.3 Time–verb–subject

If you want to stress the time element, you put this piece of information at the beginning of the sentence. However, you then need to swap over the subject and the verb so that the verb is still the second piece of information:

1	2	3		1	2	3	4
Ich	**habe**	Mathe.	→	Am Dienstag	**habe**	ich	Mathe.

11 Asking questions

Fragen

You can ask a question ...

- by putting the verb at the start of the sentence:
  Du hast einen Bruder. → **Hast** du einen Bruder?
  Bremen ist schön. → **Ist** Bremen schön?

- by using a question word at the start of the sentence:
  Wie heißt du? *What is your name?*
  Wo wohnst du? *Where do you live?*

Here is a list of all the question words in *Zoom Deutsch 1*:

wann	Wann haben wir Deutsch? *When do we have German?*
was	Was isst du? *What are you eating?*
welcher/-e/-es	Welches T-Shirt kaufst du? *Which T-shirt are you buying?*
wer	Wer ist das? *Who is that?*
wie	Wie alt bist du? *How old are you?*
wie viel	Wie viel kostet das? *How much does that cost?*
wo	Wo ist der Bahnhof? *Where is the station?*
woher	Woher kommst du? *Where do you come from?*
wohin	Wohin fährst du? *Where are you travelling/ going to?*

Answers to grammar activities

a Ich kaufe eine Tasche. **b** Ich kaufe einen Pullover.
c Ich kaufe ein Eis. **d** Ich kaufe einen Füller.
e Ich kaufe ein Computerspiel. **f** Ich kaufe eine CD.

Der Fußball ist unter dem Bett. Die Katze ist auf dem Bett. Das Regal ist über dem Bett. Der Kleiderschrank ist neben dem Bett. Die Tasche ist im Schrank. Die Schuhe sind hinter dem Bett.

a Dieses T-Shirt ist billiger. **b** Der rote Rock ist schöner.
c Der Film mit Lena ist besser. **d** Jakob ist frecher.
e Berlin ist älter. **f** Dein Haus ist moderner.

a Er; **b** Sie; **c** Sie; **d** Es; **e** Sie; **f** Wir

a habe; **b** ist; **c** hast; **d** bin; **e** sind; **f** Haben

a Ich will ins Museum gehen.
b Wir können eine Stadtrundfahrt machen.
c Man soll viel Wasser trinken. **d** Man kann hier viel machen.
e Wir wollen nach Berlin fahren. **f** Willst du Musik hören?

a Ich habe einen Ausflug gemacht. **b** Maike hat ein Eis gekauft.
c Wir haben Pizza gegessen. **d** Ich bin Rad gefahren.
e Wir haben in einem Reihenhaus gewohnt. **f** Tom hat Tennis gespielt.

a Das ist nicht interessant! **b** Susi geht nicht in die Schule.
c Meine Stadt ist nicht groß. **d** Wir fahren nicht mit dem Zug.
e Mein Bruder ist nicht frech. **f** Ich bin nicht schüchtern.

a keine; **b** kein; **c** keinen; **d** keinen; **e** keine; **f** keine

Hilfreiche Ausdrücke

Greetings	Begrüßungen
Hello	Hallo!
Good day	Guten Tag!
Good morning	Guten Morgen!
Good evening	Guten Abend!
Good night	Gute Nacht!
Goodbye	Tschüs! (informal)
	Auf Wiedersehen!

Months	Monate
January	Januar
February	Februar
March	März
April	April
May	Mai
June	Juni
July	Juli
August	August
September	September
October	Oktober
November	November
December	Dezember

Days	Wochentage
Monday	Montag
Tuesday	Dienstag
Wednesday	Mittwoch
Thursday	Donnerstag
Friday	Freitag
Saturday	Samstag
Sunday	Sonntag

Time	Uhrzeit
What time is it?	Wie spät ist es?/Wie viel Uhr ist es?
It is …	Es ist …
… one o'clock.	… ein Uhr.
… quarter to two.	… Viertel vor zwei.
… half past two.	… halb drei.
… quarter past three.	… Viertel nach drei.
… midday.	… Mittag.
… midnight.	… Mitternacht.

Numbers — Zahlen

1	eins	25	fünfundzwanzig
2	zwei	26	sechsundzwanzig
3	drei	27	siebenundzwanzig
4	vier	28	achtundzwanzig
5	fünf	29	neunundzwanzig
6	sechs	30	dreißig
7	sieben	31	einunddreißig
8	acht	40	vierzig
9	neun	50	fünfzig
10	zehn	60	sechzig
11	elf	70	siebzig
12	zwölf	80	achtzig
13	dreizehn	90	neunzig
14	vierzehn	100	hundert
15	fünfzehn	200	zweihundert
16	sechzehn	300	dreihundert
17	siebzehn	400	vierhundert
18	achtzehn	500	fünfhundert
19	neunzehn	600	sechshundert
20	zwanzig	700	siebenhundert
21	einundzwanzig	800	achthundert
22	zweiundzwanzig	900	neunhundert
23	dreiundzwanzig	1000	tausend
24	vierundzwanzig		

Dates — Daten

on the …	am …
1st	1. ersten
2nd	2. zweiten
3rd	3. dritten
4th	4. vierten
5th	5. fünften
6th	6. sechsten
7th	7. siebten
8th	8. achten
9th	9. neunten
10th	10. zehnten
11th	11. elften
20th	20. zwanzigsten
21st	21. einundzwanzigsten
22nd	22. zweiundzwanzigsten
30th	30. dreißigsten

Vokabular

A

der **Abend (-e)** *n* evening

das **Abendbrot (-e)** *n* evening meal

das **Abendessen (-)** *n* evening meal

das **Abenteuerspiel (-e)** *n* adventure game

aber but

acht eight

die **Achterbahn (-en)** *n* roller coaster

achtundzwanzig twenty-eight

achtzehn eighteen

achtzig eighty

der **Affe (-n)** *n* monkey

alles everything

alt *adj* old

altmodisch *adj* old-fashioned

die **Ampel (-n)** *n* traffic light

an to, at

anprobieren *v* to try on

anstrengend *adj* strenuous, tiring

der **Apfel (Äpfel)** *n* apple

der **Apfelkuchen (-)** *n* apple tart

April *n* April

auch also

auf on

auf Wiedersehen goodbye

August *n* August

aus from

der **Ausflug (-üge)** *n* excursion

aussehen *v* to look like

außerdem also

das **Auto (-s)** *n* car

B

die **Bäckerei (-en)** *n* baker's shop, bakery

das **Badezimmer (-)** *n* bathroom

der **Bahnhof (-öfe)** *n* railway station

der **Balkon (-e)** *n* balcony

die **Ballerinas** *n pl* pumps

die **Banane (-n)** *n* banana

der **Bär (-en)** *n* bear

Basketball *n* basketball

der **Becher (-)** *n* pot, mug

bedeuten *v* to mean

beginnen *v* to begin

zum **Beispiel** for example

Belgien *n* Belgium

beliebt *adj* popular

bequem *adj* comfortable

der **Berg (-e)** *n* mountain

berühmt *adj* famous

besuchen *v* to visit

das **Bett (-en)** *n* bed

die **Bibliothek (-en)** *n* library

Billard *n* snooker

billig *adj* cheap

das **Bio-Brot (-e)** *n* organic bread

Biologie *n* biology

bitte please

bitte schön/sehr you're welcome; (*when handing something over*) here you are

blau *adj* blue

bleiben *v* to stay

der **Bleistift (-e)** *n* pencil

blöd *adj* stupid

die **Bluse (-n)** *n* blouse

die **Bohne (-n)** *n* bean

das **Boot (-e)** *n* boat

die **Bootsfahrt (-en)** *n* boat trip

der **Braten (-)** *n* roast joint of meat

die **Bratwurst (-ürste)** *n* fried sausage

braun *adj* brown

das **Brot (-e)** *n* bread

das **Brötchen (-)** *n* bread roll

die **Brücke (-n)** *n* bridge

der **Bruder (-üder)** *n* brother

das **Buch (-ücher)** *n* book

der **Bungalow (-s)** *n* bungalow

bunt *adj* multicoloured

die **Butter** *n* butter

der **Butterkuchen (-)** *n* butter cake

C

das **Café (-s)** *n* café

der **Campingplatz (-ätze)** *n* campsite

die **CD (-s)** *n* CD

der **CD-Spieler (-)** *n* CD player

chatten *v* to chat

der **Cheeseburger (-)** *n* cheeseburger

Chemie *n* chemistry

die **Chips** *n pl* crisps

die **Cola (-s)** *n* cola

der **Computer (-)** *n* computer

cool *adj* cool

die **Cornflakes** *n pl* cornflakes

die **Currywurst (-ürste)** *n* curried sausage

D

da there

Dänemark *n* Denmark

danke schön thank you (very much)

Was **darf es sein?** What would you like?

dein/deine your

der **Delfin (-e)** *n* dolphin

denn because

deshalb therefore, so

Deutsch *n* German (*language*)

Deutscher/ Deutsche *n* German man/ woman

Deutschland *n* Germany

Dezember *n* December

Dienstag *n* Tuesday

der **Direktor (-en)** *n* head teacher (*male*)

die **Direktorin (-nen)** *n* head teacher (*female*)

die **Disco (-s)** *n* disco

der **Dom (-e)** *n* cathedral

die **Donau** *n* the Danube

Donnerstag *n* Thursday

doof *adj* stupid

das **Doppelhaus (-äuser)** *n* semi-detached house

das **Dorf (-örfer)** *n* village

dort there

die **Dose (-n)** *n* can

drei three

dreißig thirty

dreiundzwanzig twenty-three

dreizehn thirteen

dritte(r/s) *adj* third

du you

die **Dusche (-n)** *n* shower

die **DVD (-s)** *n* DVD

E

die **Ecke (-n)** *n* corner

das **Ei (-er)** *n* egg

einfach *adj* easy, simple

das **Einfamilienhaus (-äuser)** *n* detached house

einkaufen *v* to go shopping

das **Einkaufszentrum (-zentren)** *n* shopping centre

einmal in der Woche once a week

eins one

einundzwanzig twenty-one

der **Einwohner (-)** *n* inhabitant

das **Einzelkind (-er)** *n* only child

das **Eis (-)** *n* ice cream

die **Eisdiele (-n)** *n* ice cream parlour

der **Elefant (-en)** *n* elephant

elf eleven

die **Eltern** *n pl* parents

England *n* England

Engländer/ Engländerin *n* Englishman/ Englishwoman

Englisch *n* English (*language*)

entspannend *adj* relaxing

er he

das **Erdbeereis** *n* strawberry ice cream

das **Erdgeschoss (-e)** *n* ground floor

Erdkunde *n* geography

erste(r/s) *adj* first

der **Erwachsene** *n* adult

es it

essen *v* to eat

das **Esszimmer (-)** *n* dining room

etwas something

der **Euro (-s)** *n* euro

F

fahren *v* to go, travel, drive

die **Familie (-n)** *n* family

fantastisch *adj* fantastic

die **Farbe (-n)** *n* colour

das **Fastfood** *n* fast food

faul *adj* lazy

Februar *n* February

Federball *n* badminton

die **Federtasche (-n)** *n* pencil case

die **Ferien** *n pl* holidays

das **Ferienhaus (-äuser)** *n* holiday home

die **Ferienwohnung (-en)** *n* holiday flat

fernsehen *v* to watch TV

der **Fernseher (-)** *n* TV

der **Fernsehturm (-ürme)** *n* TV tower

der **Filzstift (-e)** *n* felt-tip pen

finden *v* to find

der **Fisch (-e)** *n* fish

die **Flasche (-n)** *n* bottle

das **Fleisch** *n* meat

fleißig *adj* hard-working

fliegen *v* to fly

die **Flöte (-n)** *n* flute

Frankreich *n* France

Französisch *n* French (*language*)

frech *adj* naughty

Freitag *n* Friday

die **Freizeit** *n* spare time

der **Freizeitpark (-s)** *n* amusement park

ich freue mich darauf I'm looking forward to it

der **Freund (-e)** *n* friend (*male*)

die **Freundin (-nen)** *n* friend (*female*)

freundlich *adj* friendly

frieren *v* to freeze

frisch *adj* fresh

im Frühling in the spring

das **Frühstück (-e)** *n* breakfast

der **Füller (-)** *n* fountain pen

fünf five

fünfundzwanzig twenty-five

fünfzehn fifteen

fünfzig fifty

für for

furchtbar *adj* awful

der **Fußball (-älle)** *n* football

G

die **Garage (-n)** *n* garage

gar nicht not at all

der **Garten (-ärten)** *n* garden

der **Geburtstag (-e)** *n* birthday

es gefällt mir (nicht) I (don't) like it

die **Gegend (-en)** *n* area, neighbourhood

gehen *v* to go

es geht it's OK, it's so-so

die **Geige (-n)** *n* violin

gelb *adj* yellow

das **Gemüse (-)** *n* vegetables

Genf Geneva

geradeaus straight on

gern: ich lese gern I like reading

das **Geschäft (-e)** *n* shop

das **Geschenk (-e)** *n* present

Geschichte *n* history

die **Geschwister** *n pl* siblings

gestern yesterday

gestreift *adj* stripy

das **Getränk (-e)** *n* drink

gewittern *v* to thunder

geben *v* to give

es gibt there is

die **Giraffe (-n)** *n* giraffe

die **Gitarre (-n)** *n* guitar

das **Glas (-äser)** *n* jar, glass

das **Gramm (-e)** *n* gram

grau *adj* grey

Griechenland *n* Greece

groß *adj* tall, big

großartig *adj* great

Großbritannien *n* Great Britain

die **Größe (-n)** *n* size

die **Großeltern** *n pl* grandparents

die **Großmutter (-ütter)** *n* grandmother

der **Großvater (-äter)** *n* grandfather

grün *adj* green

gut *adj* good

guten Abend good evening

gute Nacht good night

guten Morgen good morning

guten Tag hello, good day

H

haben *v* to have

das **Hähnchen (-)** *n* chicken

halb half

halb zwei half past one

hallo hello

der **Hamburger (-)** *n* hamburger

der **Hamster (-)** *n* hamster

Handball *n* handball

hässlich *adj* ugly

das **Hauptgericht (-e)** *n* main course

die **Hauptstadt (-ädte)** *n* capital city

das **Haus (-äuser)** *n* house

die **Hausaufgaben** *n pl* homework

zu Hause at home

das **Haustier (-e)** *n* pet

das **Heft (-e)** *n* exercise book

heiß *adj* hot

Vokabular

heißen *v* to be called
helfen *v* to help
hellblau *adj* light blue
das **Hemd (-en)** *n* shirt
im **Herbst** in the autumn
herunterladen *v* to download
heute today
heute Abend this evening
heute Morgen this morning
hier here
hinter behind
hören *v* to listen
die **Hose (-n)** *n* trousers
das **Hotel (-s)** *n* hotel
das **Huhn (-ühner)** *n* chicken
der **Hund (-e)** *n* dog
hundert hundred

I

ich I
die **Idee (-n)** *n* idea
ihr you (*pl*), her
im in (the)
der **Imbiss (-e)** *n* snack bar, fast-food place
immer always
in in
Informatik *n* IT
die **Insel (-n)** *n* island
intelligent *adj* intelligent
interessant *adj* interesting
ich **interessiere mich für ...** I'm interested in ...
das **Internet** *n* the internet
Italien *n* Italy
Italienisch *n* Italian (*language*)

J

ja yes
die **Jacke (-n)** *n* jacket
das **Jahr (-e)** *n* year
Januar *n* January

die **Jeans** *n sing* jeans
jeden Tag every day
jeder/jede/jedes every
jetzt now
der **Joghurt (-s)** *n* yoghurt
die **Jugendherberge (-n)** *n* youth hostel
das **Jugendzentrum (-zentren)** *n* youth centre, youth club
Juli *n* July
Juni *n* June

K

die **Kabine (-n)** *n* cubicle (*for trying on clothes in a shop*)
der **Kaffee (-s)** *n* coffee
kalt *adj* cold
das **Kaninchen (-)** *n* rabbit
man **kann** you/one/we can
der **Kapuzenpullover (-)** *n* hoodie
kariert *adj* checked
die **Karotte (-n)** *n* carrot
die **Karte (-n)** *n* ticket, card
die **Kartoffel (-n)** *n* potato
der **Käse (-)** *n* cheese
die **Katze (-n)** *n* cat
kaufen *v* to buy
das **Kaufhaus (-äuser)** *n* department store
der **Keller (-)** *n* cellar
der **Ketchup** *n* ketchup
das **Kilo (-s)** *n* kilo
das **Kind (-er)** *n* child
das **Kino (-s)** *n* cinema
die **Kirche (-n)** *n* church
der **Kirschkuchen (-)** *n* cherry cake
die **Klamotten** *n pl* gear, kit (*informal word for clothes*)
klasse *adj* great

das **Klassenzimmer (-)** *n* classroom
das **Klavier (-e)** *n* piano
das **Kleid (-er)** *n* dress
der **Kleiderschrank (-änke)** *n* wardrobe
die **Kleidung** *n sing* clothes
klein *adj* small
der **Knoblauch** *n* garlic
Kochen *n* cookery
Köln Cologne
komisch *adj* strange
kommen *v* to come
können *v* to be able to, can
kosten *v* to cost
das **Kotelett (-s)** *n* cutlet, chop
die **Krawatte (-n)** *n* tie
die **Kreuzung (-en)** *n* crossroads
die **Küche (-n)** *n* kitchen
der **Kuchen (-)** *n* cake
der **Kuli (-s)** *n* ballpoint pen
Kunst *n* art
kurz *adj* short

L

ich **lade Musik (he)runter** I download music
die **Lampe (-n)** *n* lamp
das **Land (Länder)** *n* country
lang *adj* long
langweilig *adj* boring
lässig *adj* cool, casual
Latein *n* Latin
launisch *adj* moody
laut *adj* noisy, loud
die **Lederjacke (-n)** *n* leather jacket
der **Lehrer (-)** *n* teacher (*male*)
die **Lehrerin (-nen)** *n* teacher (*female*)
das **Lernspiel (-e)** *n* educational game

lesen *v* to read
lieben *v* to love
der **Lieblingsdesigner (-)** *n* favourite designer
das **Lieblingsfach (-ächer)** *n* favourite subject
die **Limonade (-n)** *n* lemonade
das **Lineal (-e)** *n* ruler
links left
der **Liter (-)** *n* litre
der **Lolli (-s)** *n* lollipop
der **Löwe (-n)** *n* lion
lustig *adj* funny
Luxemburg Luxembourg

M

machen *v* to do
ich **mag (nicht)** I (don't) like
die **Mahlzeit (-en)** *n* meal
Mai *n* May
man one, you, they, we
manchmal sometimes
die **Mannschaft (-en)** *n* team
der **Mantel (Mäntel)** *n* coat
die **Marmelade (-n)** *n* jam
März *n* March
Mathe *n* maths
die **Maus (-äuse)** *n* mouse
die **Mayonnaise** *n* mayonnaise
Medienwissen-schaften *n pl* media studies
am **Meer** by the sea
das **Meerschweinchen (-)** *n* guinea pig
mein/meine my
meistens mostly
die **Melone (-n)** *n* melon
die **Milch** *n* milk
mit with, by
der **Mittag (-e)** *n* midday

das **Mittagessen (-)** *n* lunch

die **Mittagspause (-n)** *n* lunch break

um **Mitternacht** at midnight

Mittwoch *n* Wednesday

ich **möchte** *v* I'd like

die **Mode** *n* fashion

der **Modedesigner (-)** *n* fashion designer (*male*)

die **Modedesignerin (-nen)** *n* fashion designer (*female*)

modern *adj* modern

modisch *adj* fashionable

mögen *v* to like

der **Monat (-e)** *n* month

Montag *n* Monday

morgen tomorrow

der **Morgen (-)** *n* morning

der **Motorradhelm (-e)** *n* motorcycle helmet

München Munich

das **Museum (Museen)** *n* museum

Musik *n* music

musikalisch *adj* musical

das **Musikspiel (-e)** *n* music game

das **Müsli** *n* muesli

die **Mutter (-ütter)** *n* mother

N

nach to, after

der **Nachmittag (-e)** *n* afternoon

die **Nachspeise (-n)** *n* dessert

das **Nashorn (-örner)** *n* rhino

die **Nationalität (-en)** *n* nationality

natürlich of course

Naturwissen- schaften *n pl* sciences

neben next to

neblig *adj* foggy

nehmen *v* to take

nein no

nervig *adj* annoying

nett *adj* nice

neu *adj* new

neun nine

neunundzwanzig twenty-nine

neunzehn nineteen

neunzig ninety

nicht not

nicht so gut not so good

der **Norden** *n* north

der **Nordosten** *n* north-east

die **Nordsee** *n* North Sea

der **Nordwesten** *n* north-west

normalerweise usually

das **Notizbuch (-bücher)** *n* notebook

November *n* November

die **Nudeln** *n pl* pasta

die **Nummer (-n)** *n* number

nützlich *adj* useful

O

das **Obst** *n* fruit

oder or

oft often

ohne without

Oktober *n* October

die **Olive (-n)** *n* olive

die **Oma (-s)** *n* grandmother

das **Omelett (-s)** *n* omelette

der **Onkel (-)** *n* uncle

der **Opa (-s)** *n* granddad

orange *adj* orange

der **Orangensaft (-äfte)** *n* orange juice

der **Ordner (-)** *n* file

der **Osten** *n* east

Österreich *n* Austria

Österreicher/ Österreicherin *n* Austrian man/ woman

P

die **Packung (-en)** *n* packet

der **Papagei (-en)** *n* parrot

der **Park (-s)** *n* park

die **Pause (-n)** *n* break

das **Pferd (-e)** *n* horse

das **Pfund (-e)** *n* pound

Physik *n* physics

das **Picknick (-s)** *n* picnic

der **Pilz (-e)** *n* mushroom

die **Pizza (-s)** *n* pizza

die **Pizzeria (-s)** *n* pizzeria

die **Plastikschlange (-n)** *n* plastic snake

Polen *n* Poland

Polnisch *n* Polish (*language*)

die **Pommes frites** *n pl* chips, fries

Portugal *n* Portugal

die **Post** *n* post office

das **Poster (-)** *n* poster

praktisch *adj* practical

prima *adj* great

das **Projekt (-e)** *n* project

die **Prüfung (-en)** *n* exam

der **Pulli (-s)** *n* jumper

der **Pullover (-)** *n* jumper

Q

das **Quizspiel (-e)** *n* quiz game

R

Rad fahren *v* to cycle

der **Radiergummi (-s)** *n* eraser

rechts *adj* right

das **Regal (-e)** *n* shelf

die **Region (-en)** *n* region

regnen *v* to rain

das **Reihenhaus (-äuser)** *n* terraced house

der **Reis** *n* rice

die **Reise (-n)** *n* journey

Religion *n* religion, RE

das **Restaurant (-s)** *n* restaurant

die **Richtung (-en)** *n* direction

das **Riesenrad (-äder)** *n* Ferris wheel

der **Rock (-öcke)** *n* skirt

romantisch *adj* romantic

rot *adj* red

der **Rotwein (-e)** *n* red wine

die **Ruhe** *n* silence, quiet

S

die **Sahne** *n* cream

der **Salat (-e)** *n* salad, lettuce

Samstag *n* Saturday

Schach *n* chess

die **Schachtel (-n)** *n* box

schade what a shame, that's a shame

die **Scheibe (-n)** *n* slice

schick *adj* chic, smart

die **Schildkröte (-n)** *n* tortoise

der **Schinken (-)** *n* ham

das **Schlafzimmer (-)** *n* bedroom

das **Schlagzeug (-e)** *n* drums

die **Schlange (-n)** *n* snake

schlecht *adj* bad

Schlittschuh laufen *v* to ice- skate

das **Schloss (-össer)** *n* castle, palace

der **Schlüsselanhänger (-)** *n* key ring

Vokabular

die **Schneekugel (-n)** *n* snow globe
schneien *v* to snow
der **Schnitt (-e)** *n* cut, design
das **Schnitzel (-)** *n* pork or veal escalope
die **Schokolade (-n)** *n* chocolate
das **Schokoladeneis** *n* chocolate ice cream
schön *adj* nice
Schottland *n* Scotland
schrecklich *adj* terrible
schreiben *v* to write
der **Schreibtisch (-e)** *n* desk
schüchtern *adj* shy
der **Schuh (-e)** *n* shoe
das **Schulbuch (-ücher)** *n* school book, textbook
die **Schule (-n)** *n* school
der **Schüler (-)** *n* pupil (*male*)
die **Schülerin (-nen)** *n* pupil (*female*)
das **Schulfach (-fächer)** *n* school subject
der **Schulhof (-höfe)** *n* school yard
die **Schulsachen** *n pl* school things
die **Schultasche (-n)** *n* school bag
die **Schuluniform (-en)** *n* school uniform
schwarz black
die **Schwarzwälder Kirschtorte (-n)** *n* Black Forest gateau
die **Schweiz** *n* Switzerland
Schweizer/ Schweizerin *n* Swiss man/ woman
schwer *adj* difficult
die **Schwester (-n)** *n* sister

schwierig *adj* difficult
das **Schwimmbad (-äder)** *n* swimming pool
schwimmen *v* to swim
sechs six
sechsundzwanzig twenty-six
sechzehn sixteen
sechzig sixty
der **See (-n)** *n* lake
segeln *v* to sail
ich **sehe fern** I watch TV
sehen *v* to watch, see
sehr very
sein *v* to be
die **Seite (-n)** *n* side, page
September *n* September
die **Shorts** *n pl* shorts
sie she, they, them
Sie you (*formal*)
sieben seven
siebenundzwanzig twenty-seven
siebzehn seventeen
siebzig seventy
die **Skateboard-Bahn** skatepark
Skateboard fahren *v* to skateboard
Ski fahren *v* to ski
die **Slowakei** *n* Slovakia
Slowenien *n* Slovenia
so so
das **Sofa (-s)** *n* sofa
man **soll** you/one/we should
im **Sommer** in the summer
sonnig *adj* sunny
Sonntag *n* Sunday
Sonst noch etwas? Anything else?
das **Souvenir (-s)** *n* souvenir

der **Souvenirladen (-läden)** *n* souvenir shop
Spanien *n* Spain
Spanisch *n* Spanish (language)
spannend *adj* exciting
spät *adj* late
Wie **spät ist es?** What time is it?
einen **Spaziergang machen** *v* to go for a walk
die **Speisekarte (-n)** *n* menu
spielen *v* to play
der **Spinat** *n* spinach
der **Sport** *n* sports, PE
sportlich *adj* sporty
die **Sportschuhe** *n pl* trainers
das **Sportspiel (-e)** *n* sports game
die **Sporttasche (-n)** *n* sports bag
die **Sprache (-n)** *n* language
sprechen *v* to speak
das **Stadion (-ien)** *n* stadium
die **Stadt (-ädte)** *n* city, town
die **Stadtmitte (-n)** *n* town centre
der **Stadtrand (-änder)** *n* outskirts of town
die **Stadtrundfahrt (-en)** *n* tour of the town
es **steht dir gut** it suits you
es **steht dir nicht** it doesn't suit you
die **Stereoanlage (-n)** *n* hi-fi system
die **Stiefel** *n pl* boots
der **Stock** *n* floor, storey
die **Straße (-n)** *n* road, street
die **Straßenkleidung** *n* *sing* street wear

das **Stück (-e)** *n* piece
der **Stuhl (-ühle)** *n* chair
suchen *v* to look for
der **Süden** *n* south
der **Südosten** *n* south-east
der **Südwesten** *n* south-west
super *adj* super
der **Supermarkt (-ärkte)** *n* supermarket
die **Suppe (-n)** *n* soup

T

die **Tafel (-n)** *n* board, chalkboard
der **Tag (-e)** *n* day
täglich *adj* every day, daily
die **Tante (-n)** *n* aunt
tanzen *v* to dance
das **Tanzspiel (-e)** *n* dance game
der **Taschenrechner (-)** *n* calculator
tausend thousand
der **Tee (-s)** *n* tea
Tennis *n* tennis
teuer *adj* expensive
das **Theater (-)** *n* theatre
der **Thunfisch (-e)** *n* tuna
das **Tier (-e)** *n* animal
der **Tierpark (-s)** *n* zoo
der **Tiger (-)** *n* tiger
Tischtennis *n* table tennis
toll great
die **Tomate (-n)** *n* tomato
total *adj* totally, extremely
tragen *v* to wear
das **Traumhaus (-äuser)** *n* dream house, ideal house
traurig *adj* sad
treffen *v* to meet
trinken to drink

Vokabular

die **Trompete (-n)** *n* trumpet
die **Tschechische Republik** *n* the Czech Republic
tschüs bye
das **T-shirt (-s)** *n* T-shirt
Türke/Türkin *n* Turk (male/female)
die **Türkei** *n* Turkey
Türkisch *n* Turkish (language)
Turnen *n* gymnastics
die **Tüte (-n)** *n* bag

U

die **U-Bahn-Station (-en)** *n* underground station
über above, across, over
die **Uhr (-en)** *n* clock, watch, time
um at
umtauschen *v* to exchange
unbequem *adj* uncomfortable
und and
Ungarn *n* Hungary
unter under
der **Unterricht (-e)** *n* lessons, classes
im Urlaub on holiday

V

das **Vanilleeis** *n* vanilla ice cream
der **Vater (-äter)** *n* father
verbringen *v* to spend time
der **Verkäufer (-)** *n* shop assistant (male)
die **Verkäuferin (-nen)** *n* shop assistant (female)
verstehen *v* to understand
das **Video (-s)** *n* video
viel a lot, much

vielen Dank thank you (very much)
vielleicht perhaps, maybe
vier four
das **Viertel (-)** *n* quarter
vierundzwanzig twenty-four
vierzehn fourteen
vierzig forty
der **Vogel (-ögel)** *n* bird
Volleyball *n* volleyball
vor in front of, before
die **Vorspeise (-n)** *n* starter

W

der **Wald (-älder)** *n* forest, wood
wandern *v* to go walking
wann when
warm *adj* warm
warten *v* to wait
was what
das **Wasser** *n* water
der **Wasserpark (-s)** *n* waterpark
weiß *adj* white
ich **weiß (nicht)** I (don't) know
der **Weißwein (-e)** *n* white wine
welcher/welche/welches which
der **Wellensittich (-e)** *n* budgie
weltweit *adj* worldwide
wer who
werden *v* to become
der **Westen** *n* west
das **Wetter** *n* weather
wichtig *adj* important
wie how
Wie bitte? Pardon?
Wie geht's? How are you?
Wie lange? For how long?
Wien Vienna

das **Wiener Schnitzel (-)** *n* Viennese veal escalope
wie viel how much
Um **wie viel Uhr?** At what time?
ich **will** I want
windig *adj* windy
im **Winter** in the winter
wir we
wo where
die **Woche (-n)** *n* week
das **Wochenende (-n)** *n* weekend
der **Wochentag (-e)** *n* day of the week
woher where (from)
wohin where (to)
wohnen *v* to live
das **Wohnmobil (-e)** *n* camper van
die **Wohnsiedlung (-en)** *n* housing estate, residential area
die **Wohnung (-en)** *n* flat
der **Wohnwagen (-)** *n* caravan
das **Wohnzimmer (-)** *n* living room
wolkig *adj* cloudy
wollen *v* to want
die **Wurst (Würste)** *n* sausage

Z

die **Zahl (-en)** *n* number
zehn ten
die **Zeitschrift (-en)** *n* magazine
die **Zeitung (-en)** *n* newspaper
das **Zelt (-e)** *n* tent
ziemlich rather
das **Zimmer (-)** *n* room
die **Zitronentorte (-n)** *n* lemon gateau/flan
der **Zoo (-s)** *n* zoo
zu too
zu (zum/zur) to
der **Zug (-üge)** *n* train

zusammen together
zwanzig twenty
zwei two
zweimal twice
zweite(r/s) *adj* second
zweiundzwanzig twenty-two
die **Zwiebel (-n)** *n* onion
der **Zwilling (-e)** *n* twin
zwischen between
zwölf twelve

OXFORD
UNIVERSITY PRESS

Great Clarendon Street, Oxford OX2 6DP

Oxford University Press is a department of the
University of Oxford.

It furthers the University's objective of excellence in research, scholarship,
and education by publishing worldwide in
Oxford   New York   Auckland   Cape Town   Dar es Salaam   Hong Kong
Karachi   Kuala Lumpur   Madrid   Melbourne   Mexico City   Nairobi
New Delhi   Shanghai   Taipei   Toronto

With offices in
Argentina   Austria   Brazil   Chile   Czech Republic   France   Greece
Guatemala   Hungary   Italy   Japan   South Korea   Poland   Portugal
Singapore   Switzerland   Thailand   Turkey   Ukraine   Vietnam

British Library Cataloguing in Publication Data

Data available

ISBN 978 019 912770 2

20 19 18 17 16

Printed and bound by CPI Group (UK) Ltd, Croydon, CR0 4YY

Paper used in the production of this book is a natural, recyclable product made
from wood grown in sustainable forests. The manufacturing process conforms
to the environmental regulations of the country of origin.

Acknowledgements

The authors and publisher would like to thank the following people for
their help and advice: Marieke O'Connor, Pat Dunn (editors), Angelika Libera
(language consultant), Suzanne Prout (Ballard School) and Julie Green (course
consultants), and all participants of the focus groups held in Birmingham,
Bristol and Manchester.

Video shot on location in Berlin, with grateful thanks to Rob Cooke (Producer),
Michael O'Halloran (Cameraman), Lilja Kloth (Assistant Producer), Olaf Löschke
and Sandra Zentgraf (Production Assistants), Judith Hametner (Nina), Melvin
Keskin (Ali), Selina Mai (Kathi) and Julius Nitschkoff (Nico).

Cover: The Ampelmann is a registered trademark of AMPELMANN
GmbH Berlin www.ampelmann.de

p1ll: OUP; p1m: OUP; p1m: OUP; p1r: OUP; p4tl: OUP; p4tr: OUP; p4bl: OUP;
p4br: OUP; p6tl: OUP; p6tm: Jan Martin Will/Shutterstock; p6tr: S K D/Alamy;
p6bl: Richard Wareham Fotografie/Alamy; p6br: Paul Reid/Shutterstock; p9t:
OUP; p9b: OUP; p10: Frank Chmura/Photolibrary; p11l: OUP; p11r: OUP; p12l-r:
Imagebroker/Photolibrary, Moment/Cultura/Getty Images, Art Directors & TRIP/
Alamy, Catchlight Visual Services/Alamy, Radius Images/Photolibrary; p14tl:
Johner Images/Alamy; p14tm: OUP; p14tr: Shutterstock; p14ml: Art Directors
& TRIP/Alamy; p14mr: OUP; p14bl: Masterfile; p14bm: David J. Green - studio/
Alamy; p14br: OUP; p15: OUP; p16l-r: Cultura/Alamy, GlowImages/Alamy,
Caro/Alamy, Leland Bobbe/Stone/Getty Images; p17t: OUP; p17m: OUP; p17b:
Startraks Photo/Rex Features; p20: Rex Features; p21: Sipa Press/Rex Features;
p22: B.O'Kane/Alamy; p24tl-tr: OUP; Goodluz/Shutterstock; Howard Sayer/
Shutterstock; Monkey Business Images/Shutterstock; p24bl-br: Robert Kneschke/
Shutterstock; Monkey Business Images/Shutterstock, Monkey Business Images/
Shutterstock, michaeljung/Shutterstock; p25t: OUP; p25b: Jesper Elgaard/
iStockphoto; p26tl: OUP; p26tr: OUP; p26ml-mr: Howard Sayer/Shutterstock;
Monkey Business Images/Shutterstock; Monkey Business Images/Shutterstock;
StockLite/Shutterstock; Phase4Photography/Shutterstock; p26bl: OUP; p26br:
OUP; p27l: Allstar Picture Library/Alamy; p27m: Archives du 7eme Art/Photo12;
p27r: Reuters/Corbis; p30tl: OUP; p30tm: PhotoAlto/OUP; p30tr: photobank.kiev.
ua/Shutterstock; p30bl: bociek666/Shutterstock; p30bm: the red house image
library/OUP; p30br: Piotr Marcinski/Shutterstock; p32t: OUP; p32bl: Monkey
Business Images/Shutterstock; p32bm: Monkey Business Images/Shutterstock;

p32br: Howard Sayer/Shutterstock; p37: OUP; p38: Carlos Neto/Shutterstock;
p38b: Lifesize/OUP; p43: OUP; p44l: OUP; p44m: OUP; p44r: OUP; p45: OUP; p48:
OUP; p53: picture-alliance/beyond/Claudia Gopperl; p56: David Young-Wolff/
Stone/Getty Images; p57: Glenn Nagel/Dreamstime; p59: OUP; p61: Ciot Ciot/
Photolibrary; p62tl: Chassenet Chassenet/Photolibrary; p62tm: Grapheast/Alamy;
p62tr: Villerot Villerot/Photolibrary; p62bl: Pinon Pinon/Photolibrary; p62bm:
imagebroker/Alamy; p62br: Ianni Dimitrov/Alamy; p63l: OUP; p63r: OUP; p64t-b:
OUP; OUP; OUP; OUP; p66: LWA/Dann Tardif/Photolibrary; p69: Denis Babenko/
Shutterstock; p70l: Jovannig/Fotolia; p70m: Heiner Heine/Photolibrary; p70r:
OUP; p72tl: Cultura/Alamy; p72tr: WestEnd61/Rex Features; p72bl: Radius
Images/Alamy; p72br: Masterfile; p74l-r: Forget-Gautier/Sagaphoto.Com/Alamy;
Eric Gevaert/Dreamstime; Christopher Penler/Shutterstock; T.H.klimmeck/
Shutterstock; Jan Schuler/Fotolia; p75l-r: Joe Gough/Shutterstock, Friedhelm
Thomas/Photolibrary, Nicole Gordine/Shutterstock, OUP, picture-alliance; p76tl:
Powered by Light/Alan Spencer/Alamy; p76tr: Gari Wyn Williams/Alamy; p76ml:
Tim Scott/Shutterstock; p76mr: iStockphoto; p76bl: Keith Levit/Shutterstock;
p76br: Tim Scott/Shutterstock; p78: OUP; p80t: OUP; p80b: xyno/iStockphoto;
p81l: OUP; p81r: Cj Yu/Dreamstime; p86: Huntstock/Getty Images; p88: OUP;
p89l: OUP; p89m: OUP; p89r: OUP; p90l-r: Imagebroker/Alamy, Bernd Kroger/
Imagebroker/Alamy, Ray Tang/Rex Features, Ray Tang/Rex Features; p91t: OUP;
p91b: OUP; p92: OUP; p93tl-tr: Danny E Hooks/Shutterstock, Sonny Meddle/
Rex Features, Bildagentur-online.com/Th-foto/Alamy, Shebeko/Shutterstock;
p93bl-br: picture-alliance/dpa, Bon Appetit/Alamy, picture-alliance/dpa, vario
images GmbH & Co.KG/Alamy, Marek Mnich/iStockphoto; p94l: TS/Alamy;
p94r: picture-alliance/Image Source; p95l: Joerg Beuge/Shutterstock; p95r: Jacek
Chabraszewski/Shutterstock; p96l: OUP; p96r: OUP; p97: Imagebroker/Alamy;
p100: OUP; p101: Thomas Grass/Getty Images; p102t: OUP; p102b: Philip Lange/
Shutterstock; p105tl: OUP; p105tm: picture-alliance/Eibner-Pressefoto; p105tr:
Paul Reid/Shutterstock; p105b: Fotowahn/Fotolia; p107t: picture-alliance/
beyond/Claudia Göpperl; p107bl: Nickolay Vinokurov/Shutterstock; p107br:
afotoshop/Shutterstock; p109l: OUP; p109r: OUP; p111tl: Tony Hertz/Alamy;
p111tr: OUP; p111b: OUP; p113t: picture-alliance/Bildagentur Huber; p113m:
Losevsky Pavel/Shutterstock; p113b: Higuchi Higuchi/Photolibrary; p117t:
picture-alliance/Design Pics; p117b: Michaela Begsteiger/Photolibrary; p120tl-tr:
Karkas/Shutterstock; Grandpa/Shutterstock; Karkas/Shutterstock; Andrew
Paterson/Alamy; Photocrea/Shutterstock; p120bl-br: Karkas/Shutterstock,
Tatniz/Shutterstock; Elnur/Shutterstock; Tatiana Popova/Shutterstock; Karkas/
Shutterstock; p121l: Vovan/Shutterstock; p121r: Karkas/Shutterstock; p122tl:
picture-alliance/dpa; p122tr: Imagebroker/vario images; p122bl: picture-alliance/
dpa; p122br: picture-alliance/dpa; p123l-r: picture-alliance/dpa; picture-alliance/
Schroewig/Schoen; picture alliance/dpa; picture-alliance/Schroewig/CS; p124:
OUP; p126t: OUP; p126bl: OUP; p126br: OUP; p128: OUP; p129t: Ben Molyneux
People/Alamy; p129b: picture-alliance/Golden Pixels LLC; p132: Brian Rasic/Rex
Features; p134: OUP; p136: AMA/Shutterstock; p137l: OUP; p137m: OUP; p137r:
OUP; p138tl: Thomas Hohler/Fotolia; p138tm: picture-alliance/allOver/VSL;
p138tr: Aleksandar Nakic/iStockphoto; p138bl: Pegaz/Alamy; p138bm: Rmbssk/
Shutterstock; p138br: Jorisvo/Shutterstock; p139l: Alex Zarubin/Dreamstime;
p139r: Clearlens/Shutterstock; p140tl: © www.viennaslide.com; p140tm: Bill
Bachmann/Alamy; p140tr: Ramsey Sanford Houck/Shutterstock; p140bl: Nikada/
iStockphoto; p140br: Christoph Papsch/Vario Images; p141tl: picture alliance/
dpa; p141tr: Krys Bailey/Marmotta PhotoArt; p141ml: picture-alliance/Eibner-
Pressefoto; p141mr: picture-alliance/dpa; p141b-l: Images & Stories/Alamy,
Slava296/Dreamstime, Lya_Cattel/Istockphoto; Jeronimo Alba/Photolibrary;
p142: OUP; p143t-b: Blickwinkel/Alamy; Imagebroker/Alamy; picture-alliance/
allover; David Ryan/Lonely Planet Images/Photolibrary; picture-alliance/allover;
McPHOTO/vario images; p143bl: Prater; p144: OUP; p145t: OUP; p145b: Chris
Hepburn/iStockphoto; p150: OUP; p150t: Howard Sayer/Shutterstock; p150m:
gary718/Shutterstock; p150b: gary718/Shutterstock; p152tl-bl: Philip Lange/
Shutterstock; Jean-Jacques Cordier/Fotolia; max homand/Shutterstock; MBI/
Alamy; p152tr-br: Bratwustle/Shutterstock, Westend61 GmbH/Alamy, Cultura/
Alamy; p153: Alexander Feldmann/Corbis; p154tl: Schulranzen-Onlineshop.
de; p154tr: Tokio Hotel; p154m: Jim Parkin/Shutterstock; p154b: © 2011
Posh Accessories; p155tl-tr: Monkey Business Images/Shutterstock; Albanpix
Ltd/Rex Features, Felbert + Eickenberg/STOCK4B/Getty Images; Alex Segre/
Rex Features; p155ml: Sho Shan/Alamy; p155mr: Catchlight Visual Services/
Alamy; p155b: Lehtikuva OY/Rex Features; p156tl-bl: Lessia/Dreamstime;
Janina Dierks/Shutterstock, Ionia/Shutterstock, Sabine Lubenow/LOOK/Getty
Images; Westend61/Getty Images; p156tr-br: Mountainpix/Shutterstock; Raomn/
Dreamstime; P Narayan/Photolibrary; p157: Manfred Bail/Photolibrary; p158t-b:
Paul Reid/Shutterstock; Oliver Gerhard/Photolibrary; picture alliance/ZB; p158t:
Santa Cruz/Rex Features; picture alliance/ZB; p159t: Stefan Kiefer/vario images;
p159m: picture-alliance/Textilwirtschaft; p159b: Jonathan Hordle/Rex Features;
p160t: Culliganphoto/Alamy; p160m: picture-alliance/Denkou Images; p160b:
Alexander Chaikin/Shutterstock.

Audio recordings by Boris Steinberg at Slomophone Audio Studio, Berlin

Illustrations by: Illustrations by: Kessia Beverley-Smith, Stefan Chabluk, Bojana
Dimitrovski, Mike Hall, John Hallett, John Haslam, Tim Kahane, Matt Latchford,
Oxford Designers & Illustrators, Dusan Pavlic, Pulsar Studios, Olivier Prime,
Anita Romeo, Martin Sanders, Sailesh Thakrar, Theresa Tibbetts, Laszlo Veres.

Cover illustration by: Oxford Designers & Illustrators

Every effort has been made to contact copyright holders of material reproduced
in this book. If notified, the publishers will be pleased to rectify any errors or
omissions at the earliest opportunity.